Fundamentals of Reporting and Editing

FUNDAMENTALS OF REPORTING AND EDITING

Dr. Ambrish Saxena

KANISHKA PUBLISHERS, DISTRIBUTORS
NEW DELHI-110 002

KANISHKA PUBLISHERS, DISTRIBUTORS
4697/5-21A, Ansari Road, Daryaganj
New Delhi -110 002
Phones : 2327 0497, 2328 8285
Fax : 011-2328 8285
E-mail : kanishka_publishing@yahoo.co.in

Fundamentals of Reporting and Editing

First Published 2007
Edition-2021

PRINTED IN INDIA

Published by Madan Sachdeva for Kanishka Publishers, Distributors, 4697/5-21A, Ansari Road, Daryaganj, New Delhi-110 002, Typeset by Sunshine Graphics, Delhi, and Printed at Rajdhani Printers, Delhi.

Foreword

Kali Charan Ray, the revolutionary editor of India's freedom struggle, once said that for hundred assistant editors that India produces it hardly produces two sub-editors. What this great editor said nearly sixty years back is even more true in the present-day scenario of Indian journalism. The subbing is dying down as a work of art. Total indifference to and neglect for the art of editing and to the status of journalist doing the editing job and an equally systematic promotion for the field staff has redeemed editing to a job which no one knows and no one appreciates. Instead of sub-editors we have got rewrite man whose typical styles look attractive at the face value but lead to monotony at the end of the day. With the decline of the art of editing, the art of news gathering and news writing has also suffered. While the writing may have developed range and in certain cases depth as well it has lost sensitivity and capacity to appeal to a subtle mind.

Unfortunately, nobody seems to be lamenting the death of the art of editing. Similarly, nobody seems to be realising the fact that decline in the art of editing has made, at least print media, a classical case of what Dr. S. Radha Krishnan once said in a different context that everything is right with the body, but the soul is missing. Books like what Dr. Saxena has written are a small but determined effort in the direction of the search for soul of Indian journalism. These books do indicate the need of realising define of skills and determine the hard work that is needed to acquire these skills.

Despite a massive expansion of media education in the country, there are very few really good books on journalism of Indian origin and Indian experience. The best books still come from the West, which do not relate to the Indian context. The present-day Indian editors either have little experience of passing on the stalls of editing and reporting or are unable to translate their experience into academically relevant books. Most of Indian working journalists and editors are yet to realize the need for making a contribution to the academic world of Mass Communication. The books they write are very relevant to the subject or the event which they cover but are no great help to the teaching of the discipline. Many of the teachers of mass communication have little or no experience of working in the media industry. Dr. Saxena is one of the very few persons who combines rich media experience with rich media teaching experience. His book, therefore, is an academic contribution by a seasoned media practitioner.

The book will be a good guide to young students of journalism and mass communication. It can best be said as a beginning in the direction of creation of textual literature on mass communication and journalism as an academic discipline by those who combine experience in media industry with experience in media teaching. Only work by such people will put an end to meaningless debates by pseudo media professionals and the so-called stakeholders of media who seemingly have weird ideas about the status and role of media in society without knowing its actual purpose and potential. These persons confuse many people but their worst victims are young students of journalism and young journalists. Books by people like Dr. Saxena will certainly make media debates and media training more relevant and media discourses on right lines.

Prof. Pradeep Mathur
Course Director-Journalism
Indian Institute of Mass Communication
New Delhi

Preface

Journalism in India has witnessed many upheavals since its emergence—a quarter and two centuries back. Down the ages, decade after decade, significant changes were observed in the content and form of newspapers. Yet, right from the era of James Silk Buckingham to Robert Knight and from M.K. Gandhi to M.J. Akbar, the quintessence of journalism-skills of news reporting and editing remained unchanged. Still, a journalist ever yearns to acquire greater and greater dexterity in report writing and editing—moreover, his/her journalistic calibre is also adjudged on the basis of his/her command over writing or/and editing.

Although, in India, a considerable change in the notion and perception of news occurred after the advent and expansion of electronic media, even the definition of news has changed and the clear dividing line between news-non news, hard news-soft news and even news and advertisement turned thinner and finally it has got blurred, nevertheless the determinants of news or news value remained immutable. Proximity factor still plays a prime role, VIPs and celebrities appear as newsmakers, public interest is yet a dominant factor to decide whether the particular bit of information is news or not. This is what needs to be understood by a newsman of the new generation, particularly one who is inclined to print journalism.

Once it is decided what is to be written, we have again come back to the point how it is to be written. How it is referred to the style of writing of the reporter, the language and the expression used by the reporter, the rhetoric and emphasis of the news item. For this the reporter has to be aware of his/her tools, capable of translating all his/her knowledge and skills to a professionally done report.

This book deals with both the essential aspects of news—the

concept and the writing. Understanding of news is the first and the foremost thing that a journalist has to develop. A news has to be tasted on the basis of news value—the established parameters or the determinants of news. Thereafter the news has to be structured in the conventional format, with a certain level of flexibility available to a reporter depending on his/her creativity and wisdom. News gathering, sourcing and report writing with emphasis on lead writing are the major areas discussed in detail in different chapters.

Though the book is loaded with the reporting input, it also covers extensively all essential aspects of editing. The tools of editing, the tasks involved in editing, the administration of editing in a daily and the guidelines prescribed in the form of style sheet—all this has been discussed to a comprehensive detail. Not to forget the mention of the chapter on headline which has possibly become the finest part of this book containing editing input.

The book touches upon the basics of reporting and editing. But this is not all about this book. This is an original effort to produce a document in Indian context, a publication which takes you inside an Indian newspaper, its editorial department, its news room, its reporting section and so on. Most of the things written here are in fact the experiences of the author and so you will find nothing bookish in this book. And this is its USP.

I hope that this book will be of great utility to media students as it covers full spectrum of the topics in reporting and editing, taught in most of the undergraduate programmes in our country. An attempt has been made to reach out the students in their language and expression so that they could relate themselves with the book and its contents. No doubt the response of students will determine the success of this attempt.

AUTHOR

Acknowledgements

I have travelled a long way practicing and teaching media close to three decades. When I joined the media industry in December 1979, I had little idea of my role as a media practitioner. And when I turned to media academics about a decade ago I had little clarity about my role as a media educator and trainer. Having combined my experience and learning in the two activities—industry and academics, I find in me a changed person. This person has a clear vision, an understanding not only about his role but a determination of achieving some definite goals.

I owe to many people for my evolution; these include my seniors, colleagues and juniors who came across at different points of time. Some gave me formal lessons, some others told me the tricks of the game informally. There are few who did not do anything formally or informally but I chose to take inspiration from them. I feel obliged to all such people who have immensely contributed to my making.

I realised it quite late that book writing plays a major role in the making of an academic person. I was not inclined to book writing also for the reason that I always looked at me as an educator rather than an academician. Finally, having realised rules of the game I wrote my first book "Right to Information and Freedom of Press" in the year 2003. I also contributed to two books, one on trends in Hindi journalism and the other on the electronic media. The year 2006 proved significant as I edited two books, one on satellite radio and the other on communication theories. And the latest book on reporting and editing is in your hands.

I express my deepest gratitude to Prof. Pradeep Mathur, the media stalwart who has influenced my career the first and foremost as a journalist and then as a journalism teacher. I am grateful to Prof. Devesh Kishore, Dean, School of Journalism and Mass Communication, IMS, NOIDA and former Head-Education and

Training, EMPC, IGNOU who have provided me a great support in media education.

I owe a lot to Prof. J.S. Yadav, Director, International Media Institute, Gurgaon and former Director, Indian Institute of Mass Communication (IIMC) who provided me the opportunity of working at IIMC. I can never forget mentioning the name of Prof. Surinder J. Sharma, former Principal of Kamala Nehru College (DU), who gave me a free hand in organising and conducting teaching and other academic activities at her college for almost a decade.

One person who has influenced me most in recent years is Prof. Ashok Ogra, Director of Apeejay Institute of Mass Communication. It is difficult to believe that a person who has been the Director of Doordarshan and Vice-President of Discovery India can be so modest. Another person who has made an impression on me is Mr. Alok Verma, Director of TV Today Media Institute. He is a visionary who is determined to bring a qualitative change in media education.

Academically what I am today is attributed to Guru Govind Singh Indraprastha University. I have been associated with this university for the past seven years since the time BJ(MC) programme was launched. I have also carried on the responsibility of BJ(MC) Coordinator for three years, also contributing to revision and restructuring of syllabus of this bachelor's degree. All these years I have been seeking inspiration from the Vice-Chancellor Prof. K.K. Aggarwal who is the most dynamic person, I have ever seen in the academic field. And I want to put it on record that Prof. Saroj Aggarwal, Director-Academic Affairs, has made a significant contribution to media education by setting up the Centre for Media Studies and launching PG Diploma in Electronic media and Master of Mass Media on the Kashmire Gate Campus.

My stay for almost five years at Vivekananda Institute of Professional Studies (VIPS) gave me not only an insight into media academics but also in the administration and management of education and training. As Director I was able to do what I had visioned. I feel contended with whatever I could achieve. I express my gratitude to Dr. S.C. Vats, Chairman and Mr. Suneet Vats, Vice-Chairman of VIPS for providing me healthy atmosphere conducive for working.

Five people who actively helped me in completing this book

include Mr. K.K. Sharma, Ms Susmita Bala, Mr. S.D. Tripathi, Mr. Aatish Prashar and Mr. Prince Shadwal. Ms Bala, my wife and colleague, collected bit by bit my notes and her notes to finally convert everything in the form of a book. Mr. Tripathi and Mr. Prashar, my colleagues and friends, helped me in shaping the contents of the book. Prince Shadwal, my son and guide, helped in writing and editing few portions having spared some time from his busy film-making schedule. Mr. Sharma, my colleague and former news editor of *The Times of India*, volunteered to finally go through the made-up pages so as to make the book better editing-wise.

Whatever little contribution I have been able to make for the cause of media education is because of a good team. And the team members Mr. Amit Channa and Mr. Rajeev Panda have given me considerable strength. The most wonderful person I have come across in recent years is Mr. Pawan Koundal, DTP In-charge at VIPS. A unique combination of intelligence, skill and speed he has been instrumental in the accomplishment of many of the tasks undertaken by me. I am also thankful to Mr. Brijendra Singh who has typed many chapters in this book.

How can I forget my friend Mr. Vivek Chaturvedi who made my life miserable by issuing reminders days-after-days, months-after-months, years-after-years. The completion of this book took more than two years and Mr. Chaturvedi never let me sit comfortably during this periods. He put me so much under pressure that I was left with no option except to finish the job despite my entire busy schedule.

I express gratitude to my parents Mr. J.N. Saxena and Mrs. S.M. Saxena whose blessings have led me to success in my professional pursuits. I am also blessed by my mother-in-law Mrs. Shakuntla Kudaisya in my endeavours.

Dr. Ambrish Saxena

Contents

1

Understanding News

There is no single acceptable definition of news because the elements that constitute news are constantly changing, and so are the women and men who select it for print and broadcast. The dramatic social, economic, political and technological changes sweeping the world have a profound impact on what is considered news today just as they have on the readers of newspapers.

What may be news in one community may not be in another. For example, a newspaper in Bangalore may devote a regular section to computers and technology, while one in Ranchi may focus special attention on mines, mineral and natural resources and another in Shimla on tourism.

Reader's interest varies greatly. That is why an event that would rate the front page in a community of ten thousand may not make the calendar of events in a newspaper in a city of five lakh.

What is News?

Whatever new happens forms news. Whenever something unusual, unparallel, extra-ordinary, exceptional event, incident, happening or development takes place, the formation of news begins.

"Everything that happens" or "anything you didn't know yesterday" makes news. It is what people "talk about" or what "readers want to know." It is what a reporter "finds satisfaction in writing" or "what a well-trained editor decides to put in his paper."

Textbook writers have asserted that news is "stimulating information," "anything timely," "a timely report," "the report of an event." It is also described as "literature in a hurry" and "tomorrow's history."

News is not static. It has no rigid rules or framework. It is growing and expanding by a constantly changing direction and by producing the dramatic and unexpected.

Definitions of News

Many scholars have attempted to define news, not always successfully. One of the great city editors of all time, Stanley Walker of the *New York Herald Tribune*, didn't think there was a definition of news. News, he said, "is more unpredictable than the winds. Sometimes it is the repetition with new characters of tales as old as the pyramids, and again, it may be almost outside the common experience."

Although Walker's view of the news dates from the 1920s, his observation is still valid. Much news is routine and repetitive, although even then it may be interesting, even exciting to some people. Births, deaths and marriages are common occurrences, but despite this, they have news value. Families want to see news of the marriage of children and the birth of grandchildren in their local newspapers both as a matter of record and as news of interest to family members and friends. Deaths – obituaries – have high reader interest.

Some news is so strange that we can hardly accept it. News of medical discoveries, revelations of the secrets of the universe unravelled by theoretical physicists, photographs transmitted over millions of kilometers from distant planets—these events strain the imagination. Many people were unable to accept the idea that man actually walked on the moon, even though they were able to see the event on their television screens. Some events are so far outside human experience that they are hard to comprehend.

Joseph Pulitzer, 19th century publisher of the *St. Louis Post-Dispatch* and the *New York World*, had his own definition of news. He instructed his editors and reporters to look for stories that were "original, distinctive, romantic, thrilling, unique, curious, quaint, humorous, odd and apt-to-be talked about." Since Pulitzer's newspapers were highly successful—the World at one time had a circulation of more than a million—Pulitzer must have had a fairly good insight into the nature of news.

Charles A. Dana, editor of the *New York Sun*, had his eye on his readers when he defined news as "anything that will make people talk." Arthur, McEwan, editor of the *San Francisco Examiner* under William Randolph Hearst, is quoted as saying that news is anything that makes a reader say, "Gee whiz!" And Turner Catledge, a former managing editor of *The New York Times*, called news "anything you can find out today that you didn't know before."

John Chancellor, former senior correspondent for *NBC News*, has suggested that news is a chronicle of conflict and change.

Many editors today are more likely to define news in terms of what their readers want to know—in other words, give the readers what they ask for, whether it is local news or features or school football. Newspaper editors are depending more and more on this definition of news to make their newspapers useful to readers. They are using a number of ways of identifying reader preferences, including surveys, focus groups and various forms of contact with individual readers, to get their views on what they want to read in their newspapers.

Some editors define news as information readers ought to have and need to know to get along in this complicated and confusing world. This is a more traditional approach, and it depends on the insight of the editor. But there have always been editors who have known instinctively how to publish a newspaper that readers respond to and buy.

Here is an attempt to define news.

- News is every information received from N = North, E = East, W = West and S = South.
- News is anything timely that interests a number of persons and the best news is that which has the greatest interest for the greatest number.
- News is the timely report of facts or opinions that hold interest or importance or both for a considerable number of people.
- News is usually stimulating information from which the ordinary human being derives satisfaction or stimulation.
- News is a compilation of facts and events of current interest or importance to the readers of the newspaper.
- News is anything and everything interesting about life and materials in all their manifestations.
- News is not the event, it is the account of the events written for people who did not witness it.

- News is any printable story which in the opinion of the editor will interest his readers.
- News is the story of something that has happened or told for the first time.
- News is completely true or at least carries facts that have been presented to the reporter as truth.

Finally, news can be defined in the following manner:

- News is an account of man's changing relationships.
- News is an account of events that disrupt the status quo or have the potential to cause disruption.
- News is an event of community consequence.

Let us recapitulate the salient points of news. The news is:

- Perishable—when the event is understood and the tension is eased off—the news gets less informative and more of history.
- Of interest to a large number of people.
- Of unusual events and happenings.
- What is new to the public.
- An event put forward by a reporter—without a reporter, a news item does not exist.

Despite all these definitions and interpretations, we should remember that the general notion of news varies with people and situations. Despite this various essential points about the significance of news are universally recognised.

Nature of News

The nature or characteristics of news may be discussed likewise—

News–A Report

First, news is a story, report or accounts. At one time it was termed tidings. It may be transmitted person-to-person or by news media. The story may be oral, written, or pictorial in form. In the communication process, news is a message. The sender is a reporter who encodes it. He/she uses words or pictures to share an idea, fact, or problem. He/she is successful if the receiver gets precisely the same meaning as the reporters.

The news story may or may not be satisfactory as a message. For one thing, unless the news source is responsible, it may withhold vital facts or substitute propaganda. At the outset, then, news may not be wholly truthful.

The news editor determines the page and the position on the page for the news story. Similarly, the newscaster by the tone of his/her voice may impress the listener with the importance of the news he/she reports. These are factors in the impact of the message on the receiver.

In the communication process the receiver obviously may be a reader, a listener, or a viewer. He/she decodes the message. If it means the same thing to him/she as it did to the sender, the latter is successful.

Differences in religious, racial and regional backgrounds account for the differences in interest and attitude of news consumers. The hope of every reporter is that his/her story satisfies most of them, most of the time.

Ideas, Events and Problems

Second, news is an account of an idea, event, or problem. Man thinks, and an idea is born. If shared, this idea may become the basis for a new product or service, a new cause or conflict. It may make thinker a martyr, millionaire, or murderer.

People do things—usually together. They come together to attend weddings and funerals, to play games and make money, to discuss politics and worship God. They are thrown together by hurricanes and holocausts. All of these are events.

The ideas, events and problems provide the substance for news. People are concerned with both the causes and the consequences of what they see and feel, think and do. If substantial number of people are concerned, the idea, event, or problem may be news.

News is Real

Third, news is an account of something real. The reporter is not "a post-soaring in the high reason of his/she fancies, with his/her garland and singing robes about him/her." Nor is he/she concerned with fiction and its "softening of fancies and sentiment." The drama he/she reports is that of the real world, not a world created by the playwright.

The reporter is a fact finder. Sometimes he/she fails to get all relevant facts because of antagonism and opposition of news sources. Sometimes he/she fails because he/she does not perceive the relationship or significance of the facts.

As Coleride notes, "facts are not truths." Yet as he added, "The truth depends on, and is only arrived at, by a legitimate deduction from all the facts which are truly material." It is the responsible reporter's task to get the facts that "are truly material" and separate them from those which are not.

News is Current

Fourth, news is current, news is now—plus or minus. From the present, it stretches a little way into the past and into the future. It is a perishable product, unwanted within a matter of minutes, hours or days.

All news is timely. Its timeliness sometimes is more obvious if the reader understands the geographical setting and historical background. News happens not in a vacuum but in the world we live in.

News of any country, for instance, cannot be divorced from the environment which produced it. Sometimes climate accounts for the development of national ideals and attitudes. Sometimes natural resources determine a nation's destiny.

News Interests People

Fifth, news is an account of something that interests people.

What ideas, what events, what problems command public interest? Reporters for printed and news broadcasting media constantly seek the answer to this situation. As times change, the depth of interest in different kinds of news may vary.

Qualities of News

1. *Accuracy:* Accuracy is basic to any news item. When the reporter fails in accuracy, he/she loses credibility. The reporter should cross check the facts and information, figures and names. He/she should also check how names are spelled. People are greatly offended by misspelled names. If the reporter is paraphrasing a speech from a text given to him/her, he/she should not change the meaning

or quote statements out of context. Humours or gossips need to be excluded from the report.

2. *Balance:* Balance in reporting is as important as accuracy. If the reporter is writing about a controversy, he/she should give both sides of the story. When reporting a strike, for instance, give the claim of the authorities and also that of the workers on how far it is successful.

   A story may appear to be imbalanced, and thus biased, if it has too much of government views, or tends to give too much of foreign news which has little relevance to the readers.

3. *Objectivity:* The reporter should not mix his/her opinion in the story. He/she should report only facts and other people's opinions. He/she should be a disinterested observer, reporting events without taking sides.

4. *Clarity:* A story should be easy in understanding. The introductory sentence should be short and in active voice to the maximum extent possible. The ideal length of each para may be three-four lines containing small sentences to facilitate easy comprehension.

5. *Impact:* Whenever a reporter does a news report, he/she should consider the impact the story would have. If a reporter is writing about a dilapidated overused bridge so as to motivate the authorities to take up repairs, he may help avert a tragedy. The reporters must develop a "Nose for news."

News Elements

The qualifications, or elements of news have been interpreted vividly by writers. The intrinsic features are:

1. Conflict (tension, surprise)
2. Progress (triumph, achievement)
3. Disaster (defeat, destruction)
4. Consequence (effect on individuals or community)
5. Prominence (the well-known or famous)
6. Novelty (the unusual, even the bizarre)
7. Human interest (unusual or emotional).

Conflict: Most conflicts are newsworthy to some degree because they disrupt the status quo. Physical conflict is considered newsworthy because it may lead to injury and damage. Violence arouses emotions, not only in the participants, but also in the spectators, and can be of enormous and immediate importance.

War is a classic example of conflict. It will dominate the news. However, a fist flight between two teams at Nehru Hockey Championship played in New Delhi in December, 2005 may rate no more than a single line of type, if that is a game story. But if fans riot after the game, damaging cars, blocking traffic, breaking windows in stores and looting, as has happened on many occasions in India and abroad, particularly in football matches, the story probably will be spread all over page one because of the magnitude of the "conflict."

Wars, Murders and Violent Strikes: Conflicts of a more disruptive nature–always receive space on the front page, which leads critics to complain that newspapers devote too much space to violence. Until recently, other conflicts–political, economic, social, scientific–did not always receive similar attention. However, that has changed, and today the often impassioned debates over the safety of nuclear energy, global warming, protection of the environment and other less violent clashes often are played out on the front pages of newspapers, too.

Progress and Disaster: In conflict, one side usually wins and the other loses. For the routine struggles of life, not generally newsworthy in themselves, shining successes frequently emerge. For example, from quiet laboratories come new inventions, new advances in science and medicine and new devices to improve the quality of life that genuinely represent progress.

Sometimes Progress can Lead to Disaster such was the case with DDT, hailed as a major breakthrough in the control of crop-destroying insects. But after 20 years, it became the subject of major news stories when it was linked to cancer in humans. Saccharin was for years a seemingly harmless substitute for sugar welcomed by diabetics and persons with weight problems. But it, too, became the subject of major news stories when it was linked, in some scientific studies, to cancer. In the US, the Congress even debated banning it. The great promise of nuclear power after the splitting of the atom lost some of its luster due to an accident at the Three

Mile Island nuclear plant in Pennsylvania and nuclear radiation caused by Chernovil plant in the USSR.

Disasters, both natural and man-made, often dominate the news in a community. Take for instance, the Kanishka plane crash caused by Punjab extremists. Tornados and earthquakes strike suddenly. Lives are lost and property worth crores of rupees is damaged. Hundreds, sometimes thousands, of people are displaced. Businesses are closed. The recovery from such a disaster often becomes a story of progress. Take for example, the stories which appeared in newspapers after Tsunami in December, 2004.

Progress can be a new industry that provides jobs and brings crores of rupees into the local community. But it also can be the recovery of a child severely burnt in a house fire.

Consequence: Any event that causes or is capable of causing a sequence of activities that affect many persons is newsworthy. Obviously, certain events are of more consequence than others, and they will receive more space and larger headlines.

It should be noted that all newsworthy events, for whatever other reasons they are newsworthy, have some consequence. Conflicts have consequence. For example, one consequence of the war in Iraq was the problem of caring for the thousands of Kurdish people who were fleeing Iraq to avoid further repression by the Iraqi army.

Prominence: Names make news and big names make bigger news. The "name" must do something or have something done to her or him to be newsworthy. A prominent person may do no more than stop over in the city en route to a national conference to rate a story in the local paper, for example.

What a prominent person says or does often makes news because of its consequences. A nationally known economist's predictions could influence the stock market. A national political leader might enhance a local political candidate's chances for election by joining the local campaign for a dinner or speech.

State-level politicians have been known to fly great distances at enormous costs and considerable inconvenience just to be seen and photographed with the Prime Minister or the party president. They know it is almost certain to rate space in the state's newspapers or on local television. Prominent individuals are newsworthy for the same reason a political conference or a summit meeting of world leaders is newsworthy. The potential is there for significant change that makes news.

Novelty: Readers and editors alike are attracted by novelties in the news. They are a staple in all newspapers: the two-headed calf, the 50 kg. Pumpkin. The cat that walks 200 kilometers to find its owner who moved to another city. Novel ways of making a living, unusual habits and hobbies, superstitions—anything different—all have strong reader appeal.

The common element is simply that the event or the individual is unusual. For example, many newspapers gave extensive coverage to the legislation passed by Parliament to make reservation in admission compulsory in government-aided educational institutions in December 2006. This Act is bound to adversely affect the prospects of general category students.

Human Interest: Many stories that appear in newspapers at first glance do not seem to be news because they do not meet the tests of conflict, consequence, progress or disaster. Generally they are called "human interest" or "feature" stories. These stories may be about a famous author's battle with depression or a 105-year old man marrying a 90-year-old woman six decades after he had proposed her. There are hundreds of such stories in newspapers everyday. They have broad reader appeal.

Some events and individuals lend themselves more readily than others to human interest treatment. They may lack the basic values that would make them a news story, yet they have special qualities that have reader appeal.

Often, major news events result in a variety of human interest stories. Take reference to stories that appeared in newspapers after serial bomb blasts in New Delhi. On the eve of Deepawali in 2005. stories about the driver of the DTC bus who dared to defuse a bomb to save the lives of bus passengers and then fought for his life in AIIMS hospital caught everybody's attention. Newspapers even covered the pregnancy of the driver's wife and the birth of his child.

Where to Look for News

Reader's interest is mentioned also as an essential factor determining news value of an event. The items wherein readers take interest are listed below:

- Unusual events.

- Mysteries and the unknown.
- Prominent people, places and things.
- Statements of persons in authority.
- Whatever people are talking about.
- Ideas new to the reader.
- All events that affect the lives of readers.
- Conflicts between man and man, man and nature.
- Violence, calamities, disasters.
- Tragedies and comedies that will interest the imagination of the readers.
- Health, environment, science, money, crime, sex, humour, human interest, food, minorities, weather, entertainment.

2

News Value

How do you determine whether a current idea, event or problem is news? How do you recognise news? How can you make a distinction between news and non-news? How can you be sure that the news provided by you will interests readers, listeners or viewers?

To answer these questions, we have to examine the news value. These may be termed as appeals, factors, determinants or criteria of news.

Determinants of News

The factors on which a news report needs to be tasted are:

1. Timeliness.
2. Proximity.
3. Size.
4. Importance.
5. Personal benefit.

1. *Timeliness*

When is an idea, event, or problem news? When it is news sometimes. More often there may be something new about it—something expected, something unexpected.

Months used to separate the New World and the Old World two centuries ago. Now only minutes do. News moved slowly over the ocean waves, but it moves fast over the air waves. So news perishes more quickly now.

Today, news may travel with the speed of light. It may be

reported by broadcast media immediately after the happening. Broadcast media disseminate the news first but it cannot always tell what it means. Accordingly, printed news media excels in expository and interpretative journalism.

When does news cease to be news? Broadcast newsmen by noon may reject a news item they reported several hours earlier. Reporters of print media concern themselves mainly with the frequency of editions or issues. Fresh news becomes stale in less than a day for a daily, a week for a weekly, a month for a monthly.

Timeliness alone, of course, does not make news. The child's first tooth or his first step may interest the family or friends, not news media. News must interest enough people to make it worth printing or broadcasting.

When did it happen? When will it happen? Again and again the reporter asks these questions. The answer often helps him to determine whether an idea, event, or problem is timely enough to interest the public he/she serves.

2. *Proximity*

"Nearest-dearest." So runs an old German proverb. There is some truth in it, so far as news is concerned. We are more interested in a fire next door, murder down the street, a wedding at a local church, or an accident in the town than similar events a thousand kilometers away.

Nearness, however, is not what it once was. At least, nobody is isolated. What once was far, now may seem to be near in an age when people are setting up their own satellites into space, and attempts are being made to set up colonies of human beings on the moon or the mars.

Even in one city—New Delhi, for example, the emphasis on local news will vary. The potential readers may be the same, but the actual readers are different, hence, have a different pattern of interest so far as the nearness of news is concerned.

Both timeliness and proximity are important measures of news. Although they alone do not make an event or individual automatically newsworthy, in combination with events that have other news values they can help determine newsworthiness.

An accident today that held up local rush-hour traffic for two hours is more timely than one that happened even 24 hours before and will rate more attention in a newspaper. That same accident is more newsworthy because it happened locally than a similar one that held up rush-hour traffic in the state capital 200 kilometres away.

3. *Size*

Timeliness and nearness are important in news, but neither when nor where often is so important as the what and the who. The reporter, therefore, may ask, "What makes this story big? Who makes this story big?"

The prominence of men and women also determines the magnitude of the story. The PM or Minister plays cricket, and you can read all about this in the newspaper. You play cricket, nobody takes notice unless you achieve something big.

The noted and notorious get more space than ordinary people. The celebrity fractures a rib or argues with his wife in public he/she gets into the news.

Figures are factors in determining the size of a news story. The reporter finds out how many persons are involved or affected. If only a few, his story may be short; if many are concerned, his story may be longer.

Consider these stories: accidents—number of persons killed or injured or killed; disasters—value of property destroyed; competitive games—final score; robbery—value of stolen goods; business—profit or loss.

Size may be measured in terms of unusualness. If any idea, event or problem is odd, unusual, it may get into the news. Obviously the size of an idea, event, or problem is important in determining how much space in print or time on the air it should be given.

4. *Importance*

The successful reporter has a built-in vision which tells him which ideas, events, and problems are important and are, therefore, news. The important story is not an isolated idea, event, or problem. Its timeliness, nearness and size alone may not make it important. Yet it may be the result of a significant cause or the cause of a significant result.

Take a simple remark: "I do not choose to fight election", if made by a local leader, it would be of slight consequence. If it is made by former prime minister Atal Bihari Vajpayee, it will become news. The announcement made by Mr. Vajpayee at the BJP's convention in Mumbai in December 2005 became important because this would mean that Mr. L.K. Advani would be the prime ministerial candidate if the BJP could emerge victorious in the next elections. It would also have been interpreted that after Advani quitting BJPs president's post, Atal's announcement will open doors for the second rank leaders to take over the reign of the party.

News of today is rooted in the news of yesterday. The reporter looks for these roots in local, state, national and world history. He looks for them, in the history, labour, management, farming, science, religion, culture and government.

Readers, listeners, and viewers are concerned with (*a*) when of news to know whether it is timely, (*b*) where of the news to know whether it is near, (*c*) size of the news to know whether the what or whom in the news makes it big. But they also are interested in these questions (*d*) Why? (*e*) How?

Newsweek asserts that because of public interest in these questions, its philosophy is: "To report the news in depth; to probe the news for meaning; to project the news for probable consequences; to divorce opinion from fact."

Much that we term interpretative reporting today consists of an answer to these two questions: Why? How? In some instances, the reporter may get the answer by a single telephone call. In others, his investigation and analysis may continue indefinitely.

5. *Personal Benefit*

For immediate benefit, we read news that gives us pleasure; softness, some call it. Others say that these stories are "effective" in that they appeal to our feelings and emotions.

For immediate enjoyment, the reader is always interested in reading the humorous human interest story. Other stories promptly evoke sympathy, or anger. Still others satisfy our curiosity or give us security.

What happens when the reader reads the story of an accident, disaster, or crime? True he/she is curious about what happened. Then, he/she is concerned whether someone he/she knows may be affected.

The reader's fear grows as he/she notes that the news occurred in his own neighbourhood. It diminishes and disappears when he/she discovers that nobody he/she knows is involved. Relaxed and reassured, he/she feels secure.

Yet as the reader continues to read, he/she may vicariously enjoy the experience of the fireman who rescues children from a blazing school or of the detective who records the conversation of a top leader of Samajwadi Party by tapping his phone.

The news consumer recognises delayed benefits as well as immediate benefits. He/she knows he/she must face reality and attempt to solve the problems imposed on him/her. So, he/she reads stories that relate to the decisions he/she eventually must take.

Parents with children in school often take an interest in education news. They hear of schools in which there is the double-shift schedule. They may take steps promptly to prevent such a development in their own schools.

What Greeley said is true. Today—as a century ago—the news consumer reads what interests him/her. This interest has its origin in his expectation of some immediate or some delayed benefit.

This is the test for the typical news story: how does it benefit the reader? As the reader goes through a newspaper, he/she by-passes stories which do not interest him/her, considers those which do.

One caution the reporter may take too narrow a view of news when he/she considers personal benefits to the news consumer. The reader has an almost instable curiosity, and he/she considers it to his/her benefit to satisfy this curiosity.

Obviously, then, the reader may enjoy news of a football game, though he/she does not care which team wins. He/she may read about shares yet has no money to invest. He/she may study foreign affairs-or some news not related to his professional activities—simply because he/she likes to be well informed.

Thus, news consumer, though he/she may not realise it, feels that it is to his/her benefit to be well informed. Accordingly, the reporter who attempts a neat and narrow classification of news on the basis of immediate or delayed benefits may be in for a surprise.

Other Determinants of News Value

We have discussed five determinants of news value. But there are other factors too which are considered important. A lot depends on editors and proprietors as to how they define or interpret news value.

News Policy

If a trainee reporter accepts, first, the definition of news and second, the elements of news and the news value, he/she may be under the impression that news everywhere is the same. But it is not. Why? News policies differ.

Who presents the news? The "Who" may be a newspaper, news magazine, business paper or religious publication. It may be a radio or television channel. But who are finally the approving authorities? Obviously, the editor.

Every news media organisation has its editorial policy finalised by the editor. And the editor decides the policy keeping in view the political, business or other interests of the proprietor besides the larger interests of the people and the society.

Policies also differ because news media differ as to the:

(*a*) Basic concept.
(*b*) Content pattern.
(*c*) Space allocation.
(*d*) Journalistic treatment.

Hence, every news in a publication has to be tasted on this policy. It can get a place in the columns of that publication if it is in harmony with the policy.

Sex

Many editors consider sex a news value. This is specially true when it is coupled with prominence. The extensive coverage given to the second marriage of film actor Amir Khan which was soleminised in December 2005 is an example. The same month a sexually explicit CD of BJP General Secretary Sanjay Joshi rocked the news media which ultimately resulted in his resignation. The casting couch story about Bollywood broken by a TV channel was also a hit among readers and viewers. The sexual exploitation of children by pop star Michel Jackson remained in news till the time he was acquitted of the charge. The news media is filled with many more such examples.

Miscellaneous Values

Stories of animals often are well read, even by people who do not like animals. Write a story critical of cats and hundreds, perhaps even thousands of cat owners will respond with vehemence if not violence. Tell the story of a singing dog and you'll be swamped with requests to do stories about other clever canines. Some editors believe the only story better than an animal story is one that involves an animal and a baby, especially if the animal rescues the baby.

Many other types of stories used in newspapers are not news from the standpoint of such news values as proximity or timeliness. But they are used because they inform or entertain the reader. Stories about current fashions, trends in leisure time activities and unconventional health care fit this category.

Reporters quickly learn, by intuition or applying news values, to recognise news. They also quickly become aware that not everything that happens in a city in a day can be printed, even if it meets all the standard categories of news. From the mass of material gathered daily, only the most important, significant and interesting is offered to the reader.

To know what is the most important, significant and interesting, reporters must know their community and the readers of the newspaper. One of the greatest handicaps a reporter can have is not to know his community and the people who live in it.

News always must be measured for its comparative importance to the reader. Stories must be compared to determine their relative reader appeal, which will influence not only their length, but also where and how they are displayed in the paper. The following factors are generally considered by editors in measuring the relative importance of stories:

- The extent of disruption of the status quo.
- The number of persons affected by the event.
- The nearness of the event.
- The timeliness of the event.
- The extent of the results of the event—its consequence or significance.
- The variety of news values in the event.

Types of News

Generally, reporters and editors do not discuss news values or the relative importance of most stories, although in some cases they may. They merely apply these values instinctively in writing and editing the news. They do, however, recognise and discuss stories in other terms. They talk of "fire stories" or "accident stories," perhaps, or a "meeting", a "speech" or a "murder story" and, always, the "weather" story.

Most newspaper stories fall into well-defined types. Here are the types of stories newspapers generally recognise:

General Types

1. Personals and briefs 2. Speeches, Publications, Interviews 3. Meetings and events	Stories that are classified by a "package" in which they are "wrapped" rather than the content or subject-matter

Simple Types

4. Illness, deaths, funerals 5. Fires and accidents 6. Seasons and weather 7. Crime	Stories that generally require little interpretative writing by the reporter

Complex Types

8. Courts, trials, lawsuits 9. Government and politics 10. Business, industry, agriculture, labour 11. Education, research, science 12. Religion philanthropy, promotion	Stories that generally require interpretation from the reporter's background of specialised information

Special Types

13. Lifestyles (including social events and consumer news) 14. Sports 15. Entertainment (films, television, popular music, art, theatre, criticism) 16. Editorials and Editorial columns 17. Interpretative and investigative	Stories and articles that encompass a variety of subjects often requiring a high degree of specialised knowledge on the part of the writer

Some story types are more clearly defined than others. Many of the classifications overlap. For example, accidents frequently figure into weather stories, or a trial may also be a political story; a major sporting event could be an economics story. Because the lines of distinction between types of stories are not always clear, the reporter who masters each type will have no trouble writing a story in which several types merge.

Taking into consideration the style of writing, news reports are mainly of two types:

1. Straight news.
2. Descriptive news.

1. *Straight News*

In a straight news, hard facts are presented in an easy and clear style. The distortion of facts, making accusations, deriving conclusions or expression of opinions are not permitted in a straight news.

2. *Descriptive News*

In a descriptive news, the event/incident is thoroughly explained. The surrounding of the incident/event, its background and the possible fall-out are included in such a news item.

Taking into consideration the impact of news on people, and the time and the area covered, news may be classified as:

- Spot news.
- Spread news.

Spot News

The news of an unscheduled, unexpected, instant incident/event is known as spot news. Major accidents, natural calamities, assassination of world leaders etc., fall in this category.

Spread News

The news which affects a good number of people for a long time is treated as spread news. Such kind of news occupy major space in a newspaper.

Taking the importance of an event/incident into consideration, news may be grouped as:

1. Most important news.
2. Important news.
3. Less important news.

Depending on the nature of news and their style of writing, news may be classified as:

1. Thought based news.
2. Expression based news.
3. Research based news.
4. Sensation based news.
5. Personality based news.

With an intention to ensure a smooth working in the editorial set-up of a newspaper, news may be categorised as :

1. Local news.
2. District news.
3. State news.
4. National news.
5. International news.

1. *Local News:* News of the place from where a newspaper is published is treated as local news.
2. *District News:* News from the districts which fall in the main circulation area of a newspaper is called district news.

3. *State News*: News from different states of the country are known as state news, like states level news from UP, MP, Bihar, Rajasthan, etc.
4. *National News:* News which has a national perspective and remain equally important to whole of the country is treated as national news.
5. *International News:* News from different parts of the world fall in the category of international news. Such kind of news items originate from a place outside the country.

On the basis of subject, time/period, place and editing style, news may be put in the following four categories:

1. *Subject:* News on different subjects are grouped differently; subjects likely political, scientific, commercial, sports etc.
2. *Time/Period:* The time of the happenings is important to decide the date value of news. The latest news is always preferred.
3. *Place:* The place where an incident/event happens is always important. More than one news item can be clubbed depending on the place of occurrence.
4. *Editing Style:* News items may be grouped as variety news and developing news whenever the issue of the editing style is dominating. Some scholars have classified news as:
    1. Diary news.
    2. Hot news.

Diary News: The news of the scheduled events/incidents is known as diary news. The news of functions, seminars, public meetings, sessions of Parliament and State Legislatures etc. fall under this category.

Hot News: The news of unexpected and unscheduled events/ incidents is treated as hot news. The news reports of major accidents, natural calamities and assassinations of important persons etc., fall under this category.

Hard Vs Soft News

The most pertinent classification of news is hard news and soft news. Hard news is the serious news like fires, accidents, murders, disasters, deaths, the results of elections, the results of battles, the outcome of wars or the famine. Hard news includes news of severe weather: hurricanes and tornadoes, earthquakes, floods and other natural calamities. Soft news is the light stuff: features, human interest stories, news of engagements and weddings, sports, leisure activities and entertainment.

Hard News: Every newspaper is supposed to cover all important happenings of the day. Thus, the news which no newspaper can afford to miss is treated as hard news.

- Hard news is mostly event-centred. It is a narration of an event or happening.
- The Hard news items are centred on 'What, When, Where and Why."
- A broadsheet daily covers mainly the Hard news—i.e., all important happenings of the day.
- Hard news has a date value. No newspaper can afford to miss it or hold it.

Example: Report of an accident, natural calamity, disaster, public meeting, govt. formation, session of Parliament, introduction of ministers.

Soft News: The less important happenings of the day may be published or left out by a newspaper depending upon the space available on different pages. The news of such happenings is known as soft news.

Besides, every newspapers publishes some exclusive news. This kind of news also falls under the category of soft news.

- Soft news is not event-centred, though it can sometimes appear in a newspaper along with a hard story.
- Soft news is more of an analysis, reasons, background and interpretation.
- It deals with the lighter side of the life and is not heavy like hard news.
- Soft news doesn't have a date value in most of the cases.
- Soft news is becoming a very important segment of the daily newspaper since readers are not always interested in mere accounts of events.

Example: How a small child survived even after two days of accident? Effect of CAS on TV viewing in India.

News Vs Information

The relationship between information and news is also vital for the understanding of a reporter. The following is an attempt to make out a distinction between the two.

1. Information is the basic raw material and news is the finished product made of that information.
2. What the source provides to the reporter is information and what the reporter provides to the reader is news.
3. What the reporter collects while doing a coverage is information, and what the reporter finally presents before the reader is news.
4. Information can be useful, relevant and topical. It may be worthless, irrelevant, and even misleading. Hence, a reporter must test the information before putting it in a news report.
5. After receiving the information, a reporter has to make sure of the following:
   (*a*) Whether it is true and accurate.
   (*b*) Whether it is useful for the people.
   (*c*) Whether the source providing the information is genuine and credible.
6. A reporter has three choices before him:
   (*a*) Either to accept the information for use.
   (*b*) Or to reject it as not desired.
   (*c*) Or to use it selectively.
7. Information can flow from anywhere but news can flow only from a newspaper or any other news organisation.

Information Turning in News

A commuter rings up a newspaper office and provides the following information to a reporter :

1. An accident has taken place at Motinagar chowk.
2. The DTC bus jumped the red light.
3. It rammed into a car.

4. Five people injured. They were seated in the car.
5. The accident took place at 10 in the morning.

After receiving this information, the reporter will contact the police and DTC officials and file the following report:

Today during the peak morning hours, a DTC bus rammed into a car at Motinagar chowk causing severe injuries to the five occupants of the car. The injured were rushed to Deen Dayal Hospital.

According to eyewitness account, the bus jumped the red light to cause the accident but the DTC officials denied the charge. The police officials failed to verify the charge and said that the matter was being investigated.

3

Report Writing

The news covered by a correspondent and subsequently written in a proper manner is known as a news report/item/story. Since a news report is communicated to the audience in the narrative manner as a story is told to the people, a news report is referred as a news story in the field of journalism.

The Simple News Lead

News writing is narrative writing turned upside down. A narrative prose writer places the major emphasis on the end of the story, carefully building up a climax. The news writer does the exact opposite. In news stories, the most important fact is told first.

The two styles of writing also differ in other aspects. News writing style calls for short words, short sentences, short paragraphs and a generous use of quotes. Sentences and paragraphs in narrative writing tend to be longer, and the choice of words often is more expansive. (Both, however, adhere to the standard rules of grammar, punctuation and sentence structure).

This example will illustrate the difference in the two writing styles:

Ordinary Narrative Style

Mr. Gopinath, senior partner in New Delhi Auditors, an accounting firm with 16 offices across the country, left his office in the Chandralok, Janpath about 7:30 last night. He took the elevator to the underground parking where he had parked his car when he arrived at his office in the morning. As he approached his Sonata Car, two men came rushing out of the shadows and attempted to grab his briefcase and car keys. In the struggle that followed, Gopinath was struck in the face, but he kicked one of his assailants. The other one pulled a small revolver from his jacket pocket and fired three shots at the accountant. One bullet struck Gopinath in the left forearm and the other two went through the car's windshield. Both men fled on foot when they heard the elevator open. Several other occupants of the building rushed to Gopinath's aid. One alerted the building safety office on his cellular telephone and all exits to the building and parking were sealed off. A PCR van rushed to the scene in response to a call from the building security staff. Police and guards searched all five floors of the building but were unable to find the two men. Gopinath was taken to RML hospital where he underwent a two-hour operation to remove the bullet and repair damage to the muscle in his left forearm. He is resting comfortably, a hospital spokesman said. Police said robbery and car theft apparently were the motives for the attack. Gopinath said he had never seen either of his assailants before. And the only thing he had in his briefcase, besides some unfinished tax forms, was half a sandwich left over from his lunch.

The News Story

A senior auditor was shot in the arm last night by two men who attempted to rob him and steal his car from the parking of a building at Janpath, police said.

Mr. Gopinath, senior partner in New Delhi Auditors, was wounded when he grappelled with his assailants in the underground parking of the Chandralok building.

The assailants fled on foot when several other occupants of the building got off the elevator in the parking.

Gopinath underwent a two-hour operation at RML Hospital to remove the bullet and repair damages to the muscles in his left forearm. He is in a stable condition.

Gopinath told police the two men attacked him as he was opening the door to his car at 7:30 p.m. In the scuffle, he kicked one of the assailants. The other one fired three shots, one hit Gopinath in the left forearm and the other two went through the windshield of his Sonata car.

Police sealed off all entrances to the parking and made a floor-by-floor search but were unable to locate the assailants.

Gopinath said he had never seen either of the men before. He told police he thought they were trying to steal his car and snatch his briefcase.

The briefcase, he said, contained some unfinished income-tax forms and half a sandwich left over from lunch.

The difference between the two stories is immediately apparent. The events in the prose story are recounted in a chronological order. In the news story, they are arranged, from beginning to end, in order of their newsworthiness. The shooting of Gopinath and the escape of his assailants are the two most newsworthy events of the story. They are the first things told in the news story. In the narrative version, they are presented well into the story.

In ordinary narrative, the entire story becomes clear gradually, building up the climax. In the news story the most newsworthy fact is flashed before the reader in the opening sentence—the lead. The object of the lead is to tell the reader as quickly as possible what the story is about. This generally is done in a single sentence or two that form a single paragraph.

The narrative story will include all the minute details. The news story generally omits details or includes them in a final paragraph. This style of writing is usually called the "Inverted pyramid" because the "bottom," or end or climax, of a story told in a chronological order is inverted and placed at the top of the news story.

The style is an outgrowth of the World War, when correspondents were restricted from sending long stories by telegraph. To make certain all the essential information was sent, writers gave the most important facts first. Although the style has been refined considerably since then, most basic news stories still follow that pattern.

Inverted Pyramid

We start the normal story at its beginning and trace it step by step to its conclusion. The newspaper conversion of the lead, however, makes the news story an exception to this general rule. This lead demands that in most instances, the news story begins with its climax. Two reasons lie behind this formula:

- The desire to catch the reader's attention.
- The desire to save the reader's time.

Even a senior journalist has to think twice while writing a lead. While covering a story, he/she carries in the back of his/her mind the consciousness that a suitable beginning for the story must somehow evolve within him/her. He/she keeps a watch for those elements or element in the assignment which would make a good lead.

After incorporating the most important fact of an event/ incident in the lead, the reporter proceeds further with the remainder of the story by selecting the next most important fact or detail, then the next important, the next important after that and so on till he/she reaches the least important phase of all.

Guided by the reporter's idea of the importance of facts or details, the news story assumes graphically the shape of an inverted pyramid.

The most important element of the story is given the greatest prominence, the next most important is given somewhat less prominence, and so on down the story. The most important element remains on the topmost portion which is widest in an inverted pyramid. The story narrows down in importance and so the inverted pyramid.

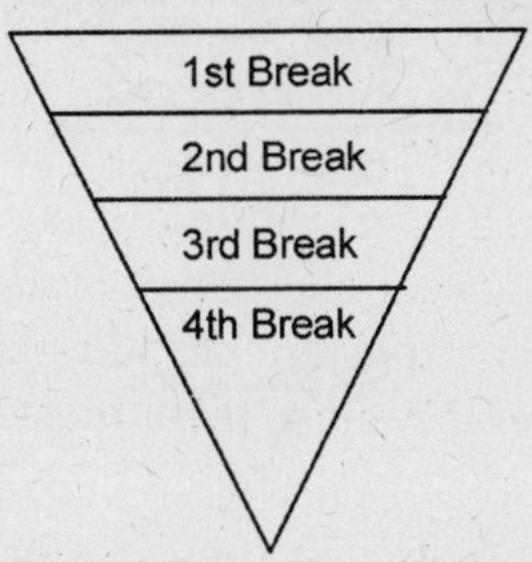

These steps can be followed in inverted pyramid.

1st Break	:	intro (Five Ws and One H)
2nd Break	:	Explanatory details
3rd Break	:	Descriptive details
4th Break	:	Additional points
Conclusion	:	Leaving the thread

The inverted pyramid can also be shown in the following manner:

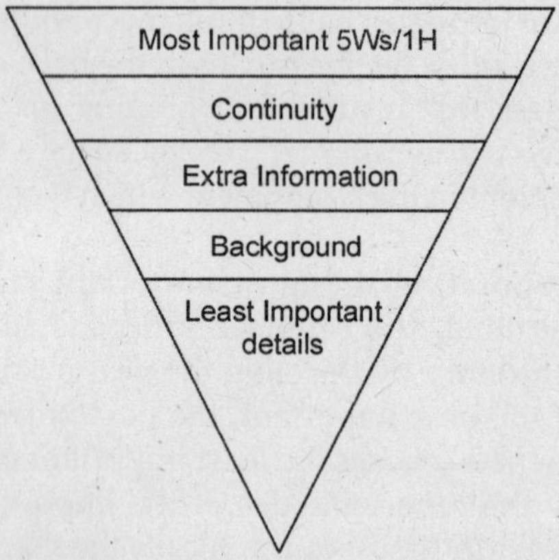

Here is another style of inverted pyramid.

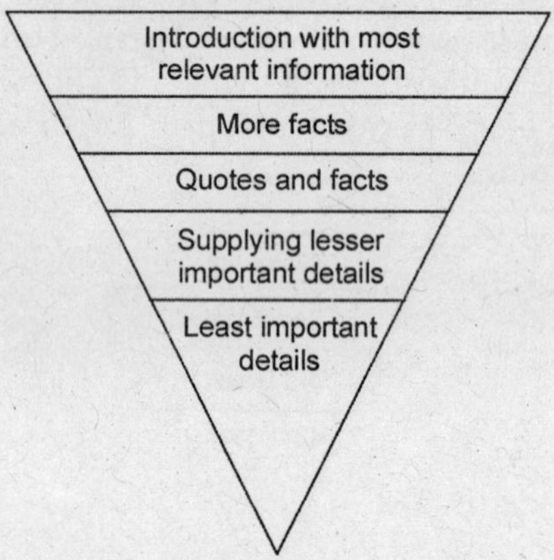

The inverted pyramid style of news story writing is of great advantage in editing. Whenever there is a need to shorten the story, the last paras (which are of least importance in an inverted pyramid style) may be cut down. This is, in fact, the technique's chief virtue from a sub-editor's point of view.

It also helps sub-editors who can easily discard as much of the story from the tail without affecting its readability.

Most newspapers receive far more news than they have space

to publish. Stories must often undergo a last minute shortening if important late news demands inclusion. The sub-editor concerned knows that he can slice one, two or three paragraphs off any story written in the inverted pyramid style without depriving the reader of the story's chief elements.

Example: From *The Hindustan Times,* New Delhi.

Fire Destroys Property Worth Several Lakhs

NEW DELHI, Nov. 11 (HTC)—A major fire gutted the first floor of a commercial building in the Chandni Chowk area of the walled city this morning. Barring a fireman, who sustained minor burn injuries, no other casualties have been reported.

At least 10 offices and stores and property valued at several lakhs were destroyed in the fire, which damaged the first floor of Rajalal Bhawan, an old single storey building next to the Moti Cinema Hall compound on Diwan Hall Road. Though the cause of the fire has not yet been confirmed, fire personnel said that a short circuit might have led to the accident.

According to the Fire Department, the fire must have started around 9.30 – 10.00 a.m., but was detected later as all the commercial establishments in the building were closed, "We got the first call at 10.25 a.m. Thirty-two fire tenders were pressed into service.

Benefits of Inverted Pyramid

According to Clark, a famous journalist of the *New York Times* "Inverted Pyramid method provides you the climax in the beginning of the story."

Daniel, journalist of *Guardian* says, "In inverted pyramid method, one should keep in mind that lead should not be of more than 35 words, otherwise it gives a bad impression."

Advantages

1. Complete story idea is put in the lead.
2. Story can be edited from the bottom and makes no effect.
3. Giving headline becomes easy.
4. A para can be inserted in between the story.

Disadvantages

1. Not good for people who love reading.
2. Discourages habit of reading.
3. Story seems to be never ending.
4. Kills the excitement behind the story.

The Five Ws

Rudyard Kipling once paid—I have six honest serving men. They taught me all I know. Their names are what, why and when and how, where and who.

Every news story should answer the questions: Who? What? When? Where? Why? And, for good measure, How? They should be answered as quickly as possible for the reader.

Some writers still attempt to cram answers to all these questions into the opening sentence, which frequently results in 60 to 70 words of almost incomprehensible prose. For example, a lead containing answers to all these questions might come out like this:

Mr. Gopinath, a New Delhi accountant, is in stable condition at RML Hospital today, recovering from a gunshot wound in his left forearm which he suffered while struggling with two assailants who tried to rob him and steal his car from an underground parking at Janpath Market at about 7:30 last night as he was leaving the building where his office is located.

Who?	Gopinath, a New Delhi accountant
What?	Was shot in the left forearm
When?	About 7:30 last night
Where?	The underground parking at Chandralok building
Why?	Two men were trying to rob him and steal his car and he resisted.
How?	With a small revolver.

But it has 68 words and it is ponderous. It would have been even longer if the fact that the assailants fled or the source—in this case, the police—had been included.

Conventional Lead

As narrated above, the old concept of lead writing requires answers to all five Ws and one H in the lead itself. Even in modern journalism, an attempt is made to honour this concept by showing adherence to five Ws and one H formula.

This lead wraps the story into a small, neat bundle by attempting to answer all or most facts of the news. All 5 Ws and one H are accommodated in the lead.

Who? What? Where? When? Why? How?

For Example

"Three young Okhla residents, Sandeep, Ramesh and Suresh, were killed last night when their car collided with a truck on the road connecting Nehru Place to Kalkaji temple, crushing them under the speeding wheels of the truck."

The lead here answers:

What happened?	An accident occurred
When it happened?	Last night
Who were involved?	Sandeep, Ramesh and Suresh
Where it happened?	Near Kalkaji temple road
Why it happened?	Collision of a car with a truck
How it happened?	Crushed under the wheels of the truck.

In the above example of 'lead' the event is fully summarised. But it is , clumsy and without punch. Then what should be done to make the lead catchy?

Modern Lead

In the modern time, it is observed that answering all five Ws and one H makes the lead heavy. The new trend is to make the lead less overloaded with facts and words. It is better to accommodate only important Ws and/or one H in the lead. Ideally there should be not more than 30 words in a lead.

As the managing editor of *The New York Times* once said—"We feel it is no longer necessary and perhaps it never was, to wrap up in one sentence or paragraph all the traditional five Ws and One H."

Thus, newspapers have changed their approach to lead with the change in the style of reporting. An up-to-date version of the above mentioned accident story might run like this:

"Three men were killed last night at Kalkaji temple road when a truck hit their car."

The move to a simpler lead pattern doesn't make the task of the news writer easier. He can no more follow the readymade formula of answering all five Ws and one H in the lead. But he is required to make a selection.

Today's new lead formula is more demanding than the old one. From among the five elements of news, the reporter should choose the one that is most relevant to report the event. Other elements are to be presented in subsequent paragraphs or to be left out altogether.

Playing Up a W

Simpler, shorter leads can be written that feature the single W that is more important than the others. Occasionally, it may be difficult to select a single W as the most important, especially if a news event is complex. However, there are some examples of how one news element can be featured effectively:

The "Who" Lead: If the "Who" is a prominent person or place or thing, it is usually the feature of the lead. The name alone attracts the reader's attention. Unless one of the other elements is particularly outstanding, the "big name" comes first as in these examples:

- Delhi Chief Minister Sheila Dikshit escaped unhurt when her car collided with a DTC bus in West Delhi today.
- President Bush on Wednesday offered to help the Iraq overcome its financial problems by writing off a $1 billion line of credit.
- Shahrukh Khan is back again. "I have fully recovered and am fit to play my second innings," announced the film star at a press conference.

A "Who" lead frequently is used even when a person is not widely known. In such cases, it is usually the person's occupation, sex, age or other distinguishing characteristics that are featured.

- A former ABS teacher went on trial on drug charges in a criminal court today and immediately was given the bad news that his supplier had pleaded guilty and agreed to testify against him.

- A Mumbai teenager freed on bond on murder charges was arrested on Friday on charges of armed robbery in the busy market of the city earlier this month.
- A senior citizen of the city was sentenced to six years in prison today for shooting a woman he allegedly pursued for 37 years and claimed to love.

The "What" Lead: If an event or action is more important than the persons involved, that element should be featured.

- Golkunda Express train hit a bus at an unmanned railway crossing near Secundrabad, killing six people and injuring 30.
- A new law requiring colleges and universities to reveal their crime statistics will give students and parents a look at just how safe the nation's campuses really are.
- A moderate earthquake shook Himalayan region early yesterday, killing 19 people and injuring about 300, panicking thousands and destroying part of a small town, officials said.

The "Where" Lead: On occasion, the "Where" is significant enough to overshadow the other W's. If it is a place where half-a-dozen accidents have taken place the same day or in a week or if it is happening in front of the house of a VIP and the people involved are less important from the point of news value, 'where' element is given importance.

In case of a particular thing happening at a particular place, the place becomes important. Here is an example:

- Many parts in east Delhi plunged into darkness for several hours following power failure last night.

Sometimes, reporters make use of 'where' to establish a mood or recreate a scene.

- The band in the Indira Gandhi Stadium strikes up a stirring march, and suddenly 8,000 people are on their feet, all eyes closed to enjoy the moment.

- Atomic Energy Commission has confirmed that there was no–radiation leak from any facility at the Indira Gandhi Centre for Atomic Research at Kalpakkam even though a team from the Atomic Energy Regulatory Board would certify the safety of the nuclear power plant before it recommences operations.

The "When" Lead: "When" is automatically included in most leads, but it is not often the most important feature. There are some instances when the writer decides to emphasise "When" in the lead, as in these examples:

- The traders of Uttar Pradesh will observe a state-wide bandh on the Independence Day to protest unwarranted curbs on their commercial activities. The decision was taken at a joint meeting of different traders' unions in Kanpur today.
- It was a black Sunday, Hundreds of people sleeping in the hangover of hectic Christmas Day 'celebrations were washed away by thundering Tsunami waves in many countries of South-East Asia, including India. The festivities of the last week of the year vanished as tourists in the sea resorts had to flee to safer places for their lives.
- In New Delhi, the Republic Day parade was over. Dozens of tiny tots were passing through the streets with national flags in their hands in a small town in Gujarat. The whole nation was paying tributes to the founding fathers on this auspicious day. But the destiny had something else in its store. The earthquake shook the earth and the tiny tots like many others in Gujarat were taken away by destiny. For the kith and kin, the Republic Day became a mourning day.

The "Why" Lead: The motive or cause of an event sometimes can be the most important element of a story to feature in the lead. Writers may avoid it because this could make for a long lead. Here are a couple of examples of strong, direct, "Why" leads:

- Saying cigarettes kill hundreds of thousands of Indians each year, an international group of doctors have declared war on smoking in a region where the Wills man still rides proudly.

- The driving of bus by the cleaner is said to be the reason for its collision with a car, killing four people in the capital today.
- To create fund for the rehabilitation of earthquake victims, the government has decided to impose a surcharge of five per cent on income-tax-payers.

The "How" Lead: There could be cases where importance will have to be given to the manner or process of the incident or happening than the other elements. This demands description. Although it can be an effective device, the "How" lead is not used as often as the others. Some reporters shy away from it because it can become too wordy. Here are several examples:

- Using fraudulent application and identification papers, thousands of people from Bangladesh who entered the North-East illegally, are seeking amnesty.
- The officials said they have been overwhelmed by fraudulent applications listing phony addresses and employment data.
- Bogus claims made by members of the Employees State Insurance Scheme (ESI) having obtained medical certificates by influencing the doctors have resulted in a loss of over Rs. 1.25 crore to the State ESI Corporation.

Crowding the Lead

The lead of a simple news story should not say too much or too little. In this type of story the best leads generally are those that emphasise a single W. If other Ws deserve attention, they can be emphasised in the second paragraph.

The shorter the lead, the better, as long as it tells the reader the most important details. Newsworthy details not included in the lead will fall properly into the body of the story. If no single element in the story seems to stand out above the others, reporters generally write a "Who" lead:

- A 32-year-old resident who murdered a car salesman

> during a test drive was sentenced to life imprisonment by the High Court today.
> Sampat was convicted of murder, robbery and theft of a motor vehicle and driving a car without the owner's consent.

Although the "Who" lead certainly is adequate, it also tends to be dull. Reporters should always examine the facts of a story carefully before writing to find an angle that will make the story more interesting. The example cited above has the potential of being more interesting if the writer had not treated it as a routine "Who" lead.

Often reporters are faced with determining who is the "Who" in a story, especially when two or more individuals or groups are involved. For example, if the police chief and the CM have a heated verbal exchange on the deteriorating law and order situation, the reporter has to determine which of the two is to be the "Who" in the lead. In this case, of course, the reporter might evade the issue and use both by writing: "Two public figures clashed today..." However, the reporter could have focused on the person who apparently provoked the argument.

Complete Reporting

Reporters should remember to answer every question the reader might have about a story. The reader should not have to make a phone call after reading a story about an upcoming event to find out what it will cost, if the event is open to the public, if it will be telecast, and when and over what channel. The complete story should give all these details.

It is not enough to identify a person by his or her address if other forms of identification are available. They all should be worked into the story at some point. It is not enough to say, "Fire destroyed the Silverline Manufacturing Company" without telling what the firm manufactured and how many persons worked for it. Incomplete reporting can produce lackluster leads such as:

- Sugarcane producers today asked the Environmental Protection Agency to lift its ban on the pesticides Aldren and Dieldrin to help fight some dangerous insects.

Although that lead is adequate, it really doesn't give the reader any indication of the seriousness of the problem and what it could mean to the state's economy.

Tasting the Lead

There is no single formula for writing leads. Every reporter has to develop his or her own way to measure how adequate the lead is after it is written. No matter what device is used, reporters must never forget that a good lead makes a direct statement of the essential facts of the story. In addition, it must say something to readers in such a way that the reader is hooked on that story and will continue to read beyond the opening sentence.

4

Writing the Lead

The newspaper story in modern society has evolved to meet the requirements of the people on a day-today basis. It relies on the elements of novelty, directness, face and variety and the strives to convey its information in the form most suitable in the changing scenario.

We can divide the newspaper story as it strikes our eye on the page into three parts:

(*a*) The headline.
(*b*) The first paragraph.
(*c*) The remainder of the story.

The Headline: The headline attracts us first. It stands out in bold letters on top of the story. Its message is tense, abrupt and often startling. It makes us stop and look. It tells us quickly what the story is about? Its primary function is to attract our attention. But we will not take up the characteristics, types or writing styles of headlines in this chapter. Headline writing falls in the domain of copyeditor and not the reporter and so we will discuss it at an appropriate place.

The First Paragraph: The first or the opening paragraph assumes utmost importance in a news story. Being the introductory paragraph, it is known as intro in the world of conventional journalism as inherited from the British.

Under influence of American journalism, the term lead has replaced intro in referance to the first paragraph of a news report.

Dateline: The intro or lead of a news report starts with a dateline. It includes the name of the place from where the news has originated followed by a mention of the month and the date.

For example: NEW DELHI, Jan 9—

As the practice goes, all capital letters are used in the name of the place, a coma is put after the place, long names of months are used in short like Oct., Nov., Dec., and Jan. A hyphen or dot is put after the date.

Recently some newspapers have started making experiments with the dateline writing. There are newspapers which mention only the name of the place and not the month and the date in the dateline. Again, there are newspapers which follow the traditional pattern of dateline writing on all pages except local pages wherein neither the name of the place nor the month and the date are mentioned.

Sometimes, datelines are written in a unique fashion as—

- On board the plane, Nov. 14—
  [This happens when PM talks to the reporters on his way back from some foreign trip. A group of selected journalists accompany the PM on such trips.]
- A place near LOC in Kashmir, Nov. 14—
  [This happens when mention of the exact place is not felt desirable from strategic point of view.]

Creditline: In this line, credit is given to the writer of the news item. The writer can be the reporter or correspondent of the newspapers or news agencies. Different newspapers follow different practices as far as mention of the credit line is concerned. While some newspapers mention the credit line before the dateline, some others put it after the date line.

For examples:

Before the dateline

HT Correspondent
NEW Delhi, Jan. 9—

After the dateline

NEW DELHI, Jan. 9 (PTI)
OR
NEW DELHI, Jan. 9 (HTC)

Different newspapers follow different patterns of creditline writing.

For Example:

- *By Our Staff Reporter*
  OR
  Our Staff Reporter.
- *Sometimes, it is covered by rule on the upper and the lower side and sometimes only on the lower side.*
  By Our Staff Reporter
  OR
  By Our Staff Reporter
- *Sometimes, the creditline is mentioned in full and sometimes in abbreviated form.*

Example—

Full—Hindustan Times Correspondent
Abbreviation—HTC

News agency, too, is quoted in different ways by different newspapers.

Example: *Press Trust of India*
NEW DELHI, Nov. 14—
OR
NEW DELHI, Nov. 14 (PTI)

Some newspapers quote the agencies in entirely a different manner.

Example:

NEW DELHI, Jan 9—The Prime Minister, Dr. Manmohan Singh said here today that he would not bow down to the pressure tactics of BJP, reports PTI.
Again, some newspapers mention the name of the news agency after the last para of the news story. Like—

NEWDELHI, Jan. 9 ....
....
....*PTI*

Byline: Whenever any correspondent or reporter files an important or exclusive story or a scoop, his/her efforts are acknowledged by giving his/her name in the creditline. This is known as byline. It is also termed as personal byline.

Mostly byline is given an exclusive display like—By Rakesh Bhatnagar.

However, it can also be given along with creditline, like:

By Rakesh Bhatnagar
Times News Network

Lead/Intro

Lead is considered the most important part of a story. The best-written lead not only satisfies the reader's initial curiosity but wets his/her appetite to read more. A reporter must see to it that his/her lead does five things—

A — Presents a summary of the story.
B — Identifies the persons and the places concerned.
C — Stresses the news feature.
D — Gives the update of the event.
E — Stimulates the reader to continue the story.

The present-day tendency is to achieve all this as quickly and as briefly as possible.

The News Lead

Not all news events fall into the single-incident story category. Many stories are far more complex and the reporter may be faced with having to juggle two or three important news elements in a lead. This complex type of story requires careful planning and organisation to make certain that the separate parts come together clearly and coherently for the reader.

Suppose the following happened during a heavy fog that shrouded New Delhi and adjoining areas early one morning:

- Dense fog blanketed the area for a 50 km radius.
- Twenty cars and trucks were involved in chain-reaction wrecks on National Highway No. 8.
- Many cars and trucks caught fire and burned.
- Twelve persons were killed.
- At least 50 others were injured and required hospitalisation.
- Jaipur-bound traffic on the Highway was blocked and vehicle were diverted to other routes.

The general rule in writing a story about a news event is to place the most noteworthy item first. This rule presents no serious problem as long as the story has only a single incident to be the focus of the lead. However, when the story has more than one significant incident, as in the above event, the reporter's job becomes more complicated. The two basic methods generally used in handling a more complex story are:

1. Summarise all features—in order of importance—in the lead sentence or paragraph.
2. Emphasise the most important or significant of the features and then quickly summarise all the other important ones in logical order in succeeding paragraphs.

In either approach, all of the features should be clearly established in the reader's mind as quickly as possible before the reporter proceeds very far into developing any open feature.

Summary or Digest Lead

This lead summaries clearly and plainly all the principal facts. It remains the simplest in construction and forms a basic part of all lead variations.

Any typical news items or despatch starts off with the digest or summary lead. The following is a fair example:

> Resenting the policy of the government of opening doors for multi-national companies in the insurance sector, the opposition invited clashes with the treasury benches. The Finance Minister proposed to put a cap on FDI and set up a regulator but the opposition members were not convinced.

This lead brings the central issued of discussion—reforms in insurance sector to the focus. It also summarises two key points—FDI limit and regulation of the sector.

Here is an example of how the details of the chain-reaction crashes might have been summarised in a lead:

> Twelve persons were killed and at least 50 injured and hospitalised when 20 cars and trucks smashed into one another and caught fire on a fog-shrouded section of National Highway No. 8 near Gurgaon early today, the police said.

That lead, like most summary leads, simply is too long. Most editors do not like summary leads because they often overwhelm the reader by saying too much.

Here is how that summary lead might have been developed. At the left is a diagram in which each geometrical shape represents a separate story feature. The diminishing size of the figures signifies the diminishing newsworthiness of the story material.

Diagram	*Written Story*
Summary of Features [1] ② △3	Twelve persons were killed and at least 50 injured and hospitalised when 20 cars and trucks smashed into one another and caught fire on a fog-shrouded section of National Highway No. 8 near Gurgaon early today, the police said.
Details of Feature No. 1, the dead [1]	A complete list of the dead has not been compiled. Mr. Hamid Hussain, SP of Gurgaon, said some of the victims were so badly burnt they may never be identified.
Details of Feature No. 2, the injured ②	The injured were given emergency first-aid at the scene and taken by ambulances to hospitals in Gurgaon and Delhi. The hospitals called in off-duty nurses and doctors to help treat the injured.
Details of Feature No. 3, the fog that caused the accident △3	"Visibility was no more than 3 to 5 metres in the two km stretch where the cars and trucks were piled up," Mr. Hamid said. Rescue vehicles had difficulty reaching some of the vehicles because of the fog and the burning and wrecked vehicles.
Other Paragraphs in Completed Story	Hundreds of rescue workers responded to repeated calls and helped pull victims and survivors from the wreckage of the vehicles. One rescue worker said the heat was so intense a car and a jeep were fused together by the melting metal. Another reported flames shooting 100 metres into the air from a tanker truck apparently loaded with petrol or diesel. (Further details of all the features should be developed in the rest of the story.)

To avoid a long summary lead, most editors would instruct the reporter to put the emphasis on the persons who had been killed and injured. Here is how that shortened lead might by written:

Diagram	*Written Story*
Outstanding Features [1]	Twelve persons were killed and at least 50 injured early today in a series of chain-reaction crashes on a stretch of National Highway No. 8 that was blanketed by dense fog.
Summary of Other Features (2) △3	Haryana State Police said more than 20 cars and trucks plowed into one another in the fog that had cut visibility to 3 to 5 metres near Gurgaon. Many caught fire and burnt.
	A complete list of the dead has not been compiled. Mr. Hamid Hussain, SP of Gurgaon, said some of the victims were so badly burnt they may never be identified.
	The injured were given emergency first-aid at the scene and taken by ambulances to nearby hospitals. The hospitals called in off-duty nurses and doctors to help treat the injured.
	(Further details of all the features should be developed in the rest of the story.)

In this example, all the emphasis is placed on the dead and injured. However, because of the unusually dense fog that caused the accidents an editor may want to emphasize it in the lead. In that case, here is how the story might by written:

Diagram	*Written Story*
Outstanding Feature [1]	A fog-blanketed stretch of National Highway No. 8 became the scene of broken and burning vehicles today in possibly the worst traffic accident in the NCR region.
Details of Feature Nos. 2 and 3 (2) △3	At least 12 people were killed and more than 50 injured in Gurgaon when more than 20 vehicles were involved in chain-reaction collisions. The fog cut visibility to 3 to 5 metres at some points.
Other Paragaphs in the Complete Story	"The fog was so thick it was impossible for the drivers to see other vehicles. Mr. Hamid Hussain SP of Gurgaon said.
	A complete list of the dead and injured has not been compiled. Mr. Hamid said some of the victims were so badly burnt they may never by identified.
	(Further details would be included in the body of the story.)

Other Leads

Combination or Scrambled Lead

There are no hard and fast rules for writing the several-feature lead. The choice of the lead usually is determined by the facts of the story. Some of the features may be summarised, but not all. Or an outstanding feature may be singled out. It might also be combined with related features. And in some cases, the reporter may decide to take advantage of the drama of an event to depart completely from the hard news lead.

Suppose, for example that the following took place during a local school board meeting:

1. The School management rejected a plea by Sikh parents to ban a controversial reading book for class VI students.
2. Decided not to appeal a court order prohibiting religious classes as part of the public school curriculum.
3. Hired a survey agency to inspect all school buildings under the Management for ensuring safety measures.

The first paragraph summarises two of the features because they deal with academic issues in the system. The second paragraph adds other features that are related because they deal with the conditions of school buildings and the safety of students. These features are equally important, but they are not as emotionally charged as the issues in the lead paragraph.

Tabulated Lead

Many newspapers use tabulations either above or within the story as a way of summarising for the reader the action reported in the body of the story. It is a way of letting the reader know a lot of information quickly. It permits the reporter to focus on a single fact. Some papers use numerals with tabulated items; others use dashes or dots.

Example:

The government has announced a hike in the prices of petroleum products. The cabinet sub-committee has taken the following decisions:

1. *Petrol prices will go up by 10 per cent and the new rate is Rs. 44/- a litre.*

2. *Diesel prices will go up by 5 per cent and it will be available @ Rs. 22/- a litre.*
3. *Kerosene has been exempted from the hike.*
4. *LPG prices might be revised soon.*

Simplified Lead Made Possible by the Above Tabulation

The government has announced a 10 per cent hike in the price of petrol and 5 per cent in the price of diesel. The new prices of petrol and diesel will be Rs. 44/- and Rs. 22/- respectively.

The Cabinet sub-committee decided not to increase the price of kerosene. It resolved to look into the revision of LPG soon.

Interpretative Lead

Rather than using the summary or tabulation lead a reporter may elect to write an interpretative lead. In this type of lead, the reporter attempts to tell readers what the facts mean. Interpretation should always be fair and objective. It should be based on the facts and the background knowledge of the event or situation, and it should be an accurate analysis of the facts. If the interpretation in simply the reporter's subjective view, then it becomes editorial opinion.

The standard straight news lead simply reports on an event, but the interpretative lead attempts to put the event into perspective for the reader. This type of lead is often used on a second-day story or by a newspaper whose rival newspaper got the story first. However, it is not uncommon for papers to use an interpretive lead when telling the story for the first time.

For example, if the Maharashtra Governor sent a message to the State Government asking to reconsider the ordinance for regularising unauthorised constructions in Ulhasnagar the standard story might begin like this.

Maharashtra Governor S.M. Krishna today asked the State Government to reconsider the ordinance prepared for regularising unauthorised constructions in Ulhasnagar.

In the rest of the story, the reporter gives the details of the Governor's observations, citing the High Court order for demolitions of unauthorised constructions.

A reporter interpreting the Governor's reluctance of approving the ordinance in the light of the High Court's directive might have written—

> *Maharashtra Governor S.M. Krishna. has sent the controversial ordinance regarding regularisation of unauthorised constructions in Ulhasnagar back to the State Government. The Governor has asked the Ranjit Deshmukh Government to reconsider the proposed ordinance before pushing it forward.*

The Governor's observations are being considered vital in view of the High Court order for demolitions of unauthorised constructions in Ulhasnagar. Mr. Krishna is of the opinion that the government should avoid confronting the judiciary on a sensitive public issue.

It should be noted that a demolition drive has been launched in Delhi by the Municipal Corporation of Delhi (MCD) under orders from the Delhi High Court against unauthorised constructions. Mr. Krishna is obviously in no mood repeating Delhi in Mumbai.

If such a lead is used, it is important to include as quickly as possible the facts and important details. Some editors try to get those details into the second or third paragraph. Others include them in the third or the fourth, depending on the circumstances of the story. In no case should they be ignored or placed much further down in the story than the fourth or fifth paragraph.

Considerable debate about interpretative reporting continues among journalists, and many newspapers still approach it with extreme caution. But it is being used increasingly in reporting government and politics, and it frequently brings cries from the persons whose action is being interpreted that the reporter is "biased".

However, the increasing complexity of modern society—not just government and politics—tends to require that newspapers explain facts as well as report them. Newspapers have a responsibility to make certain that the reporter who does the interpretation is careful and thorough and has necessary background and maturity to present an accurate and fair analysis of the facts.

Separate Stories

Elections, storms, strikes, wars and frequently big fires and other major events may demand more than one story. For example, the story about the persons killed and injured in the chain-reaction crashes cited earlier in this chapter would require a main story about the crashes plus stories on the rescue efforts; stories on the survivors; interviews with officials about the causes; a story on similar crashes, especially if others occurred in the same area; and a story on what might be done to prevent similar crashes. In each one these "sidebar" stories, the original event would need to be recapped in a brief paragraph early in the story.

Many of these stories lend themselves to strong dramatic feature leads. Often these stories are grouped in one section of the newspaper to make it easier for the reader to have immediate access to everything that is written about the event. It is not uncommon for a newspaper to collect all of its coverage of a major event such as an earthquake or major air crash in which lives are lost in a special section that is issued a week or so after the event.

Identifying the Features

It is difficult, if not impossible, to write a clear, coherent news story without identifying the features in the mass of story details the reporter has collected. Simply defined features are the highlights—the outstanding, most interesting and most significant items in any news event. The reporter has to determine which of these features are the most interesting and newsworthy.

For example, a reporter assigned to cover a speech should always look for the main arguments or contentions of the speaker to emphasise in the lead. However, the speaker's comments that the Prime Minister should resign or a fist fight's starting in the audience, be "features" that might rate even more attention than the highlights of the formal speech.

Perhaps the best guide in recognising the worthwhile features is to look for these elements first: "Who" was involved; "What" happened; "When" it happened; "Where" it happened; "Why" it happened; and "How" it happened. Obviously the news values discussed earlier in this chapter will influence the process. Reporters should always remember that the purpose of the lead is to give the reader an accurate and complete picture of what is to come later in the story.

Summarising the Features

Once the features have been recognised, the reporter's job is to decide whether to try to summarise them or select one to emphasise in the lead. Here are several examples of leads in which the efforts to summarise all of the features produced leads that really are too vague:

> Four points in favour of consolidating government and public schools were given today by Mrs. Anita Arya, President of Save Our Schools campaign., in a speech to the ...
>
> Problems of taxation and public health were debated today by the State Assembly.
>
> Four important pieces of consumer legislation were passed by Parliament today.

Each of these leads recognises the existence of several features, but the attempt to summarise them results in vague, dull and uninteresting leads. "Four points in favour" has little reader appeal and actually does not summarise those points. A brief summary of the points would make the lead more specific and catch the reader's attention.

Mrs. Anita Arya, President of Save Our Schools campaign, said at the principals', meet that the consolidation of government and public schools would:

- *Sharply reduce the cost of public schools.*
- *Bring uniform educational standards to all students.*
- *Reduce teacher-taught ratios.*
- *Reduce the number of students depending on buses.*

Another approach would be to emphasise one feature in the lead sentence and summarise the others in the next one, as in the following example:

> *The cost of public schools would be reduced sharply by consolidating the government and public school systems, Mrs. Anita Arya, president of Save Our Schools campaign, told the principals' meet.*
>
> *Consolidation would also bring about more uniform educational standards, reduce teacher-taught ratios in the classrooms and significantly reduce the number of students who would have to be provided buses.*

Combining Stories

Separate stories about a single event naturally will differ in content, although there will be some overlapping of facts in each one. As a result, some newspapers will combine the stories into one. But combined stories have a tendency to be long, and some editors prefer to group individual stories on the same page with separate headlines or group them under a single major headline. To avoid long stories, some reporters will write a lead story on the major action taken and separate shorter stories on secondary actions.

Polishing the Lead

News is repetitive and so are a lot of leads on news stories. Though every reporter quickly learns that the chief purpose of a lead is to grab the reader's attention, hundreds of them write leads everyday that begin the same way:

The MCD voted today to ....
The State Assembly voted unanimously today to.......................
The Public Accounts committee members voted 504, today to ....
The Lok Sabha today passed a bill that will.............................
The Lok Sabha today passed a bill that hikes taxes on.........
....
The Governor signed today a bill creating a ....
The President signed today a bill that will ....

The authors of such leads ignore the fact that the opening sentence of any story is crucial. The lead has to convince the reader to go on reading the rest of the story. If it doesn't, it has failed.

Reporters generally agree that the lead is the hardest part of a newspaper story to write. Some call it sheer agony, and that is often obvious in what they finally produce.

Frequently a lead will follow all the rules and principles discussed so far but still may not be interesting enough to grab the reader's attention. It may contain all five Ws, the proper identification and attribution, and it may emphasise a significant feature. In short, it may be adequate, but it may also be dull and uninteresting. It may lack originality, vividness, style, class, distinction and imagination.

A good lead is more than just adequate. It is clear and crisp. The Associated Press Rene Jack Cappon says in his excellent book, "The Word" that a good lead makes a clear statement of the essential news point and when possible includes a detail that distinguishes the story from others of its kind."

Here is well-written, imaginative lead from the AP news agency—

> *WASHINGTON (AP)—If oil were liquor, the government would know where to find virtually every drop of it.*

The remainder of the story detailed how the government had been far more successful in finding illegal moonshine stills than in finding new oilfields during the emergency crisis that gripped the United States at the time the story was written.

Here is the example of an outstanding lead:

> *On one side is a temple with a mission.*
> *On the other side is a city with a need.*
> *In the middle is the sacred Yamuna river.*

These are the ingredients of a environmentalists-state confrontation that erupted in the wake of State's permission for the construction of Akshardham Temple on the bank of the Yamuna in New Delhi and the opposition of environmentalists to any such move which could affect the lifeline of the city.

Rhetoric

Good writing demands the use of clear, crisp, colourful, precise language. When such language is combined with short sentences and short paragraphs, you have the essence of good news writing. But a reporter must always use variety in sentence and paragraph length as well as sentence structure.

The most common sentence form is subject-predicate:

> *More than half of the people killed worldwide by terrorists are Indians, a government spokesperson said today.*

It is favoured by many reporters and editors, especially when dealing with straight news. But if all leads were written that way, they would fail in their basic goal to grab the reader's attention. While this type of lead sentence often is adequate, it just as often is dull. Focusing on one of the various W's gives variety to the lead.

Reporters often turn to other sentence forms to avoid writing all leads in the subject-predicate form. Here are some examples:

Phrases

Infinitive: To halt the flow of illegal arms in Mumbai, the Coast Guard today launched a ...

Participial: Trying to save his crumbling political career, Chief Minister L.P. Yadav called a secret meeting of ...

Prepositional: In a slashing attack on the MCD for ongoing demolitions, State Congress Chief Rambabu Sharma accused ...

Gerund: Constituting third panel to investigate 1984 Sikh riots to fix the accountability and recommend relief and rehabilitation measures after 21 years is a joke, said a senior BJP leader.

Clauses

Substantive: That Parliament will vote to support the government's plan to send forces for UN peace-keeping force in Iraq is a forgone conclusion in the minds of political observers.

Adverbial: If the public does not take a strong stand against drug dealers, pushers and users, the police won't push the "War on Drugs" said Mr. S. Roy, the noted social activist.

Though there is nothing wrong with these leads, many writers avoid them and many editors rewrite them simply because they have a tendency to be clumsy. They can, if not written with great care, sound stilted and often are quite long.

Emphasising News Values

It is important for the reporter to study all the features carefully to avoid overlooking a newsworthy feature or angle that might make the difference between a routine lead and a bright, imaginative one. While it is important not to bury the news, the reporter should always seek out that special angle that might make the lead reach out to the reader. There are a number of approaches, based on the traditional news values, available to a reporter. Here are some examples:

Timeliness

The worlds "today" and "tomorrow" characterise most newsworthy leads on straight news stories. Occasionally, however, a story concerns events that happened, "last week" or even "last month" that result in a current story. In such cases the reporter should look for a "today" angle. It isn't always easy. Here are two versions of a "today" story that illustrate the point.

First Version

Chief Minister Sheila Dikshit's campaign promise last June to end her first year in office with a balanced budget for Delhi has cost more than 100 city employees their jobs.

Dismissal notices were mailed today to ...

Second Version, Today Angle Emphasised

More than hundred employees got dismissal notices today. They were the victims of Chief Minister Sheila Dikshit's campaign promise in June to end her first year in office with a balanced budget for Delhi.

Other Today Angle Leads

Today marks that giddy, impression-making first day of school for the public schools of the city.

The nation celebrated the 56th anniversary of the Republic Day today.

Proximity

In addition to striving for a "today" angle, the reporter should also look for a "local" angle to the story.

A General Lead

Fifty-six commercial properties with unauthorised constructions were demolished in South and West Delhi on the 16th day of the MCD drive being conducted as per HC directive.

A Localised Lead

Mrs. Najma Heptulla, Dy. Chairperson of the Rajya Sabha, has been nominated to the Association of World Parliamentarians.

Major national and international stories often have a local angle; there is an example:

> *The Indian Government's efforts to seek the release of Antaryami, the truck driver abducted in Iraq, have resulted in dejection.*

Antaryami and other kidnapped nationals were shown on Al Jazeera TV today with their masked kidnappers.

The wife and children of Antaryami in a Punjab village are desperately looking for his release.

Prominence

Prominent names make eye-catching leads. Here are several examples:

A General Story

New Delhi (PTI) *Sixty ministers took the oath of office at a grand function held in the Central Hall of Parliament this evening.*

The list includes...

Prominent Name Emphasised

New Delhi (PTI) *Former Chief Ministers Lalu Prasad Yadav from Bihar and Arjun Singh from M.P. along with 58 others took the oath of office at a grand function held in the Central Hall of Parliament this evening.*

Three former Prime Ministers V.P. Singh, Chandra Shekhar and Atal Bihari Vajpayee attended the swearing–in ceremony.

Various Patterns of Lead Writing

Reporters today have considerable freedom in writing leads, though there are some editors who still prefer that every story has a straight news lead. There are various approaches to writing leads. Usually, the facts of the story will dictate the type of lead and the reporter should not strain to write a lead on a story that does not justify such treatment. Here are a few of the more common forms of leads.

Question Lead

A question lead works best when a problem with reader appeal or public interest is the central point of the story. Unfortunately, the question lead is used far too often as a crutch by a reporter who does not take the time to work on another more effective approach. Some editors put a limit on the number of question leads that can be used. However, there have been some classic question leads, such as—

> *O, say can you sing "The Star Spangled Banner" without mumbling the worlds and petering out on the high notes?*

Here's an artful question lead:

> *Know anybody who needs 59 toilet seat covers? They come in all colours—blue, brown, pink, yellow.*
>
> *How about 100 units of blood plasma? Or a good glue machine? Today in Mumbai, you can get...*

The rest of the story detailed the odd collection of items the police recovered during a sting operation.

A reporter for the *San Jose Mercury News*, used a question lead effectively on his story about a new high-tech voice-controlled synthesiser:

> *So you sound great singing in the shower, but the only instrument you've mastered is the air guitar?*
>
> *The wizards of Silicon Valley have just introduced a product to turn your air guitar into a real one—all you have to do is hum and you don't even have to do that very well.*
>
> *The invention, called a Vocaliser 1000, is a voice-controlled synthesiser that works like an electric kazoo, translating phrases you sing or hum into any one of more than 50 instruments ....*

Question lead is welcome if the question asked really illuminates the story. Take for example—

> *Who would have thought that the disclosures of the Jain Commission report will prove a death blow to the Gujral Government with the United Front and the supporting Congress standing at the cross roads?*

In this case, the second para will have to explain the lead further as below:

> *This is the question in the minds of many ruling alliance MPs and other national leaders.*

Punch, Capsule or Cartridge Lead

This type of lead uses short, punchy statements to attract the reader's attention. Here is an example from a US newspaper—

Big boys don't cry. Big boys are strong. Big boys bring home the big bucks.

Big boys also suffer a higher rate of ulcers and heart attacks, not to mention incidence of violence and sexual abuse.

The story went on to detail the efforts of the National Organisation for Changing Men to "liberate males from the traps of big-boy stereotypes."

Here is another example—

Delhiites, take heart.

Reinforcements are on the way.

More than ever, today's college freshers want money and status when they get out of school.

The story went on to report the results of a survey of the goals and values of college freshers in New Delhi.

Statement or Direct-Quotation Lead

The direct-quotation lead can be extremely effective if the quote is a good one and if it is not too long. Frequently, reporters use quotes that are too long and involved. Several paragraphs may be needed to explain them to the reader. The following is an interesting quote lead on Mongol herdsmen from *The Christian Science Monitor*.

"A horse," says herdsman Davassuren, "is the most precious thing a Mongolian man can have."

Davassuren, grizzled leader of a small group of nomadic herdsmen, says he is happy these days. A gradual evolution of "perestroika"—economic reform—in Mongolia has made it possible for him to resume the life he loves, and to have as many horses as he wants.

This lead is more used in speech reporting when an epigrammatic sentence puts in the capsule form the gist of the speaker's idea. Look at the following example:

"India will not compromise with its security and will never yield to external pressures under any circumstances."

Prime Minister Dr. Manmohan Singh seemed confident and determined while making this statement at a public gathering at Ramlila Ground this afternoon.

Contrast Lead

A contrast lead reaches the reader's attention by comparing

extremes—the big with the little, comedy with tragedy, age with youth, the past with the present. Look at the following example—

> *A local public school has a problem other schools would like to have—too much money.*
>
> *The Whiteline Public School Management has agreed that the School's general fund balance of Rs. 28,00,000 is too high and the money should be spent to keep the balance more in line with other public schools.*

The rest of the story explained how the money was raised for the fund and how a committee was appointed to review ways to spend the money.

In this Associated Press (AP) lead, the contrast between birth and death during the poison gas disaster in Bhopal, adds a dramatic touch to the story updating that tragic event.

> *Bhopal, six years ago, as Rani drew her first breath, hundreds of others nearby took their last. She was bom as clouds of poison gas spewed from a Union Carbide plant and billowed deep into the city of one million people.*
>
> *The Bhopal accident was the world's deadliest industrial disaster, and its medical, legal and economic cost is still being reckoned. More than 3,800 people have died because they inhaled the gas that leaked from the plant at midnight on Dec. 2, 1984.*

And there certainly is implied contrast in this unusual rape story reported in US newspapers—

> *A 39-year-old man, jogging a Southwest Dade residential neighbourhood, told the police he was abducted by a gang of women and raped, Metro-Dade poilce said Thursday.*
>
> *"He's very hysterical, very traumatised," Rape Squad Lt. Linda Blue said.*
>
> *The victim, whose name is being withheld, is a professional man, with children, the police said ...*

Direct-Address/Direct-Appeal Lead

This lead speaks directly to the reader, often about a subject of broad interest or appeal.

This form borrows the interest compelling device of the personal letter. It addresses the reader directly or by implications as "you" and has the effect of making the reader a collaborator in what follows. It often begins with such phrases as "If you have ever thought" or "If you have ever seen or read". Here is a typical direct appeal lead.

If you think you have got it tough when you have to listen to your little sister practice the piano, take pity an Alfred Jay Smith. In the last 30 years, he's had to audition 20,500 child performance. And he likes his job.

Here is another example—

"Have you ever thought you will be living in a home where power and water supply are never disrupted, car wash and laundry services are available, gyma and swimming pool remain open for your use, your dream now comes true in Rajhans Apartment, Indirapuram, which is offering paradise facilities to its occupants.

Look at the following example in which a US newspaper advises women where to find a single man:

Go west, young man.

The June issue of Playgirl magazine, out today, has compiled a list of places just crawling with men—and man-hunting women—in six states: Alaska, Hawaii, Nevada, North Dakota, Wyoming and Montana....

Weather, taxes and other broad subjects lend themselves to the direct-address approach:

You'd better break out the blankets tonight.

The temperature is going to drop to zero, weather forecasters say.

You have less than 24 hours to file your income-tax return!

And to help you meet that deadline, the Income-Tax department has set up dozens of counters at Pragati Maidan.

"We'll take the return from anyone who is in line by 6 p.m. and make certain it has Oct. 31 mark on it", Income Tax Commission Mr. Y.P. Singh said.

Descriptive Lead

In a descriptive lead, the reporter tries to paint a word picture of an interesting person, place or event. A descriptive lead also helps create the mood for the story and for that reason should match the subject carefully. In the next example, *The New York Times* describes the scene as illegal aliens cross the border from Mexico into the United States:

> *WHY, Ariz.—It was the sweetest and gentlest of desert evenings, pitch-black except for a silver of new moon and the light from a hundred thousand stars. Nearby, a coyote scampered among the stately organ pipe cactuses, its occasional moumful howl slicing the night like a jagged knife.*
>
> *Presently the stillness was broken by a softer sound, a brief two-toned whistle. For half a minute there was nothing, then an identical whistle was heard from beyond the rise, followed by a flash of light and an answering flash, the signal that the way was clear. Within seconds, shadowy figures emerged from the desert. Smiling and talking softly, they gathered in a circle near the little-used highway.*

A story in the *Washington Post* described the change of season in the Virginia countryside:

> *CULPEPER, Va.—The dawn is chilly inside the bam, and Greg Smith's breath hangs in the air like puffs from a hand-rolled smoke. A Holstein stands motionless before him, and he strokes the cow's black and white face with a rough, stained hand. A few steps away, the sun outlines the open bam door on the earth, and there summer lingers, warm to the skin.*
>
> *It is autumn, harvest time at Ashland Farm. And while Smith still rises, with the certainty of the chime, at 5:30 sharp, the sun dawdles 60 seconds more each moming and moves imperceptibly to the south. Smith pulls a handful of brown corn silage from the trough, stirring the kemels and the chopped pieces of cob, stalk and shuck with a finger. He closes his hand tightly. When it opens again, the coarse, fluffy matter springs back to size. Perfect. The right amount of moisture to last the winter.*
>
> *It has been a good year at Smith's 1,112-acre dairy farm, so bountiful...*

The *Christian Science Monitor* used a descriptive lead in recounting the story of the first woman to drive a car across the United States:

> *It was pouring rain that gloomy June moming as a crowd gathered under umbrellas at curbazide on a New York City Street. The Maxwell, a forest green touring car with a leather-like pantasote top, was parked by the curb exactly at the place where Lincoln Center now stands. The year was 1909, the same year that Robert E. Peary set foot on the North Pole.*

Next to the car stood a dimpled and impatient Alice Huyler Ramsey. She wore a bulky, ankle-length black poncho and rubber helmet with detachable goggles. Someone had given her a bouquet of carnations. Undaunted by rain or tradition she smiled for the photographers, as did the three women next to her.

But the dimples and smile were mere camouflage. This 21-year-old Alice H. Ramsey was half steel, half lightning rod in an era when nearly all women washed, ironed, changed diapers, and cleaned their houses instead of even thinking of driving a 2,100-pound car 4,000 miles from New York to San Francisco. Ramsey didn't toy with the idea; she was doing it....

This kind of lead presents a picture. The reporter may set the stage for the action of his/her story or he/she may present in detail, one or more of his chief actors. In other words, this lead can describe the scene or it can describe one or more of the people involved.

Look at the following example—*The Indian Express* published a story (January 22, 2006) about Lahore's Kite festival as Page 1 anchor.

Mini Kapoor
Lahore, January 22

Way past midnight in this sleepless city's bustling food street in Gowalmandi, the Nite Kite Shop is running up brisk business. Visitors take breaks between handis of brain curry and glassfuls of salty tea to pick up mementos. There are just a few cities around the world that have a knack for celebrating themselves. Lahore is one of them, and akin to the miniature carnival masks of Venice, it sums up its unique joie de vivre in colourful kites. At the Nite Kite Shop, they come in small sizes and diverse colours.

So, it this it then? Will Lahore hereafter, now that Pakistan's Supreme Court has made an unambiguous statement by banning the manufacture and flying of kites, be content with these flightless souvenirs? Will those cries of "bo kata" as a kiteflyer snaps an opponent's string be echoes only from the past?

A descriptive lead describes in detail though it might not by a long one. It can have little or no action. For example, the following lead appeared in a newspaper on Mother's Day.

Every morning she is up before me to see to all my needs. She fills my world but never intrude... is ever gentle yet so strong. She is my mother.

Parody Lead

This lead attempts to play on words, using widely known provebs, quotations, song titles, currently popular sayings, book titles and other expressions to help establish an immediate identification with the reader and bring a bit of sparkle to what otherwise might have been a routine story, as in these examples:

> *Waste not, want not, the chairman of the public Accounts Committee warned the Defence Ministry today.*
>
> *He had discovered that the Department of Defence is wallowing in more than Rs. 100 billion worth of spare parts, including Rs. 300 million of equipment the military doesn't need.*

TUM ITNA KYON MUSKARA RAHE HO, the Chief Minister designate of Bihar Nitish Kumar asked the RJD chief Lalu Prasad Yadav when the latter congratulated him with unusual warmth.

Historical or Literary-Allusion Lead

This type of lead draws on some character or event in history or literature that is familiar to an average reader to attract and hold attention. The religious books and literary works often are used as reference points by writers. Here is an example of how one writer used a line from the Bible to begin a story on the demise of the World Football Leagure's Chicago franchise:

> *In the beginning, there was hope. And opulence. In the end? Well, in the end, really, there was nothing.*
>
> *It all started in a posh office building out in ...*
>
> *The following was strong. Laxman followed the footprints of his elder brother Ram to pose a grave challenge to the enemies. On the third day of Faisalabad Test Match, V.V.S. Laxman made a remarkable 90 runs while providing an unexemplary support to the captain Rahul Dravid who turned the table turtle with his magnificent century.*

In this excellent feature on *The New Yorker* magazine, Phil Casey of *The Washington Post* used this classic literary line for his opening:

> *Once upon a time, there was a unique and splendid magazine beautifully written, edited and produced, a little weekly work of art, perhaps the happiest blend of fact and fiction, reminiscence, humour, journalism, commentary and criticism there ever was.*

And when Carl "The Truth" Williams was knocked out in 93 seconds by Mike Tyson in a championship fight, a number of writers tried a variety of ways to work the truth-and-consequences theme into their leads. Here's one example:

"Truth" met consequences in the ring last night.

And it took Mike Tyson just 93 seconds to convince Carl "The Truth" Williams that the truth of the matter was that Williams was simply out of his class.

Staccato Lead

A staccato lead consists of short, clipped words, phrases and sentences, sometimes separated by dashes or dots or simply made into a list, to help create a certain mood for the story. Often this type of lead is descriptive in nature. Though it is not used as often as other types of leads, it can be effective, as in the following examples:

A garment factory was damaged. A lumberyard and department store were burnt. Vacant houses were torched.

And authorities say the men who set some of the fires went back to fight the flames. Eight volunteer fire-fighters were arrested ....

The noise begins high. UP in the rafters. It gathers strength. Spills down the aisles. Building relentlessly. It cascades over the railing. It engulfs the expensive box seats. And spills out into the playing field. A raging torrent of sound. The eardrums vibrate painfully. The heart flutters.

Pele, the world's greatest soccer player, has just received another message of love from his adoring fans.

Here is another impressive example:

Rohit has a learning disability.

Rahul has a severe speech impediment.

Reema is autistic.

They live in Sultanganj, the remotest town in the state, where the number of students who quit school almost equals the number who graduate.

But the government school system's special education students like Rohit, Rahul and Reema, defy those numbers. Their dropout rate is far below the rate for the entire school system.

> *On Thursday, 29 special education students, those with the steepest path to academic success, will wear gown to receive their diplomas ...*

To provide excitement and a word picture, short phrases are used to emphasise certain situations as has been done in the following example:

> *Boom Boom, Blesh, Dhoom Dhoom, crackers bursting marked India's victory over Pakistan in Peshhawar Test Match.*

Look at another example:

> *Ratat at at at ..... the sound of machine guns, the stench of Cordite. Death screams and artillery weapons whistles. These are sounds the people of Kashmir have become accustomed to.*

Suspended Interest Lead

This type of lead serves as a stimulator of interest. It gives the reader enough information to fullfil his desire to know. After the lead, the story usually runs along in chronological form, so that the reader must read to the very end to get at the climax. Reporters use this type of lead mainly of short bits, on the theory that if used on longer articles, readers would not bother to wait through paragraph after paragraph. Here is a typical suspended interest lead.

The quick action taken by Rahim, a vendor, saved the life of about 50 bus passengers in East Delhi this morning.

Rahim was travelling in a Central Secretariat-bound DTC bus. When the bus reached Shakarpur, Rahim discovered an unclaimed bag under his seat. He got suspicious and informed the conductor.

Initially, he was not taken seriously but his insistence attracted the attention of other passengers. Ultimately the bus was stopped and a Police Patrol Party was informed. The police party found the bag full of explosives.

Circumstantial Lead

Such a lead stresses the circumstances under which incident has happened. It crops up usually when the story has a human interest slant. Here is an example:

> *The alarm raised by a domestic help in Laxminagar last might alerted a nearby police patrol and the policeman rushed to the scene. Seeing*

them approaching, the miscreants took to their heels and thus a robbery was averted.

Oddity or Freak Lead

It is an unusual approach to capture the attention of readers. Sometimes, reporters use odd methods to attract readers. Here is an example:

Wanted: Supporters from among the opposition parties who can vote for the NDA government to save it from a possible defeat in the wake of a no-confidence motion in the Lok Sabha.

A simplified lead based on the above can be written likewise:

In the wake of a no-confidence motion in the Lok Sabha, the NDA government is seeking the support of some Opposition members.

Take another example from an American newspapers:

For Sale: one Town

Connic Carpenter, film and television actress who bought a remote hamlet in the Colorado Rockies, today put the town up for sale. Miss Carpenter said she plans to sell Echo Cross Roads and buy an island in the South Pacific...

Dialogue Lead

Sometimes, lead is written in dialogue form but in such leads, the newstory will have to be unnecessarily lengthened to explain the situation to the reader.

"There are reports of bickering in the United Front as your partners are busy in mud-slinging," The BJP threw the remark on the Prime Minister I.K. Gujral in the Lok Sabha today. "It is better to put your house in order and not to worry for us", replied Mr Gujral.

Colour or Figurative Lead

Sometimes, figurative speech is used in the lead to make it catchy. Here is an example:

The government should not feel that the Uttarakhand Movement has gone to the winds. The visible peace in the hilly region is only a lull before the storm. The warning came from the BJP benches in the Lok Sabha today.

Narrative Lead

This kind of lead starts in the middle of an event, and is full of action verbs. It carries the reader through the event and generally has a surprising twist in the end.

Here is an example—

He paused for a second to gaze upon it. Then slowly, reverentially, he reached down and laid his hand upon it feeling the skin. He squeezed it gently, amazed so soft, yet so firm.

He turned aside and carefully selected the knife. It seemed to shine with a life of its own. Sweating now, he lifted it up and then, suddenly brought it down. Red, Red it was red everywhere.

"Cut" shouted the director. Thus ended the first shot of Sanjeev Kumar. Three retakes later it was done, and what fallowed is history.

Bullet Lead

In this kind of lead, a short sentence or phrase is used in a straightforward manner. This is more used to flash a message for conveying some shattering news. Since this lead hits the readers like a bullet, it is known as a bullet lead.

Indira Gandhi is dead.

The Mahatma is no more.

When Prime Minister Jawaharlal Nehru died, the news was conveyed to Parliament by C. Subramaniam in the words.

"The Light is gone."

This phrase is a good example of bullet lead if used by a newspaper.

Contrasting Lead

This lead, highlights the change or contracts to lay the attention on the object of the story. It gives a total change of scenario in the first few words of the article.

Here is an example:

A face that never stops smiling whether he stumbles, drops things on his head or is the victim of a joke, that is Ramu the clown.

A face that merely smiles, when people ask for money, when his children cry, that too is Ramu the clown.

Blind Lead

Sometimes in a news item lead is not given much importance and more emphasis is laid on the body of the story. This is known as a blind lead since it becomes difficult to find or detect the most important point in the news item. It may be anywhere in the story or may not be existing at all.

Buried Lead

Sometimes the most important point is not given in the intro and is buried in the later part of the story. The lead element can be put even in the sixth or seventh paragraph of the story.

This kind of pattern is bit confusing and is not much preferred.

To Conclude

Occasionally, a story lends itself to special treatment in sentence structure and display to catch the reader's attention. But a reporter must be careful not to try to be too clever or too cute. There could be many examples of novelty leads many of which we have already discussed.

Most leads can be improved if the reporter stretches his or her imagination, knows what makes this particular story different and stresses that angle in clear and concise words.

5

News Sources and Sourcing

A newspaper requires everyday hundreds of stories to be printed on various pages under different sections. The same is the case with an electronic media organisation—a radio station or a TV news channel. How to get news, more and more news, is a challenge which any news organisation has to meet. This hunger for news is never ending.

Newspapers have their own sources of getting the news which are authentic and reliable. Newspapers depend on them and get the news that they want. Those manning these sources of news are trained people who work in a highly professional manner.

News Channels

The editorial department of a newspaper receives news through a variety of sources and channels.

1. From local sources through the newspaper's own reporters, who gather news from regular beats, flesh it out with background from the newspaper's library and do most of the writing in the newspaper office under the direction of the news editor or the chief reporter.
2. From national and foreign sources through the wire services and syndicates such as the Press Trust of India (PTI) and the United News of India (UNI). In addition, commercial syndicates provide many of the features and columns used. Some of this material is received by wire and except for copyreading, is ready for publication.

   Many feature services send material to their client newspapers by mail if it does not fit into the immediate-news category. The news editor or the chief sub-editor incharge of a desk is responsible for handling this material, although the task may be assigned to a copy editor. Credit is given by use of the name or initials of the press service that provided the material on each story used. The press service or syndicate may be credited in a byline, or the initials may be included in the dateline, which is the line at the beginning of a story giving its place of origin: New Delhi (PTI)

A local story needs no dateline, although some papers use it. Some papers reserve the right to combine stories from various services to which they subscribe. In these cases, the story usually carries a byline, saying, "Compiled from News Agencies."

3. From state and regional sources through correspondents. Much of this material is written and ready for publication, although many chief sub-editors incharge of 'Stale News'page either rewrite the stories or heavily edit them. Occasionally a correspondent simply dictates his notes to a state desk reporter who will write the story. Such stroies often have "Special to the (name of newspaper)" preceding or in the dateline. In addition, some reporters gather stories by telephone from news sources such as police and city officials in communities in the newspaper's circulation area.
4. From various individuals and organisations, such as chambers of commerce; public information offices of various social and educational organisations; public relations agencies through the mail, by telephone or during personal visits. Most of this material is rewritten by the city staff under the direction of the city editor.

News Gathering

Most news gathering is straightforward and uncomplicated. A reporter may be assigned for specific jobs like covering a cricket match, a convention of a political party or a labour strike in a factory. During such a course, a reporter has the background information, attends the event, observes it, makes notes, asks for further information from sources available at the location and writes the story. Or he/she may take an interview, check facts and write down the story.

But often it is not that simple. A reporter may face access problems or several other obstacles. There is no law in the country to enforce an individual to disclose whatever he/she knows about an event to a reporter even if the event has significance for the public and the people involved are public figures. A source can prefer silence for valid reasons: the news can endanger his/her business plans, might cost him/her money, might invade his/her privacy, or he/she might not have the authority to disclose it. If the reporter believes his/her audience should not be denied the information, he/she should find ways to dig for facts.

The reporter should locate alternate sources. It is rare that newsworthy facts are corked up in only one flask.

He/she may publish a story reporting the source's refusal to talk. That itself is newsworthy. However, this is a dangerous weapon and should be used with scrupulous care. For example, if he/she writes about a man's refusal to disclose who used the pistol owned by him in a murder case can directly implicate him as the murderer.

There are cases where reporters have masqueraded as gardeners or waiters to get access to news sources. There is the famous case of a Delhi correspondent creating a violent scene on the road and getting arrested for doing a story on the uninhabitable conditions of jails in Delhi. In one case, a reporter hid in a closet of a city council meeting to listen a session discussing a proposed tax revision. The councillors could not make out how the reporter got the proceedings of the meeting with so much accuracy.

Competition is yet another hazard faced by reporters in the process of racing against time. Often some reporters stoop to the act as thieves stealing another's report. There are occasions when correspondents have agreed to become syndicated to make out a better story. This is particularly so when one reporter cannot cover an event by himself.

Some editors lay down firm rules against syndicating of any kind with competitors. Often this arrangement dulls the initiative and reporters get lazy. Their reports also will become routine. When an important news source is willing to talk to only one reporter a pool management is unavoidable. The story of swearing—in function of President Johnson into office on the plane immediately after the assassination of John F. Kennedy was reported to the world by one correspondent who represented the entire media of the world.

Types of News Sources

For the coverage of any event, incident or happening, a reporter has to bank on his/her sources. These Cources can broadly be divided into two categories:

External/Identified/Known/Scheduled Sources

In this category, all such sources can be included which are available and accessible to a reporter.

The reporters mostly cover public meetings, functions, seminars, lectures, or any other similar kind of programme. These are scheduled programmes where the date, time, venue, agenda or topic of discussion, occasion, everything is predecided.

The organisers of any such programme are supposed to inform the reporters with a request for coverage. The reporters can ask for more details from the organisers, else they can try to collect information from their own sources, i.e., library, reference sections etc.

Press conferences and press briefings are also regular sources of news. These are scheduled events and the hosts will always approach the reporters for attending them. Not only the date and venue are conveyed to reporters, the hosts also provide logistic support to them, so as to ensure proper coverage.

The sources in all the above mentioned events/programmes, are identified and can be quoted by the reporters in their writings if it is desired The local office-bearer of the city unit of the Congress or the BJP will be a source for the public meeting to be addressed by a senior leader of the party. The principal/director of the college or a senior functionary of the NGO/social service organisation will be a source for the seminar to be organised for discussing some social/contemporary issue.

If the reporter has taken pains to cover a public meeting or attend a seminar (which he/she should do in any case), he/she will not find it difficult to write the report. If the reporter fails in reaching the spot for the coverage, he/she has to again depend on the organisers concerned for getting the oral input or the printed release.

Press conferences and press briefings are addressed by the persons in authority—an administrative or police officer, a minister, a spokesperson, an industrialist or big businessman, or an eminent personality. These are considered official and authentic sources mostly known to common people.

In fact, a lot of information flows from government sources. For instance in a district, DM/Collector is the most important and reliable source for the reporter. The government information officer in a district further carries forward the information received from the state headquarters through the DM. In case of development programmes and schemers, Chief Development Officer/District Development Officer becomes an important source.

In crime related incidents, top police officers like SSP or SP, CP, DCP or ACP and middle level police officers like Inspector or Sub-inspector are vital sources. The way violence is increasing in our society and terrorist strikes are becoming routine, the importance of police as source in constantly increasing for reporters.

The sources in this category are mostly the people who hold positions and who are mostly known in large sections of society. However, sometimes the spectators in a public meeting, participants of a seminar, beneficiary of a government welfare scheme and eyewitness of an incident can also be an important source. But a reporter should always be careful of the credential of such a source before using him/her in the report.

Because all details in a news story are facts gathered by the reporter, the information in every story should be traceable to its source. The source should be named and statements should be attributed to the person who made them. Here is an analysis of a news story showing how the facts in the story were drawn from various sources:

Source of News	*News Type: Crime*	*News Content*
Police	The son of a businessman knocked down two police officers with his car during a dramatic chase after they tried to arrest him in drug charges on Thursday.	What took place

(*Contd.*)

Source of News	*News Type: Crime*	*News Content*
Police	Sahil, 28, a resident of Srinagar was jailed following arrest. He was charged with two counts of aggravated assault on a police officer, one count of evading arrest and one count of soliciting to purchase drugs.	Identification of man arrested and charges
Police	Munirka Police had raided a known drug house in Vasant Vihar and arrested four other people on drug charges when the incident occurred about 8 p.m.	Specific details
Police	Sahil allegedly purchased what he believed to be coaine from undercover officers, then ran to his Sonata when they attempted to arrest him, CBI officer Dasgupta said.	More details
Police	Officer Raman Kumar opened the passenger door just as Sahil slammed the car into reverse. He was dragged 10 to15 feet before he fell to the ground. The car struck Officer Sukumaran who was behind the vehicle, "a glancing blow and knocked him down," Dasgupta said.	More details
Police	Sahil wrecked his car about a half-block away, then tried to escape on foot before he was caught by police.	More details
Hospital officials and police	Raman and Sukumaran of the Special cell were treated at AIIMS Hospital and released.	Details of injuries
Police Dept.	Police Officer said that Sahil is accused in a drug case registered by Mumbai police three years agos.	

The outstanding news value of this story is conflict—a police raid, an attempted escape, two police officers injured. It is timely because it happened on the day of Publication. It was given more length and displayed prominently because of the unusual aspect of the man's attempt to flee and the injury to the police officers. In addition, the on-going "war on drugs" by police had strong reader appeal.

Internal Confidential Sources/Personal Contacts

These are the sources developed by the reporter on his/her own. They are termed as contacts of a reporter. Any reporter would have a variety of reliable and highly placed contacts. These contacts are sources of exclusive information for the reporter.

These sources may be in the government, public or private sector business or just anywhere. A reporter has to work hard to develop a source in any office or department. For this purpose, reporters keep an eye on insiders who form the dissatisfied lot, or who are moved by vengeance or vendetta. The radicals who want to change the system or the potential whistleblowers can also agree to be the source for a reporter.

These are the exclusive sources who act in close confidence with the reporter. These sources can be tapped till the time the natural trust is maintained. If the source has some vested interest, the reporters are mostly ready to oblige. This could be even in the form of some payments which undoubtedly cannot stand on the moral ground or the professional ethics.

However, most of the confidential sources are good people who join hands with the reporter (in anonymity) for some good cause. An insider can decide to act as confidential sources for some reporter and this has to be his/her well thought of decision. But in many cases, the concerned people might not be aware of the fact that they are being used as source by some reporter. For instance, a valuable tip-off may come from an ordinary person such as the bodyguard driver or domestic help of a VVIP.

Some of the personal contacts of a reporter may like to be quoted for the story as it gives them publicity. In case of a critical story, they may not risk their neck. In such a case, the reporter has to put this in the story—

According to sources..........................[instead of writing official or authentic sources].

Tapping the News Sources

A reporter faces a lot of obstacles in newsgathering, the most serious one is tapping sources for news. Knowing the source and having access to it is a challenge before a reporter. There are everyday informants to help the reporters and who among these informants can turn to regular and dependable source is something to be explored by the concerned reporter.

In the case of both identified and confidential sources, a reporter has to work a lot to tap the source. There are more visible and less visible sources, close and accessible and difficult to access source, routine written source and unconfirmed oral source, well-placed or a passersby source.

Sources could be diverse. From legislators to ministers, secretaries, political appointees to corporators and MCD officials, everybody qualifies to be a source. But there should always be a testing period for the source as a reporter would like to wait till the credentials of the source are proved.

A reporter should be careful enough not to make any promise to the source. For example, a reporter collects some information from a source, uses it for writing a news report and submits the report to the chief reporter. The report is finally not cleared by the news editor and so doesn't appear in the newspaper. If the reporter has made a firm commitment to the source about the publication of the news report, he/she will find it difficult to save face in case of non-publication.

A reporter faces some other problems as well. Sometimes, the source goes missing at the hour of need, an overtalkative source can confuse, a sophisticated source can come out with modest information less than what is desired, a fresh source may indulge in gossip and rumours. While quoting numbers to the source, a reporter should always be careful.

Credibility of Source

Often, government sources are reluctant to talk to news reporters if they consider some information sensitive. And one wonders if there is any information they do not consider sensitive. If a reporter wants to know something from the secretary of a ministry but the secretary does not cooperate with him, he/she will go to other officials in the ministry. If none of them talks, he/she may be tempted to talk to the Personal Assistant or some other staff or even to some friend or relation of the secretary.

The ideal relationship between a reporter and his/her sources is that of mutual trust. Mutual trust comes from the past behaviour of both parties. If the reporter does not enjoy the trust of his/her sources, he/she will not get their cooperation. And if he/she cannot trust them, he/she cannot write his/her story on the basis of what they tell him/her.

A reporter should rely on the source only when his/her

credibility is established. It the source is genuine and has provided the correct and accurate information, the reporter, would be able to fiie an authentic report. It is the responsibility of the reporter to ensure the truthfulness of a report by having reliable sources.

Protection of Source

A reporter should treat his/her sources as sacred. He/she should give his/her sources proper respect so that the bond gets strengthened and the reporter continues to get important, relevant and news-worthy information.

When the information has been supplied by identified or known source, he/she must be quoted in the news report. But the problem arises when the source is a personal contact of the reporter. In such a case his/her identity should not be disclosed.

Sometimes there may be pressure on the reporter from the government or the judiciary to disclose the source. But it is the professional and moral responsibility of the reporter to protect his/her source. Protecting one's source is a cardinal principal of journalism.

It may be noted here that there is no legal protection or immunity granted to a journalist for the non-disclosure of source. If in a legal case, the court of law asks a reporter to disclose the name of the source, he/she has no option except to oblige the court. Else he/she has should be ready to face the wrath of the court.

If a reporter fails to protect his/her source, he/she may loose, his/her credibility as a journalist. Disclosure of the name can put the source in trouble, even his/her life can be in danger. Hence, no genuine reporter should/will take the risk of revealing the identity of the source.

Sourcing

All news material published in a newspaper must be authentic. Authenticity is best achieved by factual presentation. This will mean supplying all facts relating to an incident, event or happening and as many facets of the reality as possible so that the reader has no doubt as to its veracity.

Sourcing is essential to ensure factuality, to locate accountability and to give a sense of confidence to the editor. It is not always easy. All statements made to the reporter or reaching the newspaper directly and duly signed can be attributed to some persons. Reports are generally based on the reporter's direct experience or on statements made by others.

This takes us to what are called on-the-record statements. A person says something and agrees to be quoted. In such a case, the reporter is free to submit his report, subject, of course, to a knowledge of the laws of libel, invasion of privacy and his own judgment of what is newsworthy. There is, however, a difficulty here. Somebody (*a*) may say that someone else (*b*) is a cheat.

It is a fact that A said something. Whether what he/she said is true or not is the reporter's business to cross check. B may simply deny it, which means loss of credibility for the reporter and the newspaper. On a private level, people may sue the reporter/newspaper.

Generally, there is no trouble about on-the-record statements. The reporter checks facts and also checks with other persons mentioned in the statement. For instance, he/she would check with B about what A has said.

There are occasions when the reporter is sceptical of an on-the-record statement because it seems on the face of it implausible. Suppose he/she sees extraordinary activity in the Naval headquarters and also military aircraft flying southwards. If he/she is politically conscious, he/she would connect it with some conflict. The reporter calls the Naval headquarters and is told that there is nothing unusual in such a movement.

Yet something tells him/her that all is not normal. Here, he/she is torn between his/her duty to disclose to the public vital information and silence (or denial) by official sources. So the reporter tries other methods—of intuition, logic and risk. He/she looks for circumstantial evidence. He/she may tempt a naval rating to disclose the destination and through clever questioning of officials make useful deductions even from their silence.

Generally, the case for sourcing or attribution is put thus by Alfred Friendly, one-time Managing Editor of the *Washington Post*:

> "Direct attribution is the best way of handling news and information about an event or conditions or situations of which we do not have direct eye-witness knowledge ourselves. This is always that best way, in as much as it provides the reader

> with a knowledge of the source, enabling him to evaluate the credibility for himself. It involves no pretence of having direct knowledge which we do not have. It avoids the risk of having the newspaper used to disseminate material for which the author is unwilling to take responsibility."

It is also necessary to examine off-the-record statements where the person explicitly forbids publication of information he/she has disclosed. If the reporter agrees to that condition, he/she is morally bound not to publish it. If he/she violates the assurance, he/she loses potential or actual source of information. Off-the-record statements may be made because the source wants to protect an innocent individual or throw a veil over corruption or crime.

There are instances of what American newsmen call "smart diplomacy." Presidents and other dignitaries calculatedly leak stories to assess public reaction to a measure they propose to adopt. Ivan and Carol Doig speak of John Kennedy leaking a story regarding the appointment of his brother as the attorney general. When the reaction was not negative, he made the appointment, sparing himself the plight of having to reverse his own decision.

Quite often reporters insist on being told in advance whether the information the source is giving is off-the-record. This is not always an easy operation. Reporters and their usual sources have a lot of give and take which they must honour. Clever reporters give away less. They do not accept favours from sources so that their freedom to report is in no way undermined. Sources, too, do not antagonise the reporter because it is through him they reach the audiences. Both need each other. The reporter, because of his/her media connection, has an edge over the source, however, in this see-saw.

The strategy a reporter should adopt must thus be: As soon as the reporter knows that the source is about to disclose important information, he/she must stop the source and warn him/her that the information would be published. Even if the source refuses permission, the reporter, having got an inkling of what is about to be disclosed, can work on other clues and approach other sources. But where the reporter agrees to keep information off-the-record, he cannot and must not disclose the source even if he comes into conflict with the law. In some countries the reporter retains the right not to disclose his/her source.

While most information in a news story is traced to a source, facts which are general knowledge or which can be verified readily need not be attributed.

There should be a clear demarcation between information the reporter is giving on his own and information he attributes to a source. Otherwise, identification of source becomes difficult. The lead paragraph in a recent report on Dr. Gautam Goswami says: Dr. Gautam Goswami has been reportedly placed under suspension," the second paragraph however sounds emphatic adding: "the suspension order, issued by the Union Home Minister, did not give any reason." If the reporter knew that the suspension order was issued by the Home Ministry why he had to say "reportedly suspended." Such a confusion in sourcing will alienate the reader's trust.

All reporters need to check facts given out by a source. They should not take them readily as true. According to John Griffith and Edward G. Weston, authors of Programme Newswriting, "a compulsion to verify information from every source is a healthy quality in a journalist." Suppose you ask the police officer for the name of a suspect and he gives you with an air of assurance the name of someone else, you are sure to land yourself in the dock if you do not cross-check.

Thus the copy editor and the reporter preceding him must check on facts given by the source and more importantly the authority and credibility of the source to give such information. In all countries, certain officials are designated "official spokesmen" and the nature of information they can give is well defined.

From experience reporters know that some persons, because of their situation and office, are in a position to release information with the stamp of authority. A post-master general can authoritatively disclose information on the number of new post offices to be opened. A secretary for agriculture on the other hand is not the proper authority to say if India is signing a new defence deal with the United States.

To put it briefly, a source acquires authenticity from the office he or she holds. There may be cases, where sources lose their credibility and, therefore, authenticity when they pass on information which is found to be unreliable and is contradicted later. For instance tourists, Africa watchers, or China arrivals cannot be incontrovertible sources of information. Or, take a refugee from Afghanistan. He may be one of the few thousands who fled that country, but he need not necessarily be politically aware enough to interpret the situation in his country. Such sources are unreliable. Fred Holliday says that most of the stories on Afghanistan are manufactured in the United States, Britain and Pakistan.

It is advisable for governments not to withhold information on flimsy or technical grounds. Such a course drives the reporters to monitoring unreliable sources. The reader respects a source because the source has the authority to give information or is in a position to come into possession of such information. The reader doubts information which is gathered from sources who have no means to gather or the authority to give such information.

The reporter must never take all information from a source unquestioningly. He/she must explore the motive of the source in giving such information, always reading in between the lines. Suppose a reporter asks the police commissioner.

Is it true that 15 persons died in police firing yesterday at 10 a.m.?

PC : There is no truth in it.
REP : Then how many died?
PC : Nobody.

The Police Commissioner is telling a lie about the number of deaths and yet getting away with it because it is true that nobody died in the police firing at 10 a.m. However, 30 people were killed in the firing at 9.45 a.m.

Need for Attribution

Sourcing or attribution means acknowledging the source in the news report. Attribution is necessary in all kinds of news reports except in the case, where the information is common knowledge or indisputable.

A news report is based on two things—

(*a*) Reporter's direct experience.
(*b*) Statements made by others.

(*a*) There is no difficulty about reporting on realities the reporter has witnessed. He/she can attend any public meeting, seminar, function etc., and file a report. He/she may witness any accident site and write a report on what he/she has seen.

(*b*) On many occasions, the reporter is not on the scene and has not witnessed the happening. In such a case, he/she has to depend on the information given or statement made by others. He/she has to identify his/her source in the news report and thus attribution becomes necessary.

Attribution's importance does not reduce even if the reporter is a witness to something. For example, a *Public meeting*—while writing a report on a public meeting covered by the reporter himself/herself, he/she would like to add the statement by the organisers of the meetings as also the reactions expressed by those attending the meeting.

For example: *Accident*—A reporter might visit the spot where the accident has taken place and write a report based on what he has seen or experienced. But at the same time, he/she has to put in the news report the statements made by eyewitnesses and the information given by police authorities.

Identification of Source

Attribution is done by quoting eyewitnesses, government spokesperson, or an individual making the statement. Whenever such a person figures in the news story, he/she must by identified by name and designation. Statements or versions not so identified will automatically get attributed to the reporter or the newspaper.

Sourcing is essential to ensure factuality, to locate accountability and to give a sense of confidence to the editor. It is not always easy. All statements made to the reporter or reaching the newspaper directly and duly signed can be attributed to some persons.

Example—Press releases, press statements.

However, the problem arises when the source prefers to remain anonymous and insists on not to be quoted. If the source is one of the contacts of the reporter, the latter would himself/herself like not to disclose the source's identity. Under the circumstances, there are two courses available to the reporter.

1. He/she may attribute the information as according to sources, reliable sources, confidential sources, sources who preferred to remain anonymous, etc.
2. Using the information given by the contact as a tip-off, the reporter can further investigate the matter to collect evidence in support of the information. In such a case, no attribution would be required.

How to Attribute?

The attribution should be in the lead for controversial or accusatory information, but in many other cases it can be delayed so that it doesn't clutter the lead. Police stories often have attribution in the lead, especially when you get information by telephone or if the information is accusatory.

1. *Example*: *A 15-year-old boy was stabbed twice in the chest Thursday afternoon when he apparently tried to break up a fight in a crowded parking lot near Nehru Place, authorities said.*

Police and school official said the stabbing, believed to have occurred after one student took another's tiffin, was the first they could recall at ABC school.

Here general attribution is in the lead, but the specific attribution is in the second paragraph. Also in the following example, the name of the research organisation is mentioned in the second paragraph. Perhaps long name of the organisation is too cumbersome to be used in the lead.

2. *Example: U.S. college students, criticised as over materialistic in the 1980s, are showing increased interest in social causes such as the environment and less interest in making money, a new study says.*

The 25th annual survey of college students, conducted by the American Council of Education and the University of California, Los Angeles, shows steadily changing attitudes.

Off-the-Record

This is something related to sourcing or attribution. Most of the times, the source talks to the reporter on-the-record providing the latter the required information. But when the source insists on not to be quoted, he/she is said to be talking off-the-record.

When the source has provided some information to the reporter and agrees to be quoted, he/she is said to be talking on the record. This is the most comfortable situation for the reporter but he/she has to adopt a cautious approach. It is his/her responsibility to cross-check the facts because publication of any wrong information will mean loss of credibility for the reporter and the newspaper.

Though on-the-record statements are the best, one needs to check the contents of the statement for their veracity, for libel or violation of right of privacy.

Off-the-record statement can be given in two situations—

1. Where the source is willing to provide the information, is also interested in the publication/broadcasting of the information but is not willing to be quoted.
   In such a case, the reporter should be ready to oblige the source. He/she writes the report by referring to source as "reliable" or "authentic".
2. Where the source is providing the information willingly but this information is said to be for the personal consumption of the reporter and not for publication.

The second situation is more complicating. Any off-the-record statement can be made by a politician during an interview, a press conference or an informal chat. But any statement is to be treated as off-the-record only when the person explicitly restricts publication of information he/she has given.

We need to examine the role of the source as well as that of the reporter in the case of an off-the-record statement.

Role of Source

A source can make an off-the-record statement—

(*a*) for wooing the reporter, winning his/her confidence and buidling a strong relationship with him/her, or

(*b*) for saving his/her skin from any possible fall-out of the publication of the information, or

(*c*) for maligning the image of any of his opponents without himself/herself coming into light.

Role of Reporter

If the reporter has agreed not to quote the source or not to publish the information given by him/her.

(*a*) he/she can decide to honour his words because if he/she violates the assurance, he/she loses potential or actual source of information, or

(*b*) he/she can ask his/her source as to why he/she chooses to speak only off-the-record, And if he/she is not convinced with the explanation, he/she can make his/her own judgment on the issues involved such as public good; and subsequently can decide to publish the information, or

(*c*) he/she can ask his/her source to allow him/her to be quoted. And if he/she fails, he/she may look for another source who agrees to be quoted on the same subject.

6

Reporting for News Media

Newsgathering and newswriting is a professional job undertaken by reporters at various levels in different media organisations. Reporters or correspondents work in city reporting rooms, bureaus, state and regional offices, district headquarters, blocks and even village level. While many of them are highly placed covering Parliament and diplomatic missions, many of them even work as stringers or part-timers from remote locations.

Reporting is an essential activity in all kinds of media organisations—daily newspapers, weeklies and other periodicals, news agencies, radio and TV channels and cyber media. The imgredients or elements of reporting remain the same everywhere though the organisational and operational part of reporting has some differences. In any case reporting assumes more importance in dailies than periodicals.

Much has been written about report writing in previous chapters but little has been discussed on the conceptual part of reporting. We shall discuss in this chapter, the principles of reporting which include objectivity and the social accountability in reporting, also the intricacies of reporting in different media.

Principles of Reporting

Principles of reporting are difficult to elaborate as no distinguished journalist or scholar has attempted to define them. However, an attempt has been made here to identify some important principles—

1. Objectivity
   - Non-partisan
   - balanced.

2. Accuracy
    - Relevant details
    - Truthful facts.
3. Substantial
    - Research based, in-depth
    - Informative, educative.
4. Focussed
    - Issue based, to the point
    - Crisp, not too long.
5. Socially responsible
    - Reasonable, rational
    - Safeguard of people's interests.

Objectivity in Reporting

Objectivity in reporting is a concept not covered by any legal regime. There is no law laying down the principles of objectivity. Media organisations have voluntarily accepted objectivity as a sacred media tradition. Because it will not be fair to common people if issues pertaining to them are not dealt with properly.

We can always trace the birth of objectivity to the birth of news agencies whose primary obligation was reporting only facts. However, facts themselves sometimes could lead to social conflict. In such cases, objectivity alone does not save a situation, but it can certainly lead to responsibility. This is where responsibility too should be an important element of journalism.

The advances in communication and information technologies have imparted greater power to communication and therefore, a sharper edge to its consequences. A moving and talking picture of an event is a hundred times more impactful than a printed word or a still. This has imparted a new urgency to the entire debate of responsibility and the need to draft and re-draft existing codes of ethic. Today, the magnitude and the economics of mass media operations have resulted in primacy being accorded to market objectives. Consequently, there has been a reshuffle in media priorities.

In India, the growth of investigative journalism, after the internal emergency, led to a new phenomenon. This new phenomenon has done a lot of service to Indian public life, but no less dis-service, too.

We witness a decline in professional and ethical standards in newspapers, half-baked investigative reporting and poor editing. The former director of PII calls it partisan reporting in Indian newspapers.

Some of the findings of the Press Council call for a return to objective journalism. The Council mildly criticised the *Times of India* for its reporting of Indira Gandhi's assassination. The Council advised that in reporting on or writing about communal or other sensitive matters, newspapers should exercise proper restraint and caution.

These are other examples as well, *The Illustrated Weekly of India* was sued by former Orissa Chief Minister, J.B. Patnaik for damages worth rupees one crore. *The Sunday Observer* was in trouble for linking the sister of a famous film actor with the Prime Minister of Pakistan in a romantic manner.

The United States was rocked in the 1980s, by a woman (Janet Cooke) who wrote a piece of fiction in the *Washington Post* and managed to win the Pulitzer Prize for the story. In fact, it was the Post which later found that the piece was a fiction.

Social Responsibility

Objectivity in reporting leads to social responsibility or to put it the other way round a socially responsible press has to ensure objectivity in reporting. In principle it sounds nice but the present day practices in media compel us to rethink.

Take for instance the case [June 2006] of Batuk Nath Chaudhary, a teacher in Patna, who fell in love with his student. To teach him a lesson, his wife called press people and publicly humiliated him before the camera. Later, television channels were charged with abetting the public humiliation of Chaudhary. Patna SSP Kundan Krishna accused the media of overstepping their limits.

This was not the first incident when television channels were accused of engaging in pro-active roles in their bid to capture sensational images. Within two months of this incident, another incident happened in Gaya. On the Independence Day in 2006, a contractor with the state run Sudha Dairy set himself on fire, allegedly egged on by TV cameramen.

Manoj Mishra, allegedly protesting against non-payment of

bills, succumbed to burn injuries. The police registered a case against unnamed media personnel for 'abetment'. Gaya Superintendent of Police told *The Indian Express* the television teams present there coaxed the man to immolate himself. One cameraman soaked the man's towel in diesel and coaxed him to light it up assuring that it will be put off after they record pictures.

No doubt, concepts have started changing, new trends have set in and objectivity and social responsibility are being reinterpreted. All this is happening under growing influence of television. The news channels in India, particularly Hindi and language channels, are redefining reporting, whether good or bad for journalism is yet to be analysed.

Reporting for Different Media

The planning, organisation and action in reporting as also selection and presentation of news vary from medium to medium. Some differences are so loud and clear that even a common sensible user of news can make out. While print media focusses on contents, television in packaging. While print media concentrates on sensitivity, television on sensation. While print media maintains a balance, television creates a hype. No doubt, these are exceptions on both sides.

For a learner, understanding of reporting in a daily newspaper should be the first and foremost task. The reporting network in a newspaper is vast and complex and its handling demands lots of expertise. One who has done reporting in a daily for few years can be fitted into any news organisation, particularly the scribe who would have started as a trainee in the City Reporting Room.

Daily Newspaper

The reporting network in a daily newspaper includes city reporting room in the city from where the newspaper is published, bureaus in the national capital and the state capitals and reporting offices and correspondents in districts and towns close to the place of publication which are considered the main circulation areas of the newspaper.

The thrust of reporting is on the coverage from the districts, cities, villages where the newspaper is largely circulated. The reporting is mainly community oriented and even small incidents and happenings become major news. The emphasis is on extensive and widespread coverage in the defined area and so the number of news reports in an issue are many in number and small in size.

For a better understanding, you can take the example of *Amar Ujala* and *Dainik Jagran* published from Bareilly, Meerut and so many other places, or *Hindustan* published from Varanasi and Agra besides other places. English newspapers like *The Indian Express* have also their publications from different cities. But for a better understanding of the network and nature of reporting, you need to look at publication operating as an independent unit serving the people in a small region.

News Magazine

Reporting is not the thrust area in a news magazine which focusses more on follow up, analytical and research-based stories. Whatever reports are filed, most of them are clubbed to make one major story or few can be taken as leg stories with a major story. Obviously, the job demands more editing skills than reporting qualifications.

A news magazine has a bureau in the main office i.e., the place of publication. There are not more than two or three bureaus or offices of the magazine in the country. Since a news magazine is either weekly or fortnightly correspondents in the bureau have enough time to finish the reporting assignments given to them, even if it involves travelling to different locations.

For a better understanding, you can take the example of *India Today* and *Outlook*. You can even find in these magazines that on many occasions important stories are assigned to those whose names appear in the print line as assistant, associate or joint editors and not to correspondents. This proves the point that the dividing line between reporting and editing is not as sharp in a magazine as it is in a daily newspaper.

News Agency

News agency is nothing else but a reporting network. Its reporting infrastructure is very vast, so widespread that no part of the country remains uncovered. While a daily newspaper might have its correspondents in 10 to 15 districts, a news agency has its correspondents in more than 500 districts of the country.

A news agency has a bureau at its headquarter or main office, bureaus in state capitals, bureaus/regional offices in major cities and stringers in every district of the country. For coverage from abroad, correspondents are posted in major cities in the world which include Washington DC, London, Brussels, and West Asia. Besides, a news agency in India enters into an agreement with one or the other agency of Europe or the United States for getting international news.

For a better understanding, you can take the example of PTI and UNI, the two indigenous news agencies. Almost all the news organisations as also number of non-media organisations subscribe to the services of PTI and UNI. These subscribers might be based in any part of the country yet they find the news reports of these agencies useful.

The news agency reports are mostly concise, straight, informative and factual. If you want to look for objectivity in reporting, look at agency reports. These reports are free from any bias, having no tilt towards this side or that side. They have a national canvass yet a local flavour fulfilling the needs of newspapers right from Cochin to Guwahati.

Pool Reporting

This is a centralised system of reporting. In this system, a News Pool is created in the News Room, wherein news stories received from different sources, are compiled, edited and made available for further use.

News Pool can be created in any media organisation—Newspaper, New Agency, Radio or Television. It helps in the handling of a large number of news items and controls the inflow and outflow, smoothly and effectively.

Pool in Newspaper

The Times of India has a New Pool, named as "Times News Network" and *The Indian Express* has a news pool "Express News Service". The central pool of these newspapers is in Delhi office. The reporters and correspondents posted at all the publication centres, including Delhi, submit their selected copies in the News Pool. These copies are selected on the basis of their national and international importance.

An Asstt. Editor can be made incharge of the News Pool. He/she and his/her subordinate editorial staff shall assess the news value of the stories, edit and headline them to finally despatch them to different publication centres with necessary instructions for their use.

News Pool system is effective in newspapers which have chained publication i.e., publication of a newspaper from a number of cities in the country. In today's time, most of the multi-edition English, Hindi and language newspapers have created news pools. The news pool helps *The Hindustan Times,* Mumbai, to exchange news from Delhi and vice versa, *Hindustan Times,* Lucknow, to exchange news from Patna and vice versa and so on.

The success of the News Pool depends on the contribution of correspondents working with a particular edition and the motivation of the News Editor to get the relevant stories done by respective correspondents. For instance, if a correspondent posted at the Nagpur edition of *The Indian Express* covers a story on the farmers' suicide in Vidarbha region, he/she should always keep this in mind that his story will possibly be carried in all the editions of *The Indian Express*. The News Editor should also make it a point that this story is definitely sent to the News Pool as contribution from Nagpur.

News Pool can prove effective when correspondents at different locations file reports on the same subject or topic, and the Pool Editor decides to club these stories to make one major story. For instance, if the Surat based correspondent files a report on floods with *The Times of India*, Vadodara and the correspondent in Panchmahal files a report on floods with *The Times of India,* Ahmedabad. These two reports having been sent to the News Pool will definitely be converted in a major story on foods in western and central Gujarat. [Take reference to floods that hit Gujarat in July/August, 2006]

Example: On August 15, 2006, Kochi correspondent filed a report that IT majors Charter Mercantile Agency and Affiliated Computer Services were forced to down shutters after officials threatened them with criminal prosecution for working on a national holiday. The same day Kolkata correspondent filed a report that BPOs functioned as normal with the State Government maintaining that they will never be asked to close even for a day as it would amount to 'closing a power plant on a holiday.'

The 'Express News Service' clubbed the two reports to highlight the contradictions in the Left parties. The news report was headlined as "On August 15, tale of two Comrades: Kerala shuts down BPOs, Bengal says will never do that."

Pool in News Agency

Like a newspaper, a news agency can also create a news pool at its central office. Sometimes an agency can have two news pools—one at the state level and the other at the Central level.

The Central News Pool is to receive news items from the state offices, regional offices, stringers at district headquarters and also from correspondents abroad. The stories are then selected on the basis of their news value, edited and sent to the subscribers for use.

There is also an example of a few agencies joining hands to create a pool. This was done by non-aligned countries under the banner of Non-Aligned Movement (NAM) and the pool thus created was named as Non-Aligned News Agency Pool. The basic objective of this pool was the exchange of news reports among non-aligned countries so that they do not remain dependant on western news agencies.

Pool in Radio

News Pool can also be created in radio and TV news networks. For instance in All India Radio, News Pool is created in the General News Room (GNR) and Hindi News Room (HNR). The contributors to these news pools are Delhi based correspondents, Regional News Unit (RNU) correspondents, stringers, correspondents abroad and News Agencies—PTI and UNI.

In AIR, every story has to be routed through News Pool. Any story to be included in a bulletin has to be picked up from the Pool. These are two News Pools—News Pool 1 and New Pool 2. Pool 1 carries reports originating from India and Pool 2 comprises reports originating from outside India. The Pools are named as per the shifts like Morning Pool, Day Pool, Evening Pool, etc.

Rewrites

Rewriting is a common practice in the editorial department of a newspaper. It takes place at various levels. On many occasions, the sub-editors/copy editors take information over the phone from reporters on regular beats and then prepare a news story, often with the reporter's byline on it.

These copy editors work with one on more reporters who may be covering the scene of a major fire, bridge collapse or other disaster. The reporters on the scene phone the information to the rewrite desk, where the facts are woven into an accurate and interesting story. Papers in smaller cities use this system of rewrite only occasionally, usually for last-minute stories gathered right on deadline.

"Rewriting" can also mean producing a new story from a clipping taken from another publication or a press release. It can also mean rewriting a story because the editor did not like the way it was written originally. Most editors will give the story back to the reporter who wrote it for rewriting. However, if the reporter is not available, a rewrite person may handle it.

Often the persons assigned to rewrite on larger newspapers are among the best writers and most capable members of the editorial staff. They usually work with reporters on the beats. The job of rewriting less significant stories from clippings and press releases frequently goes to the newest reporter on the staff.

In rewriting a story from another newspaper or other source, the reporter must first verify the facts in the clipping and then attempt to get additional facts to use in the rewrite. The object is to have the story appear to be a new one, not simply a repeat of the original story.

To accomplish this, a reporter may start the rewrite by (1) playing up an additional newsworthy fact or facts, or (2) reorganising the story if no new facts are available. In the second case, the story often is shortened unless it is about a very important news event. Obivously, the first method is preferred, but sometimes there simply are no new facts to add to a story. In any event, the rewritten story, especially the lead, should be as different as possible from the original one.

Here are two leads for the same story. The first one appeared in a morning newspaper:

> *Washington—Syrian President Col Gaddafi appealed to the United States in a live televised message on Saturday to ask Israel to withdraw its troops from Lebanon as soon as possible and avert "death, destruction and misery."*

Because there were no new facts to add, an afternoon newspaper used a slightly different approach to the story:

> *Damascus—In an address aimed at the American Presidency this evening, Col Gaddafi of Syria pleaded for understanding of his country's increasingly difficult position in the Persian Gulf crisis; but he repeated his call for the removal of Israeli troops from the Middle East.*

Press Releases

Hundreds of press releases are received every week by most newspapers. They come from private industry, civic groups, religious organisations, educational institutions and just about anyone else who has some information they want to give to the public. Many of them are extremely well written by very talented public relations writers. Others are, quite frankly, badly written.

In many cases, the press release contains no news or information that is of any value to the newspaper's readers. The careful editor has to get them checked by a staff member and then rewritten for publication. However, at some newspapers, both large and small, press releases find their way into print as originally written.

Often the task of rewriting a press release can be easy because the real news may be buried down in the third or fourth paragraph after the public relations writer has plugged his or her client shamelessly in the lead. However, a number of press releases are well written and the task of rewriting them can be tough. A person on rewrite handling a well-written press release needs all the skills and imagination at his or her command to improve what is basically a good story tc start with.

Here is an example of how a press release was rewritten to emphasise the most important news element. The original lead on the press release reads:

> *A spokesperson of Delhi Government said today that in order to execute the High Court order and in pursuance of the guidelines given by the Central Pollution Control Board, the Cabinet has*

approved setting up a Rs. 1.2 crore sewage treatment plant near Rajghat. The work on the project will commence within one month, expected to be finished by the year-end.

Based on the above press release (60 words), a newspaper wrote a story in the following three paragraphs:

- *Another sewage treatment plant will come up on the embankment of river Yamuna near Rajghat within six months time.*
- *Delhi Cabinet approved the project under pressure of a High Court order which indicted the Dikshit Government for a sharp decline in the water quality of the Yamuna. The Central Pollution Control Board had also criticised the government for unabated river pollution.*
- *However, some people have expressed apprehension asking why the existing sewage treatment plant failed to deliver. [Approx 70 words]*

In the following example, an awkward direct quote lead was rewritten to take the emphasis off the president of the company and focus on the news element. The original lead on the press release was.

"For the first time in 19 months, the company's earnings have risen above the annual dividend rate of Rs. 90 a share," R. Krishna, President of the Sunlight Company, announced today.

The rewritten lead put the company's name at the start of the sentence rather than at the end and told what the actual earnings were for an average share of common stock:

The Sunlight Company today reported that the average earnings of its common stock rose to Rs. 90 a share for the 12 months ending January 31—an increase of Rs 4 a share over last year.

Consolidated net income for the electric utility totaled Rs. 1020 million for the period—up nearly Rs. 155 million, R. Krishna., company president, said.

Although many reporters object strongly to being assigned rewrites, it can provide excellent experience in handling a wide variety of news as well as human-interest and feature stories.

Follows–Ups

There are broadly two kinds of stories done by a reporter—

1. Stories which appear for once and die the same day, example, story based on a press conference, coverage of a function, seminar, etc.
2. Stories which have an element of continuity and where developments are bound to take place. These kind of stories are known as follow-up stories.

Thus, a follow-up story can be defined as a story linked to a major parent story, reporting the developments taking place over a period of time. In other words, it is an updating of an earlier news story in which the latest developments are reported.

Though follow-up stories can be done in any area like political, civil administration, civic or education; but crime and legal proceedings provide the most fertile ground for follow-up stories.

Example: If a murder has taken place, the follow-up stories can be done on the police action/inaction, whether the culprits have been arrested or absconding, whether they have been remanded in police custody or judicial custody, whether the investigations have been completed and charge-sheet has been filed, whether the court has fixed the charges. Then the proceedings of trial, examination of witnesses, arguments/counter arguments by advocates and judgment of the court, all this can be covered in follow-up stories.

Follow-up stories have a two-fold objective:

1. They keep the readers informed on any particular issue or on a major happening and thus take care of their anxiety.
2. They keep a watch on the police/administrative authorities, politicians or other people (as the case may be) and put them under pressure by giving the indication that all their actions/inactions are being monitored.

A follow-up story naturally features the new developments, but the reporter must summarise enough of the background of the original story for the benefit of readers who did not see it and to refresh the memories of those who did. Because this summary refers to an earlier story, it is called, a "tie-back".

The tie-back of one or two short paragraphs follows the lead or second paragraph, but no set rules govern its length or position in the story. One sentence or phrase within a paragraph or within the lead itself may be sufficient to make new developments clear. If the story remains prominent for several days, the tie-back becomes shorter and shorter because chances decrease daily that a reader has missed all the earlier stories. However, in some stories, several paragraphs may be necessary, particularly when the follow-up is published some time after the original story appeared.

The follow-up is handled in the same manner as the rewrite; the reporter uses the facts already in hand and diligently seeks new developments. Except for the tie-backs, follow-ups are written in the same form as a news story.

Most rewrites are brief and about rather insignificant items, as a general rule. The pressure to conserve space is so heavy that information previously seen by a large number of readers must be condensed as much as possible. However, if a big story—a natural disaster such as a flood or earthquake, for example, breaks on the competitor's time, the story is not rewritten, in the usual sense of the term. In fact, reporters are sent to cover the story along with the competition, only they have longer to write it.

Subsequent stories will be follow-ups, just as they are when the newspaper's own first account deserves later developments. Most stories of importance are pursued through later developments for days or weeks and on rare occasion, even years. Reporting of the Watergate scandal in the federal government covered more than two years. A fire or a storm is followed by accounts of relief and reconstruction. Crime is followed through the trial and sentencing. Gradually, the force of the first explosive event plays out, and the follow-ups dwindle away.

Sometimes the follow-up can develop into a much larger story than the original one. A short story may be followed by a longer, more detailed account over several days or weeks until a major story develops. Bank failures, embezzlements of public funds or investigations by Joint Parliamentary Committees may be the basis for stories that will build slowly.

The Developing Story

Another type of follow-up that offers problems of rewriting is the story requiring "latest developments" changes in several editions of one day's newspaper. If a major court trial is in progress, for instance, the newspaper may want an up-to-the-deadline report of the trial in every edition. A newspaper with three editions (NCR, city, late city) will have a different deadline for each edition, and it may require the rewriting of one story (or parts of it) three different times to include the latest newsworthy features in each edition. This type of story is called "developing story", or running story.

It is also a follow-up because it includes developments later than those in the previous story. Moreover, it is something of a rewrite, although it usually does not entail rewriting the bulk of the previous story. A new lead, including latest developments properly linked with previous developments, may be all that is required. Inserts, or "adds", for the original story may fill the need. As much of the original story as possible is left undisturbed.

Developing a story is a common practice in news agencies. With a view to catering to their subscribers—mainly news organisations—more efficiently, they keep on revising the stories where constantly new developments are taking place. For example, Sonia Gandhi's refusal to become prime minister and the following deadlock in 2004 and the Diwali blast in Delhi in 2005 where causalities kept on increasing.

In developing stories, news agencies have the practice of issuing FIRST LEAD, SECOND LEAD, THIRD LEAD, LEAD ALL or NEW INTRO.

Developing stories have got new meaning after the arrival of TV news. The news channels keep on updating most of their news items to give a fresh look to their bulletins.

Embargo

- Embargo means prohibiting, forbidding or restricting something. This word is mostly used in trade or commerce but it is also part of the journalistic terminology.
- Sometimes, on top of the news reports, EMBARGO is printed in bold letters, which means that a particular news item is not to be published or broadcast before the identified time.
- *Example*: *Embargo* [Not to be carried before 8 p.m.]
- This is a style mostly followed in news agency copies or in the press releases or other news material released by the Press Information Bureau (PIB).

- The most common example of *Embargo* is the speech given by the Prime Minister from the Red Fort on August 15, or the President's Address to the nation on the eve of the Republic Day.
- The benefit attached to an *Embargo* item is that the editorial staff get the news material in advance, prepare the stories well in time and go ahead with the publication or broadcast as soon as the deadline is over.
- The dissemination of any information carried by an *Embargo* item is wrong, both professionally and legally.

7

Reporter and Reporting

Everyone who works for a newspaper is there to make it possible for a reporter's stories to get into print and be delivered to the readers. Most of the public attention is focused on reporters mainly because they are the 'point' men and women of the news business. A newspaper's reputation often is based on the public perception of its reporters.

No doubt, reporters take up major responsibility in a newspaper. They collect information from international, national and local arena and present that in a structured form for the consumption of readers. Accordingly reporting is organised at various levels in a newspaper, particularly local reporting assumes utmost importance.

Reporter—Backbone of a Newspaper

It is said that a reporter is both eyes and ears of a news organisation. It is not possible to strictly prescribe qualifications which a good reporter must possess. However, novice reporters must train themselves informally for the job so that they would be able to discharge their responsibilities with confidence, courage and competence.

A reporter should be well-read. He/she should equip himself/herself adequately with all aspects of his/her beat. He/she should cultivate wide contacts with all kinds of sources in his/her beat, sometimes even outside his/her area of activity. He/she should be able to find out information, he/she should have a bend of mind for research.

A reporter should be a perfect talker. He/she should have patience and the ability to get along with any kind of people in difficult situations. To be a successful reporter and to accomplish his/her job competently, he/she must be able to perceive, calculate, predict and plan his/her actions appropriately in anticipation of a news event.

A Reporter Defined

John Hohenberg has this to say as regards the professional requirements of reporters.

"He is diligent without being a busy body, penetrating without being offensive, persuasive without being a confidence man, perceptive without being a reader of tea leaves, thoughtful without being pedantic, skeptical without being a confirmed cynic, thorough without being a stenographer, careful without being hesitant, determined without being argumentative, well-unanswered without being a doormat. He does much more than report the news. Journalism would not be his profession if it were a mere recording network of events. He is a primary force in our daily life, a force that transmits, explains and sometimes originates a worldwide flow of current events and ideas. He exerts a vast and incalculable influence over the people within the range of his communication. He is no demigod. He is reporter on your daily newspaper."

Tools of a Reporter

In order to excel in the profession of reporting one should have certain indispensable tools of the craft with him. What are they? Seasoned journalists who might have made their mark in the field may say that there are not much. It is certainly an exaggeration.

Education

The first tool, of course, is a sound general education. One who lacks in broad eduction may be good for reporting small local events but evidently not suited for an international arena where what is needed is a profound knowledge of history, geography, economics and politics.

Experience

A crime reporter with enough contact with police, lawyers, and court officials may be an asset to any newspaper in that particular field. But he is highly unsuitable to cover the State legislature or Parliament. The basic point is apart from good education, *experience* is one vital aspect which makes a reporter excel in any field. A well-educated man may be able to turn his talent in any field whereas the ill-educated will end up where he has begun. James Reston, the celebrated American columnist of the *New York Times* started his career as a sport reporter. He later became one of the top columnists, every word of whose was read avidly by Washington diplomats. A reporter should be a student throughout his life and never refuse to learn.

Knowledge

A good general education does mean knowledge of different languages also, particularly in a country like India. When a country has more than a couple of dozen languages the reporter with knowledge of a few of the important languages has an edge over his rivals who are not multilingual. A reporter in the capital city of our country with speaking knowledge of different languages can build up rapport with news makers by speaking in their own mother-tongue. A dignitary, especially one from outside the Anglo-American world, would be flattered to hear a reporter speak in his own mother tongue, whether it be Arabic, French or German. A news-maker will be more at home with correspondents who speak in his own language and might reveal more of his mind than otherwise.

DTP Skills

Knowledge of computer, particularly DTP, is essential for reporters these days. Earlier, the essential tool used to be the typewriter. Another contemporary device is the moblie phone wherein you have the facility of audio video-recording. This saves the reporter from taking notes all the time. He/she needs not to depend on his/her memory any more and can easily do factual and accurate reporting.

Physical Tools

A reporter should always carry a standard size notebook and a pen so that he/she can easily take notes in case of need. Yet another helpful aid will be a diary in which important future events are noted. Also a diary with telephone numbers, addresses, e-mails etc., of important persons. In today's time most of the above-mentioned jobs can be performed in the mobile handset.

A Reporter in Action

A reporter must go by the slogan "Get it first but first get it right." Unfortunately in today's mad race for TRPs, TV reporters will hardly pay attention to any such advice. Print media reporters have both will and time to cross-check the facts before filing a story.

A reporter must recognise a story, must spot a story. In handling a story, he/she must know the facts to seek, their order of importance and where to find them.

A reporter must have the ability to express himself/ herself both in writing and speech. The need for effective oral expression exists because the reporter interviews so many people in the course of his/her work and very often he/she has to give details of the story on the phone to the news desk where it is necessary that every word is clear and unambiguous.

A reporter must be able to work at top gear and must not break under the pressure of time. He/she must be able to handle accidents, disasters and other spot stories in the minimum possible time.

A reporter should have ability to build contacts. He/she must maintain a long list of friends who may be of help when stories break. He/she should know the persons in authority who could be contacted in case of need and appropriately quoted in the news report.

A reporter should be able to select the relevant facts and present them in a manner that they provide a comprehensive story. Sometimes people might try to feed him/her with mistakes or wrong versions to an event, may be to suit their objectives. But the reporter should be cautions and use only what is relevant.

A reporter should be friendly with the sources but should not be intimate as such relations can restrain him/her from honest reporting. An independent and courageous reporter can almost always get whatever information he/she needs on adequate ethical terms without paying too much a price.

A reporter should eliminate from his/her mind any temptations or favours. Temptations taint his reporting and take away his independence. The best way to avoid favours is keeping a safe distance from dispensers of favours like politicians in authority.

Precautions Required in Reporting

A reporter should be cautions enough in reporting and filing stories. On the job, he/she has to look into the following:

Accuracy

For a news reporter facts are sacred, comment is free. In the first place, the reporter must pay utmost attention to details, secondly, he/she must be a compulsive note-taker (audio video recording can be a substitute). Thirdly, he/she must check and double check, ask questions relentlessly and query when in doubt.

One of the *Washington Post* reporters who investigated the Waterage scandal once said—"We never accepted a statement of fact as true until we had at least two witnesses we could trust without a vestige of doubt."

Even when the information has been collected through authentic sources a cross-checking will help. No distortion of facts is acceptable, whether it has taken place because of a lapse on the part of the reporter or a deliberate action of the reporter under influence of some ill-motive. In any case, the reporter should be cautious to save himself/herself from misleading information.

Emphasis

A reporter should select the key facts and throw away those which are not needed. He should avoid overplaying facts of secondary importance at the expense of the primary. Some reporters use this tactics in subtle ways of highlighting certain points which he/she thinks will go against someone he/she wants to let down.

For instance, in 1985 a Kerala minister mentioned about the need for an agitation against the Central Government for wresting more industries to Kerala. He stated that Punjab was getting more benefits from the Centre because of its agitation. While reporting the speech, some reporters worte that the minister had exhorted the people for a Punjab model agitation.

This was a clear case of giving wrong emphasis. Rival politicians took up the issue and argued that the minister was instigating separatism. Ultimately, the minister was compelled to resign.

Estimation

While estimating crowd, a reporter should not depend on one's own guess work. He/she should ask a few other witnesses and also the organisers, if possible, and come to a nearly correct assessment.

For instance, in the case of public meetings the assessment of the participants always varies, while one reporter will put the figure as 10,000, some other might he putting it as one lakh. The same happens in the case of natural calamities like Tsunami where estimation of deaths becomes difficult.

Problems in Newsgathering

News is a business and newsgathering is the job of the reporter. Naturally, the reporter often faces problems and unavoidable pressures in the process of newsgathering.

Skepticism should be a quality of the reporter and he should never accept an information without questioning. Why does he/she give this piece of information to me? Has he/she anything to gain by its publication? Is it factually correct? Can I counter check the truthfulness of the information? Who is affected by its publication? These are some of the questions which should come to the mind of the reporter in the process of newsgathering.

Newspaper publication was a mission in the pre-independent India. The sole objective at the time revolved round the freedom of the country. Most of the leading politicians at that time were publishers of newspapers because that was the only channel of communication with the masses of people. Once we gained independence the situation has changed. Politicians left the field of journalism once their mission succeeded. Businessmen made their apearance as owners of newspapers.

Gradually, a new dimension was setting in the style and functioning of newspapers. Every newspaper worth the name had separate division for editorial management and business management. Survival was possible only as a business proposition for modern newspapers due to various reasons. Technological invasion on the production process, incresssing news collection expenses and various other factors made newspaper publication a big business.

With this transformation papers came under pressure from the government which had control over the newsprint and also issued import licences for printing machinery. The government emerged as the biggest advertiser in the country.

The newspapers have grown to such a large size that the subscription alone has become insufficient for subsistence. Thus has come their heavy dependence on advertising revenue.

Writing about pressures in the process of newspaper publication—particularly newsgathering—we have to start with the newspaper management itself.

The owner of the paper lays down policies keeping in mind his business interest. If he/she is too much concerned about the business promotion there will be too many dos and don'ts for the reporter to observe. Pressure from advertisers also influences newspaper management. It is possible that an advertiser may be spending several lakhs of rupees for advertising in a paper and there is a possibility of such clients trying to pressurise the correspondents through the advertising section or the top management. The fact is the advertiser needs the newspaper more than the newspaper needs the advertiser. If this is borne in mind there will not be much difficulty in resisting pressure from advertisers.

More dangerous is the pressure which may come to the reporter on account of his own actions or for other reasons. A reporter should keep in mind that he/she should be friendly with every news source but never intimate. If one tires to be chummy with the Prime Minister, the chief minister or other ministers what often happens the reporter will tend to accept and report official views rather than seek qualified information. Friendship can taint the reports if the people involved are the reporter's friends.

One universally prevalent dubious practice among newsmen is that of accepting considerations from news sources. Offer of free foreign trips by diplomatic missions, dinners and parties at posh hotels, free supply of Scotch and other expensive whiskies, valuable gift items and other presentations are the things which will influence the reporter while gathering news from the providers of these items. We often hear a reporter saying that "I will get the news only on its merit and no consideration can taint or colour my reporting." But it seldom turns out to be true as gratitude plays its role.

News is public property when it relaters to public events or public men. The reporter should, however, bear in mind that the private life of public men belongs to them and not to public and the reporter has no right to invade the privacy. The public men also have no moral right to suppress or withhold a public information. The reporter should be very careful not to land up in libel or defamation cases by encroaching beyond the line of fair comment and criticism.

Examples:

A member of Parliament elopes with his secretary. He wanted to keep this a secret. The reporters get the details and publish stories about it. Marriage is a personal affair. But this private behaviour of a public figure is a matter of concern for the public.

A photographer following a couple on their wedding trip gets a photo of them swimming naked is an offence and violation of privacy.

Public figures, either in government or in other institutions and activities in which they seek public attention, are generally judged to have given up privacy in their public activities, but not in their private life.

One reason why the reporters do not observe an individual's right to privacy is that privacy and the right of the public to information may be at odds. What might be called good taste in journalistic behaviour may come in conflict with the mandate to report what ought to be reported.

Matter of taste is ill-defined because yesterday's vulgarism can be today's routine usage. The modern trend in reporting is if an obscene or a vulgar word is necessary to bring out the accurate meaning of an event it should be printed.

Guidelines for Reporters

The following can be guidelines for reporters:

1. A reporter must be honest while making a comment or criticism. Honest expression of opinions or judgments on

all kinds of public actions by public men can be defended as fair comment and criticism. But it must be reasonable and fair.

A reporter can call a man a disreputably bad tennis player if his performance does not come anywhere near the expected level. But you cannot say of him as a man who beats his wife every morning.

2. A reporter must verify facts before publication. He/she should not write anything to malign somebody. The truth of a statement can be a full defence against most of the libel actions. In certain cases, absence of malice also will have to be established.
3. A reporter must present a true account of the proceedings of Parliament and State Legislatures. The press is given freedom of reporting the proceedings but this freedom could be enjoyed by a reporter till the time he/she is reporting the facts accurately and substantially.
4. A reporter must report the fact correctly otherwise he/she can land himself/herself in trouble.
5. A reporter should respect the right to privacy of an individual. However he/she has to use his/her discretion whether or not to publish a private action of a public figure.

Qualities of a Reporter

1. *News Sense*: It is the basic quality of a newsman. A reporter should have a sense to capture a news, asses and evaluate it, then to produce it.
2. *Clarity*: A reporter should have clarity of mind and expression. He/she should have an ability to understand a newsworthy event or incident clearly and then present it with a clear expression.
3. *Objectivity*: A reporter must ensure that whatever he/she has written is correct and accurate. He/she should check and recheck his facts till he/she is satisfied.
4. *Alertness*: A reporter is always on duty like a policeman. He/she should keep eyes and ears open and should always be alert whether or not he/she is on duty.

5. *Speed*: In today's world, speed matters everywhere. So a reporter should also be speedy. He/she should think fast, decide fast and write fast for he/she has to meet deadlines or may have to go to another assignment.
6. *Curiosity*: A reporter should always be curious to know more and to dig the facts on a particular subject. He/she should also possess a reading habit to update his/her knowledge.
7. *Patience*: Patience is a quality which always pays. The reporter should not get provoked while waiting for somebody for long or facing unpleasant situations while doing a story.
8. *Punctuality*: A reporter must be punctual particularly those who are doing spot stories. If a reporter fails to honour time, he/she is always taking the risk of missing the happenings he/she intends to cover.
9. *Scepticism*: A reporter should not believe anything just on hearsay. A successful reporter should continue to doubt the truth of a story unless the facts are verified and confirmed.
10. *Imagination*: A reporter should always be imaginative. Imagination gives an insight to a reporter to write well and increases his creativity as well.
11. *Discipline*: A reporter should be disciplined, dedicated and committed to his/her job. An indisciplined reporter may spoil the whole of his efforts.
12. *Initiative*: A reporter should be dashing and energetic. He/she should be habitual of taking initiative and should be in the lead while working on some assignment.
13. *Mobility*: A reporter should be mobile. He/she should enjoy moving around and should not hesitate travelling distances to get stories when required. He/she should go to his news sources as often as possible for such constant contacts help him/her to get news.
14. *Diligence*: A reporter should be a hard worker and habitual of working without being tired. He/she should be dedicated to the task and should not give up by the time it is finished.

Tips for a Reporter

Dos

1. Search for stories vigorously.
2. Follow the story aggressively.
3. Maintain effective communication with people around the story.
4. Develop mutual trust with the source.
5. Always adhere to your deadline.
6. Keep an eye on the interests and requirements of your readers.

Don'ts

1. Don't get tired, work hard.
2. Don't hesitate in revealing facts.
3. Don't disclose your story before publication.
4. Don't take sides, remain unbiased.
5. Don't take facts in story without verification.
6. Don't accept favours, be strong.

Responsibilities of a Reporter

Reporting is both-an art and a craft. It can be learnt and acquired by hard work, sheer determination, imagination and, of course, by constant practice. But for a reporter, professional capability is not enough. What is more important is that he/she should perform his/her job with a sense of responsibility. We can discuss the responsibilities of a reporter in the following manner:

1. *Responsibility Towards Newspaper*: A reporter should thoroughly study and understand his/her newspaper or periodical and its requirements. He/she should make an earnest effort to gather the information which can fulfill the requirements of his/her newspaper.
2. *Responsibility Towards Readers*: A reporter should understand his/her audience i.e., the readers of his newspaper/journal. While doing the news coverage, he/she should always keep in mind the aspirations, interests, needs and tastes of his/her readers.

3. *Responsibility Towards Editor*: A reporter should always seek guidance from his/her editor in the performance of his/her job. Editor is considered the professional head of the newspaper and so a reporter should always be ready to seek guidance and instructions from him.
4. *Responsibility Towards Proprietor*: Though a reporter is not directly linked with the proprietor, he/she is expected to guard the business and other interests of the owner of his/her newspaper. He/she should be sensitive and cautious enough not to write anything that harms the interests of his/her proprietor.
5. *Responsibility Toward Profession*: A reporter must be honest to his/her profession. He/she must observe ethical standards and perform his/her job with sincerity and dedication. He/she should also have a command over the language in which he/she is writing the report.
6. *Responsibilities Towards Society*: A reporter should perform his/her job with social commitment. He/she should always keep in mind the larger interests of the society. He/she should promote harmony in the society through his writings.

Functions of a Reporter in a Democracy

In a democratic set up, a reporter has an added responsibility of focussing his/her writings to strengthening of democracy. At whatever level the reporter is working whether as a special correspondent covering Parliament or as a stringer covering comparatively insignificant local happenings, he/she can make a contribution to cementing democracy.

When a reporter is covering political institutions or political functionaries at Central, state or local level, he/she should report the matters in a manner that people's faith in the democratic process doesn't diminish. The reports should be written more for the political education of the people than making a mockery of the political system.

On many occasions, political corruption, embezzlement or misappropriation of funds is repoted in the media but in such a case, the motive of the reporter should be to detect the loopholes, thereby pressurising the government for taking steps to rectify the system. People on the wrong side should be attacked but not actually the political system in which we are living. No doubt, the reporter can always write and suggest improvements in the system.

To understand this point, we can take the example of Operation Chakravyuh and Operation Daryodhan. If certain channels showed some MPs taking bribes for asking questions in Parliament or irregularities committed in MPLAD fund, the motive was not to tell the people that parliamentary democracy has failed but to alert them of those few politicians who were trying to hijack the system to their benefit.

A reporter at a local level also makes a significant contribution to the cause of democracy even if he/she is not directly involved in reporting big political institutions. A city reporter might be covering local politics, civil administration or crime in city, but he/she can contribute by talking about the orientation of local politicians, the development work done or neglected by the district development officers, success of the police in combating crime or failure in giving the people a sense of security.

A city reporter may even be covering the Municipal Corporation, the deliberations taking place in the elected House, conditions of government hospitals and educational institutions. In any such reporting, his thought—process and style of writing will determine what the society and the country is going to gain by his/her journalistic contribution.

The basic job of a reporter is to inform—informing the people on the issues and problems they are concerned with, also information about governance and development. The information empowers the people who then become more knowledgeable and vigilant in the discharge of their democratic duties and responsibilities, as also pulling their elected representatives.

In the collection and dissemination of information, a reporter also makes use of government information and put it in the columns of his/her newspaper. In the process, he/she is able to communicate useful information to the people, which in many cases would be extending them various benefits. At the same time, he/she helps the government in taking all that information to the people which could build its positive image.

Thus, a reporter acts as a bridge between information holders and informational seekers by performing the job of information collector and disseminator. This is undoubtedly the greatest service a reporter does for the sake of democracy.

Reporting Set-up in a Newspaper

Reporting infrastructure in a daily newspaper can have the following broad classifications:

1. News Bureau.
2. City/Local Reporting.
3. Outstation Correspondents.
4. Correspondents abroad.

1. *News Bureau*

A daily published from New Delhi, Mumbai, Kolkata or any other part of the country definitely has a news bureau in the national capital, New Delhi. Many newspapers also have a news bureau in the capital of the state from where they are bringing out the newspaper.

Bureau in News Delhi is responsible for coverage of Parliament, various ministries and departments, PMO, diplomatic missions, national headquarters of political parties, visits of foreign dignitaries, and national-level organisations and institutions like the Planning Commission and the Election Commission. Bureau in the state capital covers Assembly, State Government, CM and other ministers/ministries, state headquarters of political parties and other state-level events/incidents/happenings.

2. *City/Local Reporting*

Chief Reporter
↑
Senior Reporter
↑
Staff Reporter
↑
Trainee Reporter

Local reporting means coverage of incidents, events, happenings or any other newsworthy development taking place in the city from where the newspaper is getting published, for the benefit of citizens. Thus, local reporting is city centric reporting. It is reporting of the local concerns for the local consumption.

For local reporting, a daily has a City Reporting Room comprising few reporters, mostly of middle and junior level. The set-up of a City Reporting Room has been shown on the right side.

Local Beats

The areas covered by city reporters include local politics, district/civil administration, police, law and order and crime, health, hospitals and public health, civic bodies and civic issues, schools, colleges and other educational institutions, district level/lower level judiciary, local festivals, congregations and religions meetings, cultural and entertainment programmes.

One area or more than one areas of similar or almost of the same nature constitute one beat. For instance, crime is one beat wherein a reporter will be covering crime incidents, accidents, traffic, security, terrorists' attacks, other law and order problems, police set-up and responsibility of police officers at various levels.

There is no hard and fast rule with regard to the number of beats you might find in a daily newspaper. On an average, one can find ten beats being covered by city reporters. Depending on the size of the city reporting room, a reporter can be assigned one or more than one beat. Normally, you can find five to ten reporters working in the reporting room of a daily.

The distribution of beats takes place on the basis of the importance of beats and the seniority and capability of reporters. For instance, politics and district administration beats are retained by the chief reporter himself/herself, crime and legal beats can be given to middle level reporters and health and education can be given to junior reporters.

Functions of Reporting Room

City reporting room comes to life every evening from 4 to 10 when reporters reach office after day-long hectic schedule. During day time the reporters are in the field attending press conferences, seminars and functions, meeting the people, authorities and sources, roaming around in search of news and desperately looking for some scoop.

In the evening, the reporters file their reports, have professional exchanges, decide about their assignments and seek instructions from the chief reporter. They also interact with their editorial counterparts—sub-editors/copy editors who edit their copies and finalise the city/ local pages. They even talk to the news editor and seek his/her guidance or advice.

Reporters remain under pressure to meet their deadlines. They are mostly seen busy with their mobiles or office phone to collect information for their half-baked stories or simply doing public relationing. They also devote a lot of time in meeting the visitors who might be their contacts or persons with invitations for press conferences etc. or the common men with some vital clues to something great.

In the reporting room, a large number of stories originate from the bulk of press releases received in the newspaper office everyday. While it is customary to take the press releases issued by government information agencies, on many occasions press releases are found carrying some useful information for the readers. Also, press releases are a great help to reporters for filling up space in the columns of newspapers.

Besides filing their exclusive and investigate stories, reporters are either writing the general story or the simple story types. As part of general stories, they write personals, briefs, fillers, stories based on speeches, publications interviews, or meetings and special events. As simple story types, reporters file stories on illnesses, deaths and funerals, fire and accidents, or seasons, weather and natural disasters.

Writing of all these story types and the local beats shall be discussed in the following chapters:

Functions and Responsibilities of Chief Reporter

Chief reporter is incharge of City Reporting Room. Hierarchy-wise he/she is equivalent to the chief sub-editor working in the News Room. He/she is answerable to the news editor and finally to the editor of the newspaper.

Chief reporter is responsible for the local coverage. His/her basic job includes:

- Organising working in the reporting room.
- Distribution of beats among the reporters.
- Giving assignments to reporters on a day-to-day basis.
- Discussing story ideas with reporters and granting a go-ahead.
- Monitor working of reporters to ensure accomplishment of the given jobs.

- Leading the team of reporters from the front providing all possible help, guidance, tips and even contacts in case of need.
- Resolving differences of reporters arising due to professional rivalry among them or in the wake of overlapping of beats.
- Making sure a comprehensive and all-inclusive coverage from the city better than the rival newspaper.
- Bringing innovative ideas to local reporting.

For discharging his/her functions effectively, the chief reporter normally conducts morning meetings. Depending on the practice in a newspaper, this meeting may be attended also by the News Editor. Morning meeting is basically organised for the following purposes:

- Doing the post-mortem of the local reporting pages to find out what the newspaper has missed and where it has scored on that day.
- Making an assessment of the local coverage in comparison with the rival newspapers on that day.
- Reviewing and finalising assignments for that day, including the need of a follow-up story if something has been missed out.

The relationship of the chief reporter and the news editor is very important because only their combined efforts can lead the newspaper to success in the city. The chief reporter consults the news editor on all important stories, thereafter the display of major stories is decided. Very important local stories are always carried on the front page. The news editor can even instruct the chief reporter with regard to any developing or follow-up story.

The basic responsibility of the chief reporter is two-fold:

- To plan and organise local reporting in a manner that each segment of readers in the city is catered to effectively.
- To score over rival newspapers in local reporting and to ensure that the newspaper is not missing out any important happening of the city.

8

Writing General Stories

In newspapers, editors and reporters label stories by subject—crime, politics, education, culture, health, religion, sports, business, entertainment etc. In journalistic language, these are called beats. This is a convenient way for the staff to classify stories. It is a quick indicator as to which department/section like the city reporters' room or news bureau will handle a particular story and where it probably will appear in the newspaper.

Three types of stories, however, are most general in nature because they are not confined to a particular subject. They are personals and briefs; speeches, publications and interviews; and meetings and occasions.

All are different types from the viewpoint of categories. But all are used in connection with every subject covered by a newspaper. A personal item may grow out of a court/legal story and a speech story could originate from a politician (political beat) or businessman (business/economic beat).

It is important that these general types of stories be considered before the reporter studies the various reporters' room or bureau beat stories dealing with specific subjects.

Personals and Briefs

In today's time, a newspaper has to be personal if it wants to be successful and compete with rival newspapers. This can be done by publishing news related to birthdays, anniversaries, obituaries and wedding announcements.

The readers are always interested to know who got married, who came to visit, who won the students' union elections and who are the Arjun awardees of the year. No doubt, names make news.

Most newspapers, especially community or neighbourhood newspapers, carry numerous short stories, often no more than a sentence or two, that are generally called "personals" or "briefs", could be part of 'News in Brief'. Others use them as individual stories with their own headlines.

As a general rule, metro newspapers carry briefs or personal items about only the most prominent persons. Frequently these items are collected in a column. However, community newspapers usually carry briefs and personals about practically everyone in town.

Many community newspaper editors say that personals are the best-read stories in their newspapers. Personals may be grouped into a column with a single headline, or they may be scattered through the regular news sections. The use and placement of briefs or personals is unlimited.

Briefs and personals serve several important purposes: They provide information on activities of various citizens as well as social, civic and religious groups in the community, and they can be used to facilitate make up by filling in small spaces left after longer stories are placed on pages.

In any case, they should be written with the same care and effort that go into the main story each day. A mistake in a name, an address or a fact in a personal item is just as serious as a similar mistake in any page—story.

Personals and briefs are classified as a separate story type. Actually, they are a type only in the sense that they emphasise personalities and are short. Otherwise, they are relatively unimportant in news value in relation to the news value of the front-page stories. In subject-matter, personals and briefs range the entire spectrum of human activity. In some newspapers they are considered to be merely elementary stories that the trainee reporter is often assigned to write. However, every regular reporter knows their value and collects them.

Personals

Names make news. And they do not always have to be prominent names. Newspapers have always recognised the news value of names of quite ordinary persons. The names of visitors; guests; committee members; and those sponsoring or attending dinners, banquets, conventions and so on are usually listed by newspapers as fully as space permits.

Announcements of trips, visitors, parties, newcomers and many relatively minor events that take place in any community are considered to be personals. The lifestyle pages or family pages often use many such items, but other personals are used throughout the paper as one, two and three-paragraph stories with headlines.

News Value of Personals

It is often difficult to classify personal items by the standard tests for news value-disaster, progress, conflict and so on—though a careful study of them will show that in a minor way they may fall into these categories.

Personals, as a class of story, would seem to be a composite of all the news values. Individually, they may be of little consequence except to the persons immediately involved; yet collectively they record life in any community on a very fundamental level. They contain virtually all-human interests—gossip, birth, death, illness, conflict and the rest. They give the readers of any newspaper a daily look at the activities of their fellow citizens, not just the prominent ones. And they are well read.

The most common characteristic of most personals is that they are quite local in nature. If a member of a Lions Club is planning an event—New Year party or fashion show—it is local news of a personal type. A similar event in a community 50 kilometres away would mean nothing.

The personal, then, is a standard item in the columns of newspapers in smaller communities. It is usually unnecessary to belong to an organisation or take part in a major news event to be mentioned in the news columns of a small town newspaper—daily or weekly.

A shopping trip to a nearby city or the purchase of a new tractor may be sufficient for one to get his or her name in the local newspaper in many small communities. In the large city dailies the personal is somewhat confined to the more or less prominent persons, the activities of local groups and clubs, and the personalities of so-called high society.

Sources of Personals

Most personals are telephoned, mailed or brought to the newspaper office by interested persons. Hostesses report their party plans, themes and guest lists. Mothers announce vacation plans for their children. Dinners, parties and other social events are reported by life-style reporters of the paper. There could be press releases from vacation hotels, convention centres and other tourist attractions reporting the local persons who visited there recently.

Every regular beat yields personals and briefs to the alert reporter. Public officials and employees go on business trips and vacations. Behind the public front of every person on every beat are many personal items of interest. Hobbies along with other recreation and sports activities, are fertile fields for personals. On a rare occasion a personal item can lead to an even bigger story.

Writing Personals

The personal should be written as a straight news story. It should have a well-written lead and contain all the necessary information to make the story complete. The lead requires:

1. The five W's. These are essential in all stories, of course, though some of them may be implied in the lead.
2. Identification of the person or persons mentioned. If a long list of persons is given (for example, the names of new club members), do not try to use them all in the lead. Write a more general lead and include the names in the second paragraph along with their identification. But if the item reports the activities of only one or two individuals, each should be identified. Wherever possible, a descriptive identity should be included to intensify reader interest. The descriptive identity, lacking in the first of the following personal is underlined in the second item.
   - Mr. Ram Nath of Patparganj is making a month-long auto trip of Punjab. Mr. Nath who recently launched a company to create awareness on AIDS, is making a month-long trip through the G.T. Road in Punjab. He will interact with truck drivers during the trip.

Here is how to handle a personal with a long list of names:

- Eight members of the Rotary Club will exhibit their paintings in Town Hall next week. They are: (List the club members. If descriptions of the paintings are available, include that. But do not include any if you cannot include all of them).

Stressing an Interesting Feature

Reporters should always look for interesting features when writing personals and not be satisfied to use only the basic five Ws. To say that "Shankaracharya will leave for New Delhi on Tuesday" is interesting to friends and members of his Math. But what he is planning to do in New Delhi? Is he on a religious mission? Is he meeting any minister? Will he be doing some charity work. The reporter may find an interesting feature on this.

The following is an example of how a personal item might be improved by adding a few details:

Initial Item

- Shruti, a student of BJMC at VIPS, has got the first position in GGSIP University merit list once again.

Improved Item

- Shruti, a V Semester student in one of the affiliated colleges of GGSIP University, has been placed on top fourth time in a row. She is the daughter of Mr. Prabhu Dayal, a government servant.

In writing a personal, every effort should be made to avoid referring to persons by such terms as "widely known", "popular" and "beloved". (In newspaper offices, such words are called "puffs"). This is not only poor writing, but also editorializing and should not be permitted in personals or briefs, just as it should not be permitted in any straight news story.

Briefs

It is often difficult to distinguish between a personal and a brief. Perhaps the best distinction between them is that briefs generally do not pertain to persons. The change in city library hours, the post office's holiday schedule, dates for obtaining new auto licenses, announcements of minor fund-raising events and dozens of other short but newsworthy items would be classified as briefs.

Briefs are usually one-or-two-paragraph stories dealing with incidents or occasions having broad or limited appeal. Naturally, the wider the appeal, the more prominently they will be displayed in a newspaper.

Briefs may be rewrites from other papers or new stories picked up by beat reporters or phoned in by interested persons. They are used because they are news, and they may be grouped together in a "News Briefs" column or used as fillers throughout the paper.

It is difficult to establish a dividing line between a brief and a longer, more important story. An event worthy of no more than two paragraphs in some newspapers may be "blown up," with the inclusion of more details, to five or six paragraphs in other newspapers. The size of the community and its newspaper, the availability of local news and the interest of the readers are factors to be considered by the reporter. A story's relative significance—the proportion of readers it will interest—is the major space-measuring device for the reporter.

Here is an example of a brief from a neighbourhood newspaper:

- Public Library will launch membership campaign in the city next week. The counters at all the branches of the library will remain open from 10 a.m. to 5 p.m. for this purpose.

Like a personal, a brief is obviously a single-feature story—and hardly more than a lead at that. The five Ws, with the proper emphasis given on the most important W, usually compose the whole story. Further explanation of one or more of the Ws may call for a second paragraph.

Careless reporting, notably the lack of an inquiring attitude, sometimes makes potentially long stories into briefs. If the trainee reporter becomes too "brief" conscious, feeling that every story should be told in two paragraphs, he or she may fail to ask the kinds of questions that could develop a possible front page story. On the other hand, insignificant news events should not purposely be blown up or overplayed.

Fillers

The standardisation of advertising format, the trend of six-column makeup and the availability of DTP software have reduced some of the need for fillers. However, many editors still are faced with problems and often tiny spaces need to be filled.

Some newspapers use briefs and personals to fill these spaces. Others keep on hand a supply of very short items to "plug" these holes. Such fillers are usually inserted without headlines.

Fillers come from a variety of sources, but the most common source is a news feature service (syndicate). Some special interest groups include them in their press kits or publicity releases.

A number of newspapers develop their own fillers from government reports, census data, history books and encyclopaedias. They are selected with some care to present unusual facts, "fascinating" information or descriptive items highlighting the local community. Many newspapers coordinate fillers with the general subject of the page or section of the newspaper in which they are used. Fillers about food are placed on the food pages, and so on. Humor and quotes from famous people also are used as fillers.

Here are some examples:

- "A little learning is not a dangerous thing to one who does not mistake it for a great deal." —William Allen White.
- Life has its disappointments but there is no reason to be one of them.

It is worth mentioning here that the use of fillers has reduced to a great extent in view of make-up devices available in DTP software.

Speeches, Publications and Interviews

News stories generated by speeches, press conferences, interviews and articles in professional journals or magazines add reader interest and often excitement to every newspaper. These stories may be vastly different in subject-matter, but they all have something in common.

Basically, they are one-source stories that are a collection of direct and indirect quotations from the source. In most, only a minimum of material is provided by the writer through research. Rarely do they include any interpretation on the part of the writer. These stories require skillful handling to keep them from being dull.

Speeches

While speech stories are common in Indian newspapers, they often are neglected as "just another routine story" unless they are speeches given by prominent public figures. Many of these stories are poorly written because the reporter lacks interest in the assignment.

Covering a speech and writing a story about it can be exacting. It takes considerable skill to report a 7,500-word speech in 300 words and still give the reader an accurate report of what was said. It takes time, thought, hard work and writing talent.

For example, a reporter assigned to cover a meeting in New Delhi, where the Speaker of the Lok Sabha was to release the book 'Fatigue and Famine' took the assignment unwillingly. But it was a "must" assignment. The meeting, sponsored by a people's rights group, drew a stellar crowd of MPs, MLAs and Ministers to Vigyan Bhavan across the street from Rashtrapati Bhavan. The Speaker didn't like the book and said so pointedly. The reporter, casting around for a way to handle what was basically a rather dull event, decided to use a feature lead. Here it is.

- The Famine struck the capital today—across Rashtrapati Bhavan.
  While two ministers, several three and four-time MPs, some MLAs and few bureaucrats looked on, India's fate was seen doomed in 45 minutes, with time for questions and answers....

The remainder of the relatively short story focussed on direct quotes from the reviewer as he told why the book was, for him at least, dreadful. The final paragraph gave some details of the group and its membership to help the reader understand why there were so many prominent individuals in the audience. A basically dull assignment was turned into a lively short feature because the reporter used his imagination.

Some reporters dislike being assigned to cover speeches because speakers often are not very good and what they have to say is not very interesting. Yet every speech, no matter who is giving it or what is said, offers a chance to a reporter to show his or her resourcefulness and talent as a writer.

All speeches, whether formal addresses on special occasions or impromptu remarks during an unstructured gathering, are handled very much alike. The reporter must consider the following three elements:

(*a*) The speaker.
(*b*) The audience.
(*c*) The speech.

A fourth consideration is the possible interpretation that any of the three elements may need. The proportion of the story to be devoted to each element varies with the comparative importance of each, but no speech story is complete without all three. Generally, in speech stories the emphasis should be put on what is said.

The speaker should be properly identified in the lead. Sometimes this can be done with a title or a short sentence. If more identification is needed, it can be in the body of the story. This is an amplification of the basic principle of identifying persons named in the news.

The reader needs to know who the speaker is and why his or her statements are worth quoting. Even a description of the speaker's distinctive characteristics and manner of emphasising certain points is sometimes woven into the story to give it more colour.

The audience also should be described. How many people were there? Who were they? Why did they meet? The reporter looks over the crowd, talks with the leaders, and reads any available programme carefully to help answer those questions. The names of persons in the audience need not be given unless it would be of interest to the reader to know the names of a few of the more prominent ones, but the reporter should tell whether they are bankers, teachers, doctors or engineers. These facts are implied, of course, at regular meetings of civic clubs and similar organisations, when nothing more than the name of the organisation is required. Audience reaction is also frequently worth noting.

The speech—what the speaker had to say—is the most important of the three elements. "What is the most important thing the speaker said?" is the first question that a reporter should ask when starting to write the story. Two reporters covering the same speech may not agree on what the most important thing is. Here are leads on two stories covering the same speech by former Finance Minister Mr. Jaswant Singh:

- Mr. Jaswant Singh, former finance minister, attacked the UPA government for excessive taxation, while addressing members of the BJP executive in the Capital today. He said that both direct and indirect taxes should be rationalised in a manner that people's interests are not sacrificed.
- Mr. Jaswant Singh, the last Finance Minister in the NDA government, attacked the UPA government for delaying the process of tax reforms, while addressing members of BJP's elite group in the Capital today. Mr. Singh who himself was not able to implement the recommendations of the Kelkar Committee, asked the government to make the tax structure rational.

Some interpretation of one or more of the three necessary elements may be needed. Perhaps the audience is not as representative as it appears to be for the occasion. Applause may be staged by partisan supporters of the speaker. Perhaps the speaker has affiliations or a record that should be presented to clarify his or her significance. Perhaps the speech content should be related to larger national movements, editorial campaigns or other programmes. Frequently the speech will have significance in local issues. For example, if the speech concerns public reaction and if the community is campaigning for removal of encroachments in the DDA Park, a story ignoring this relationship would be inadequate and non interpretative. Interpretation, however, must avoid editorialising. The interpretative reporter is not authorised to express an opinion. Interpretation must be merely the presentation of pertinent facts to give the reader a clearer picture.

Getting the Speaker's Words

Ideally, a reporter should obtain an advance copy of the speech. However, many speakers do not provide advance copies, so the reporter has to attend the speech and make extensive notes. Most reporters do not take notes of everything the speaker says. Usually they make notes only on the important statements and arguments or points made by the speaker.

A careful reporter will make every effort to place only the speaker's exact words within quotation marks, particularly in matters that may be controversial. Many reporters like to tape a speech while taking notes to make certain the quotes are exact. Because direct quotations tend to add emphasis, the reporter should avoid quoting routine, obvious or minor points from speeches. Accurate paraphrasing is usually sufficient to convey the less important elements of a speech. However, a reporter should not paraphrase too much. Direct quotes should be used liberally throughout a speech story. Under no circumstances should a reporter turn in a speech story with few or no direct quotes.

A speech may have one or several features just as any other type of story. In organising the material, the reporter should look for the central theme, the logical division and unusual or provocative quotes. A good speech will have all of those elements. However, the reporter does not have to play up the central theme if some other aspect of the speech may have more reader appeal.

Speech Story Lead

On most speech stories, the lead should feature the most important point the speaker made. That is the whole point—to focus on the most newsworthy element of the speech. It can be done by using direct quotations, indirect quotations or interpretation. Summarising the entire speech in the lead is acceptable; however, it can result in a long and dull lead. Summary leads should be used sparingly on speech stories. Here are several examples of speech leads:

- Mr. Vijay Kumar Malhotra, general secretary of the BJP, said that the opposition would not sit at rest till the time the tainted minister was removed. He was commenting on the Speaker's observations that the opposition was not allowing proceedings in the Lok Sabha to be conducted smoothly. Addressing a meeting of party MPs, Mr. Malhotra said that parliamentary democracy could not succeed if the government continued to ignore the opposition and the Speaker was always seen taking sides.

- "Communalism is a disease that infiltrates everyone's life", Salman Rushdie, author of the '*Satanic Verses*', told a symposium of political activists here today.
  "Almost everybody is infected or affected by the disease," he said. "We are fooling ourselves if we think we are not."
- Secretary of State James Baker warned Iraq on Monday the United States may attack if it continues to occupy Kuwait.
  "Saddam Hussein must realise there is a limit to the international community's patience," Baker said in a tough talk to the World Affairs Council in Los Angeles. "Let no one doubt we will not rule out a possible use of force."

Here are some exceptions to the rule of featuring the most important point the speaker made in the lead: (1) If the speaker is very prominent, his or her name may be featured in the lead without focussing on the most important thing said; (2) if the occasion itself is important or embraces several speeches; (3) if the entire programme is keynoted or has a central theme.

The following examples illustrate the exceptions:

- Mother Teresa, Kolkata's "Saint of the Gutters," opened the United Nations' Conference on World Hunger today. The Nobel Peace Prize winner told delegates from 130 nations that...
- Delegates to the United Nations' Conference on World Hunger today heard Mother Teresa, Kolkata's "Saint of the Gutters," describe how millions of people are starving each year.
  The Nobel Peace Prize winner spoke at the opening session of the conference, which was attended by representatives from 130 nations.
- The responsibility of rich nations to help feed the world's starving masses was the theme of the speakers who took part in the opening of the United Nations' Conference on World Hunger today.

These exceptions, however, are not strictly speech leads. They are leads for meetings and conventions. They bracket several speeches and lay the ground-work for speeches to follow. They should be used sparingly because they tend to be more general than specific.

Body of the Speech Story

The body of the speech story should be direct quotations, indirect quotations and interpretative summaries of the speech. They should be fairly well balanced, but the writer should remember that direct quotes often carry more impact than indirect quotes or summaries. Readers respond more favourably to direct quotes because they give a story more authenticity.

Quote-Summary-Quote Story

Newspaper reporters have over the years developed a popular form for stories containing a large number of direct quotes. Commonly referred to as a "quote-summary-quote" story, it can best be described in this example:

- Changes in society are creating strains on family relations that could eventually threaten the existence of the family unit, one of the nation's psychiatrists said here today.
  "I think there have been a lot of subtle changes such as the effect of affluence on young people," Dr. Sanjay Chugh said.
  "Those who don't have to work to help support the family have more free time, become bored more easily and may be more likely to use drugs or look for other artificial highs."
  Dr. Chugh spoke at a workshop on "Parenting in a Changing Society" at New Delhi Mental Health Institute. He is a senior faculty member at the school of Psychiatry in the Indian Institute of Medical Sciences.
  Other important changes in society include the changing role of women and the rapid advances in technology, he told the 250 persons at the workshop, sponsored by the Health and Family Welfare Department.
  "One of the biggest problems facing families today is the loss of a clear definition of roles," he said. "Instead of staying home to raise the family as their mothers did, many women today have to work full-time. And the number of

> single mothers who have to work has increased dramatically over the last decade."
>
> These changes have had a major impact on the family as a unit, he said.
>
> "In fact, sometimes it means not having a family at all," he explained. "When a couple meets in college and they each have an agenda that often precludes having a family, their relationship tends to be viewed with less of a commitment to permanence."
>
> Most people have conflicting ideas and feelings about such issues as commitment to work and family, he said. "And it is important for them to sort out these ambivalent feelings so they can more easily resolve conflicts with others," he added.
>
> Dr. Chugh said he was concerned about the impact of our rapidly changing technology on the family as well.

Take note of how the writer attributed all statements to the speaker. Attribution (the source or authority) is always a problem for news writers. Some tend to overuse it, others don't use it properly. In this example, the writer was careful to use attribution throughout the story to remind the reader that the speaker, not the reporter, made the statements.

Obviously, attribution is not needed in every sentence if the story is carefully organised so there can be no doubt who is being quoted. Attribution can be omitted with a quoted statement if the source of the quote is clear. Generally speaking, however, every paragraph containing indirect quotations should include some attribution.

Story Contents

A speech story should include:

Facts

1. Speaker
   - (*a*) Present position
   - (*b*) Experience
   - (*c*) Description (if apropos)
   - (*d*) Unusual speaking characteristics

2. Audience
   (*a*) Name and type of organisation
   (*b*) Number present
   (*c*) Purpose of meeting
   (*d*) Reaction to speech
   (*e*) Description
   (*f*) Important persons present
3. Speech
   (*a*) Theme
   (*b*) Divisions
   (*c*) Title
   (*d*) Quotations

Sources

1. Speaker, various Who's Who publications, members of group before whom speaker speaks, observations of reporter.
2. Officials of organisation, observations of reporter.

Publications

Thematic journals on Science and Technology, IT or medicine could provide good news stories about important advancements in the respective field. These stories often make the front pages of the daily newspapers.

News magazines also are a source for news stories. Celebrity interviews in *India Today* or *Outlook*, or *Femina* or *Filmfare* and other magazines often result in news stories carried by national newspapers and news agencies. News and opinion magazines publish articles that frequently are the source of important news stories. Even newspapers with national circulation are sources of stories picked up by the news agencies and used by other newspapers. Many newspapers try to localise those stories if there is a logical tie-in.

Thousands of issues of specialised publications, trade journals, academic journals and regional and local magazines are checked regularly by reporters searching for news and feature story ideas. In some cases, a story may have only local news value. However, in many cases the story may have state, regional or even national significance.

Here are examples of stories published in a national daily based on stories appeared in some medical journals.

- We should live so long. Or should we?

Today's "Science" says 75 is about as high as we can expect to push the average Indian lifespan. Average now: 65

But is living longer something to look forward to?

- Hard work and long hours do not, by themselves, hurt a woman's chances of a normal pregnancy and delivery, new research suggests. The study of more than 5,000 women—which focussed on female medical residents working about 70 hours a week—casts doubts on previous studies suggesting long hours, night work and prolonged standing might lead to premature delivery and other problems. Finding women "who work longer hours, suffer more sleep deprivation and are under more stress than residents" would be hard, says the report in *ICMR Journal of Medicine.*

Reporting articles such as above should not be confused with a book review or with a critical analysis. The news story based on an article is not an evaluation of the ideas in the article. It is simply a news story based on what the article says, nothing more. The reporter should follow the same general principles and form that are used in reporting a speech.

There is very little difference between a story on a speech and a story on a published article. As in a speech story, the content of the article and not the fact that the article has been written is usually the substance of the lead. The remainder of the story can be handled effectively as a quote-summary-quote story. And, of course, a description of the publication in which the article appeared (name, type of publication, frequency of publication) may be necessary, just as a description of the occasion (audience, time of presentation) is necessary in reporting a speech.

Personal Interviews

Virtually all stories in a newspaper are the result of interviews, which is why a reporter has to know what to ask, whom to ask and how to ask to be effective. Even reporters who witness events must ask questions of persons involved and others to obtain additional facts and quotations for a story. Police, hospital officials, witnesses and others are questioned for facts about a road or train accident or a fire for example. A Rotary club president is interviewed about a programme featuring a prominent speaker or unusual events. A public authority is asked to reply to charges made by a political opponent.

Reporters should never stop asking questions—interviewing. Without asking the right questions, a reporter simply cannot write a complete story.

Interviews directly related to a news event or a public issue are done to collect facts rather than to draw out the personalities of the persons involved.

Here is an example of a major news story developed out of an interview:

- RIYADH, Saudi Arabia, April 1, The commander of the American forces in Iraq said today that his troops could obliterate Iraq, but cautioned that total destruction of that country might not be "in the interest of the long-term balance of power in this region."
  "President Bush has stated again and again, our argument is not with the Iraqi people, and that would cause thousands and thousands of innocent casualties," the commander, Gen. H. Norman Schwarzkopf, said in an interview.

However, many interviews are conducted specifically to develop a profile or intimate close-up of a famous or infamous, or at least interesting person. The subject of the interview may be a prominent scientist, nationally known novelist, professional athlete, or popular television or movie performer. Or it may be an interesting local person, someone with an unusual hobby or someone who is thrust into the news—a lottery winner or loser.

Here is an example—

- Abhijeet Kale, an assistant in a private firm, who won the biggest lottery jackpot in Indian history, won't fritter away his 5 crore rupees.

> "I've always wanted to become a rich man", Kale, 32 of Vile Parle, said today".
> His annual salary is Rs. 1,50,000 after taxes, he'll get 3.27 crore rupees.
> Kale says he'll take care of his parents and wife and may leave for a world tour.

In the personal interview story the reporter is trying to make the subject come alive on paper. In addition to basic biographical information, the reporter tries to capture for the reader the subject's mannerisms and personality as well as to elicit answers to questions that will give the reader additional insight into that person. To do that successfully, the reporter has to be able to ask good, often provocative questions and to observe the subject carefully. Additional information often is collected from the subject's family, friends, co-workers, admirers and even detractors, if there are any.

Advance preparation is essential to any successful interview. Without it, a reporter will be hopelessly over his or her head. An experience of the writer of this book can illustrate this point beautifully. On a reporting assignment, one of the fellow reporters asked a superstar of Indian cinema to name a few of his hit films. The reporter was not aware of the actor's achievements which obviously caused him considerable embarrassment.

Every reporter must know at least some important bits of information about the person he or she is going to interview if the story is to be a major personality interview. Various Who's Who publications may provide a brief biography. The newspaper's library may contain photographs and biographical data in news clippings or press bureau material. Countless other reference books covering major personalities in practically every field are available at most libraries. Often only one or two reference books may be of help. If no standard reference material includes information on the person the reporter has to interview, a telephone call to someone in the city may supply the needed background. With even a brief information, the reporter can begin to formulate a few questions that can be asked in an interview.

Planning Questions for Interview

In general, questions should pertain to the work, life or personal interests of the person interviewed, but the questions should be planned to bring answers that will interest the general newspaper reader. Questions should be timely and, to whatever extent possible, local. Comments of a prominent person on a current national event in the person's field are timely.

If there is a local angle to the national event, then questions about the local situation should also be asked. Of course, if the person has absolutely no knowledge of what is happening locally, his or her time should not be wasted by asking question about such subjects. Obviously, visitors to the city would not feel competent to comment on a strictly local issue.

Questions should be tailor-made for the subject's profession or background. If a television star is not particularly known as a political activist, do not spend a great deal of time asking him or her political questions. Most readers are not interested in how their favourite star votes. They usually want to know what the stars are really like. Are they as nice as they appear on television? Are they as tough? Are they like the characters they play?

In preparing questions, the reporter should keep in mind that one question should lead to another. The interview should move along in a conversational, informal manner while the reporter jots down on paper, tape-records or commits to memory the answers and attitudes revealed. Constantly taking notes in inadvisable except for dates, figures and the like, although in some cases it may be permissible to keep a pencil busy throughout the interview.

If a reporter wants to use a tape recorder during a private interview, he or she should ask the person concerned for permission. However, in the case of a mass interview with the electronic media, no special permission is needed because radio and television reporters will be recording the interview on tape. The reporter should always be aware of whether note-taking or recording makes the interviewed person self-conscious and "quote timid"; if so, the use of pencil or tape recorder should be limited.

As soon as possible after the interview, however, the reporter should type up the interview notes because the exact responses of the interviewee are then still fresh in the reporter's mind.

The reporter should watch as well as listen. The interviewee's mannerisms, dress, distinctive features and other personal characteristics make copy for the personal interview story. No matter how important the interviewee's statements, there is always room for a few phrases describing him.

Some reporters bring themselves into the personal interview. However, the circumstance of the story rarely justify extensive personal references about the reporter. The reader wants to know about the subject of the interview, not the reporter.

Because of the increasing role of science and technology in our lives, reporters may find themselves having to interview persons in highly technical fields. Faced with such an assignment, a reporter has to make advance preparation. A reporter has an obligation to the interviewee to do some homework.

The library usually is the best place to start. A speech the person gave may have been reprinted in Vital Speeches. Articles the person has written may be listed in the library catalogue. General or special magazines may have carried earlier interviews with the subject. Reporters frequently are criticised by interviewee for not being prepared or for pretending to know about a topic or issue when they do not.

The following 'Interview Bill of Rights' could be a guide for the reporter and the interviewee:

Rights of the Interviewee

- The right to an objective listening to the facts presented.
- The right to an accurate representation of his or her position.
- The right to a fair and balanced context for all statements.
- The right to know in advance the general area of questioning and to have reasonable time for preparation.
- The right to reasonable flexibility as to when to have the interview. (Just as there are times when a reporter cannot be interrupted near a deadline, there are times when others cannot be interrupted.)
- The right to expect the interviewer to have done some homework.
- The right to withhold comment particularly related to, information governed by some regulations, competitive secrets, matters in litigation or negotiation, information that could damage innocent persons.
- The right to an assumption of innocence until guilt is proven.

- The right to offer feedback to the reporter, especially to call attention to instances in which the story, in the honest opinion of the interviewee, missed the point or was in error, and to have this feedback received in good faith.
- The right to appropriate correction of substantial errors without further damage to the credibility or reputation of the interviewee's organisation.

Rights of the Interviewer

- The right to access to an authoritative source of information on a timely basis.
- The right to candor, within the limits of propriety.
- The right to access to information and assistance o adverse stories as well as favourable ones.
- The right to preparation on a story the reporter has developed exclusively, until it has been published or until another reporter asks independently for the same information.
- The right not to be used by businesses for "free advertising" on a purely commercial story.
- The right not to be reminded that advertising pays the reporter's salary.
- The right not to be held accountable for ill-treatment by another reporter or another medium at another time.
- The right to publish a story without showing it to the interviewee in advance.
- The right not to be asked to suppress legitimate news purely on the ground that it would be embarrassing or damaging.
- The right not to be summoned to a press conference when a simple phone call, written statement, news release or interview would do just as well.

Conducting the Interview

Most reporters begin personal interviews with a brief period of small talk to establish rapport with the interviewee. This often is the most critical part of the interview. Those first few minutes often determine the tone of the interview.

A good reporter will move quickly into the questions prepared for the interview. The questions should be arranged in order of their importance. The general questions should come first. The tough, intimidating or offensive questions should be asked near the end of the interview. If the tough questions are asked at the outset of the interview, the interviewee may refuse to answer and terminate the interview immediately.

A reporter should listen carefully to everything the person says and be prepared at any point in the interview to ask the subject to clarify an answer. When in doubt, ask for the correct spelling of all names mentioned in the interview and for verification of important times, dates, places, addresses and statistics. The interviewee's memory may be hazy, and the reporter must not be too timid to ask for verification of the facts presented.

Interview Problems

Special problems can arise during interviews. The most common are off-the-record comments by the subject, sources who do not want to be identified in print and requests by the interviewee to read the story before it is printed. Before agreeing to any of these requests, a reporter should know the newspaper's policy on each. It also would be helpful to the reporter to know the law on the protection of confidential sources.

There often is a credibility problem when unnamed sources are used in stories. Several readership studies show that readers often do not believe stories in which the source of information is not identified. Some readers have told researchers they suspect the reporter may have made up the information when a source is not identified.

The problems created when sources demand to read a story before it is printed seem to grow annually. Most newspapers refuse to allow sources to read stories in advance. However, it is common practice among reporters to check quotes, especially those dealing with highly technical or scientific subjects, with the source. A reporter should never agree to let a source read the story in advance without checking with the editor first.

Telephone Interviews

Many interviews are conducted by telephone. It saves time for the subject of the interview and the reporter. However, many reporters consider the telephone to be ineffective for conducting personality interviews because they are unable to observe the interviewee's reactions to the questions. Reporters also say they are unable to observe the interviewee's mannerisms, dress, distinctive features and other personal characteristics that add a special dimension to personality profiles.

A reporter should prepare for a telephone interview the same way he or she prepares for an in-person interview. When conducting a telephone interview, the reporter should observe all the simple courtesies used during in-person interviews. The reporter should give his or her name and make certain the person knows the information being collected will be used in print.

The reporter also should (1) speak clearly and calmly and avoid long, rambling questions; (2) avoid irrelevant or obvious questions; (3) save the tough or embarrassing questions for the last; and (4) try not to obtain so much information in the telephone interview that the interviewee grows impatient.

Interview Story Forms

In the personal interview, the reporter finds that a variety of approaches will apply, depending on the person interviewed and what is said. But all interview stories have one thing in common: many direct quotes. A reporter can make use of the quote-summary-quote form in the body of the story, and in that regard the interview story is somewhat similar to the speech story. The lead can be a summary, an outstanding feature, a quote or an anecdote, or, to set the scene, it can be descriptive.

The lead, of course, can contain the substance of the interview, but often a striking word picture of the speaker is more desirable if his or her personal characteristics are particularly impressive. By all means, somewhere early in the story, the importance of the interview must be established, although it does not have to be in the lead or first paragraph.

Another story form that has gained considerable popularity in interviews, especially in same magazines, is the "question-and-answer" structure. Newspapers, however, use this form sparingly because it generally requires large amounts of space. In this form, the reporter simply writes a short introduction similar to an editor's note, giving a brief biographical sketch of the interviewee, and then reproduces the questions and the interviewee's answers. Often these interviews are done on tape recorders and are simply transcribed and perhaps edited for style and length.

Meetings and Special Events

Dozens of meetings are held everyday in smaller communities and hundreds in larger cities, often producing important news stories. The public's business is conducted at meetings of governmental bodies. Civic, religious, social, business and professional organisations meet and frequently generate news, which is why meeting stories are a staple in every newspaper.

There are so many meetings; they simply cannot all be covered, so editors have to decide which ones to cover and how to cover them in ways that would be both informative and interesting for readers. Editors consider such questions as:

- Do we write an extensive advance story about what is expected to happen, and then a brief follow-up after the meeting?
- Will a brief advance story do, with a detailed report on what actually happened?
- Do we rely on a press release for our advance, and in some cases, the follow-up?
- Do we assign a reporter and perhaps a photographer?

There are almost as many answers to those questions as there are editors and meetings. But, as a general rule, editors consider meetings of non-governmental organisations particularly newsworthy if:

- There is a prominent speaker or significant programme that would interest readers.
- There will be a large number in attendance.

Meetings about real issues often make important news. But significant stories can and do come from what may appear to be just another routine meeting. For example:

- The City Business Circle met for lunch yesterday and heard an interesting talk by Mr. Subramaniam.

It is important for reporters to keep in mind that when reporting on a meeting, the most important aspect is to tell the reader what took place and why she or he should care.

Once an event has occurred, there is no news value in the simple fact that it happened. Even at meetings where little or nothing goes on, the reporter should look for a news peg or interesting fact for the lead.

Even when writing an advance story about a meeting, the reporter should look for something interesting to put in the lead. Never settle for "A meeting will be held...."

Types of Meeting Stories

The Advance

Most groups rely on newspapers to publicise their meetings through a story or stories printed in advance. Some groups mail or phone in announcements of upcoming meetings. Often the information they provide is incomplete, and the reporter has to call a representative of the group to obtain additional details to write a full and accurate story that will interest many readers—not just members of the organisation.

Information needed for a meeting story includes the correct, formal name of the organisation (and local chapter name if it is part of a national group); the exact time, date and place; and details on the programme such as speakers, entertainment, election or installation of officers. The more the reporter knows about the organisation, the easier it will be to write an interesting and informative story. Compare these two meeting leads:

Weak Lead

In the backdrop of MMS incident, parents will meet in the auditorium of DPS tomorrow at 11 a.m. to watch a presentation by AIIMS doctors on the importance of sex education in schools.

Better Lead

A team of AIIMS doctors will make a presentation on the importance of sex education in schools at a meeting of parents tomorrow. The meeting scheduled in the DPS auditorium at 11 a.m. is taking place in the backdrop of MMS incident.

Avoid starting meeting stories in the following ways:

- There will be a meeting of the Senior Citizens Club at noon...
- At 7:30 p.m. Wednesday, members of the Rotary Club will...
- An evening of fun awaits members of the youth club when they meet in the Fun and Food Village on Monday.

The first example is not written in news style; the second one focuses on the time element, which rarely is the most important fact in the story; and the third-one is editorial in nature. How can the writer be sure everyone will have fun?

In the body of the story, the reporter should avoid editorial comment on the caliber of the programme, such as "an excellent talk was given by" and a "thrilling presentation of magic gimmicks." Such expressions as "All members are urged to attend" and "The public is cordially invited" should be omitted. If the meeting features a speaker and the club or organisation would like others to attend, include that the "meeting is open to the public."

The Follow-Up

Most meetings worthy of more than a bare announcement will have produced something of substance on which the reporter can build the story, including:

1. A definite action—passage of a law, adoption of resolutions, announcement of plans, endorsement of candidates or issues.
2. One or more speeches.
3. Discussion and debate—conflict, difference of opinion, voicing of views, criticism.
4. Personnel—election of officers, nominations, new members, resignations, membership drives, visitors, prominent members or guests, interesting personalities.
5. Miscellaneous features—music or other entertainment, unexpected interruptions.

The lead on the follow-up story can vary greatly from a summary of the entire meeting to a single outgoing feature followed by a summary of other features. In many cases, reporters attempt to develop a general theme for the entire story if there seems to be a central theme to the meeting:

- An urgent appeal for raising a fund of Rs. 1 crore for improving the civic conditions in the city was made at the meeting of the MCD in New Delhi today.

The remainder of the story would be built around the central theme of the civic conditions and its effect on the city and its need for more help from the government.

A reporter should not try to develop a theme, however, if one does not logically exist. Often some feature that is far from the main purpose of a meeting will be the most logical lead because it has stronger reader appeal. The reporter's responsibility is to the reader, not the sponsor of the meeting. The story should be written with that in mind. At the same time, the story should not present a distorted view of the meeting.

It is important that the story be told in a logical order, with the most important thing that happened at the meeting being told first. The story should not be written in chronological fashion, and it should never sound like the minutes taken by the club secretary.

Here is an example of a story coming out of a meeting on public health issues.

- Getting a move on could be the key to staying out of a nursing home for people over 60—India's fastest-growing age group.
  Just two 40-minute exercise sessions each week—emphasising flexibility and stretching—will spur major health improvements within three months. A yoga expert reported at a meeting of the Indian Public Health Association on Wednesday in New Delhi.
  "Most research on exercise and the elderly looks at people under 60. But they tend to be fairly healthy," says Ram Nath, Head of reputed Yoga Kendra.
  "It's the over 60 that get the chronic conditions, and will become a real public health concern as their numbers continue to grow."

Conventions

Conventions have always provided newspapers with a wide variety of stories and, increasingly they are becoming the focal point for major newsbreaks. Planners often schedule a particularly newsworthy speaker to attract the attention of newspeople as well as delegates. Speakers frequently use the convention platform to announce new scientific discoveries, plans for world peace, or formation of a new political party or pressure group.

Handling the stories generated by a large convention can be a major undertaking for any reporter. A big-scale convention is in reality a series of meetings that offer the reporter a wide variety of features and frequently requires the writing of multiple news stories. It is not uncommon for several staff members to be assigned to a large convention. If the convention is a major event—a political party convention or the national meeting of an organisation that might attract several thousand delegates—a special convention staff of a dozen or more reporters and photographers under the direction of a special editor may be assigned.

Many newspapers make special efforts to "cover all angles" of a large local convention, frequently devoting more space to it than that warranted by its appeal to local readers. This type of treatment can be justified on several counts. Each of the many delegates is interested in the coverage and is a potential buyer of the newspaper and, furthermore, newspapers generally give broad coverage to such meetings as a matter of civic spirit. Conventions are important to the economy of any city, and the newspaper joins other organisations of the city in welcoming the visitors and promoting the city as a convention centre.

Of course, a large convention also has many angles of local interest. Although it may attract little attention in the largest cities, several hundred visitors in the average city will create news in itself. Even the smallest of conventions might attract prominent visitors, newsworthy speeches and discussions, resolutions on important issues, unusual persons or incidents and participation of local persons. Any of these should generate considerable local reader interest and make the convention worthy of coverage.

Preliminaries

If the editor of a newspaper decides to give the maximum attention to a convention, a reporter may have weeks—perhaps even months—to begin preparing for the event. Long before the opening of the convention, the reporter may write stories almost daily to feature all phases of the upcoming event.

Most organisations planning a convention will have a publicity committee or manager to work with reporters, providing them much of the information needed to write stories. Often complete press kits are given to reporters to help them cover the event. A kit usually includes the complete programme, pictures and biographical sketches of the speakers and officials of the organisation, a history of the party/group, an explanation of important subjects on the programme and a variety of other material that could be used for stories.

Some publicity managers also provide copies of speeches in advance. But they insist that a story on the speech not be printed until it has been given. A copy of the speech can be extremely helpful because it gives the reporter time to read and digest the speech completely before writing the story.

Even with a copy of the speech in advance, a reporter should attend the meeting to make certain the speech actually was given and to record any material the speaker might add. On some occasions, often with permission of the speaker, a newspaper will publish an advance speech story in its editions on the day the speech is to be delivered. In those cases the lead usually contains the phrase "in a speech prepared for delivery at the (name) convention today."...

All this help from publicity representatives does not relieve the reporter of the responsibility for gathering material for stories on the convention. If a publicity manager is not available to help, it is the reporter's job to get as much material as possible about the convention in advance by writing or phoning officials of the organisation and the speakers. Reporters should also work with the local convention bureau or the hotel or office serving as convention headquarters to gather information about the convention.

Sometimes the number of speakers and the variety of sectional meetings of a convention are so large that the newspaper must omit details of the less important ones. As in every other story, it is important for the reporter to develop a keen sense of what really is news when gathering and writing convention stories.

Presenting Convention Features

In preparing a number of advance reports on a convention, the reporter must plan stories to avoid repetition of the same features. Each story should have something new in its lead, but the time, date and place of the convention should be repeated somewhere (not necessarily in the lead) every time.

The first story lead generally announces that the convention will be held in the city. Often it emphasises the approximate number of persons who will attend along with the time, date and place of the convention. Story leads of follow-up stories will highlight different phases of the programme (speakers, discussion, officers, entertainment).

A summary of other features (minus details) will be included in the body of the story. If a summary of all other features runs the story length beyond the space allotted for it, some of the less important features usually are omitted. It is also acceptable to play up—in the lead—features that have been summarised in the body of the preceding stories even though they are not new developments.

From the day before a convention opens—especially if it is a major one—until the day after it closes, there is a real rush. Often photographers and other reporters team with the reporter in-charge to gather speeches, conduct interviews and search other significant information that was unavailable in advance.

In addition to reports on business and the speeches of the convention, many newspapers seek out human-interest stories on interesting delegates, unusual events in connection with the meeting, comments from delegates on the convention and the city, or other material.

All aspects of a convention may be put together in one long story, or they may be divided into a number of stories. The larger the convention, the more stories, generally speaking. If the stories are divided, one main story will be devoted to the major—most newsworthy—event of the convention and include such essential information as number of delegates and other general information.

Other stories will present reports from sectional meetings within the convention, interviews and other sidelights. The exact manner in which the convention is covered depends on its size, overall newsworthiness in relation to all other news that day and the amount of space available in the newspaper.

Special Events

Fairs, festivals, dedications, exhibitions and other large events that attract a great number of persons offer much the same sort of problems, as do convention stories. Each presents the possibility of some significant straight-news reports as well as dozens of features. Advance preparation is necessary to obtain details.

Several stories, each playing up a different feature, are required before the event takes place, and adequate coverage of all features is necessary while the event is in progress. If the programme of the special event is simply substituted for the convention programme, the whole assignment involves the same procedure.

9

Writing Simple Story Types

Few trainee reporters or staff reporters start writing major stories for a newspaper. Even on small community newspapers, the front-page story generally goes to the experienced reporter and the beginner gets simpler stories.

The classification of stories as simple or complex is a convenient and arbitrary division that most editors use when making assignments, even though there is no real technical significance in this classification. To most editors, single-incident stories—automobile accidents, deaths, illness, funerals, minor crimes—would fall into the "simple" classification. Those stories requiring little interpretative writing and little background might be added to the editor's list—an award or public appointment, for example.

However, it should be noted that any single story may turn out to be either simple or complex, depending on the facts and their news values. For purposes of proceeding from the less difficult to the more difficult stories, the "simple" or "complex" classification has proved useful.

Illness, Deaths and Funerals

The obituary is one of the most important stories in any newspaper. It is read and reread, clipped, bound in plastic and often pasted in the back of the Ramayan or Gita in a household.

To a reporter, the obituary may be routine but not to the family. The newspaper will be remembered for the careful, accurate way it reported even the smallest details during the family's time of sorrow.

Let the obituary be inaccurate—a name misspelled, facts

incorrectly reported, survivors omitted—and the family will never forget it and never forgive the offending newspaper. Everything in the newspaper will be suspect in the eyes of that family whose members constantly will remind relatives and friends that the newspaper had left out the name of his beloved baby sister in the list of survivors, or made some other grievous error and cannot be trusted.

Writing obituaries requires a special sensitivity. That is why many newspapers, even small ones, use experienced reporters to write all obituaries. However, some still give the new reporter the job of writing them, even those of very prominent residents, as a test. How a new reporter handles obits often determines how rapidly he or she will be given other assignments.

News Value of Obits and Other Stories

Why are obituaries and stories about illness and funerals so important? Evaluating their news value shows they all fall on the disaster side of human experience. They are disruptions of the status quo, and they are of consequence in the community. The removal of almost any human being from the local scene requires social and economic readjustments among relatives and friends. His or her place must be taken; his or her job must be filled by another. The home may be offered for sale; the widow or widower may move to another city; the daughter or son may withdraw from college. All such changes touch the lives of others.

Factors of Magnitude

The importance of the news story is determined by several factors. Illness is measured by its gravity, approaching death as its climax. And both illness and death are measured by the number of persons affected in the community. Thus the prominence of the person and the name of the illness may determine story importance. A rare disease or accident, even one involving someone who is comparatively unknown, is interesting because it is unusual.

Even more important may be stories about the threat of epidemics of quite common diseases. Since prominence usually means being well known, in addition to holding a position of importance, the community is more generally affected by matters involving prominent persons. Multiple deaths or cases of illness extend importance of the news. Although the story of illness or death (and of the funeral) may frequently stand stripped of its disaster appeal, its news importance may sometimes be heightened by prominence, novelty, consequence, human interest and even conflict.

Illness

Illness—grave illness—is reported less frequently than its news importance justifies. Patient, family, physician and hospital are often unwilling to have the illness known. Physicians and hospitals usually tend to avoid publicity even in the case of very prominent persons. Family and patient may wish to avoid unnecessary alarm to friends, employer or employees, and sometimes the family wants to hide information from the patient. Often if the person is very prominent—a public official or a major entertainment figure, for example—the illness may not be disclosed to assure the person's privacy.

Illness can affect business matters, contracts, perhaps even diplomatic negotiations, as well as various other obligations. Always in the background is the thought that tomorrow or the next day the patient may be well and the less uproar about the matter the better. If the patient's family, physician and hospital all refuse to give a statement on the illness, the reporter should use whatever information is available with extreme caution.

Illness is not easy to report properly. Highly technical or tenuous conditions may characterise the illness itself. The physician might not know the exact nature of the illness. The nature of the illness itself might be so technical that it is extremely difficult to translate into language the average reader can understand. Some medical schools, however, now have special courses to teach medical students how to write and speak in non-technical language.

The reporter should always keep in mind the emotions and the sensitivities of the patient as well as the family. Once the brief bulletin on the patient's condition is announced, little substance is left for the reporter to take hold of and expand, as a general rule. However, if the person is prominent—a major entertainer, or chief minister or central minister—the attending physicians sometimes will hold a press conference and explain the nature of the illness and the patient's condition.

In the prolonged illness of such a prominent person, regular medical bulletins will be issued and the comings and goings of delegations, friends, relatives and others as well as their public statements may provide copy. The illness stories of lesser known persons will usually be brief, however, unless they suffer from a rare or unusual ailment.

Although a list of patients admitted to and discharged from hospitals often is published each day in newspapers in many smaller communities, the reporter gives individual attention to only a few. In addition, "tips" sometimes will lead the reporter to interesting stories about illnesses.

Story Content

Many accounts of illness contain only one, two or three paragraphs and are usually handled similarly to a personal. The following information is usually given:

1. Name and identification of the person who is ill.
2. Cause of illness.
3. Condition (fair, serious, critical—an accurate quotation from the doctor or hospital).
4. Name of hospital (government or private hospital).
5. Duration of illness.
6. Members of family at bedside.
7. Effect of illness on person's public position (especially in the case of an elected official) or business.

The "Who" is the most important "W" in most illness stories and should be in the lead. For variety, or if the disease or operation is unusual, the cause of the illness or the condition of the patient may be featured. However, if the story is a follow-up, the condition of the patient is usually the feature. Note these examples:

Who

Railway Minister Lalu Prasad Yadav was taken to AIIMS today for observation after suffering several dizzy spells while working in his office at home.

Cause

A severe nose infection caused Mr. Lalu Prasad Yadav, Railway Minister, to suffer several dizzy spells while working in his office at home, doctors at All-India Institute of Medical Sciences, (AIIMS) said today. He will remain in the hospital for three days.

Condition (a Follow-up)

Mr. Lalu Prasad Yadav, Railway Minister, is in good condition at AIIMS, recovering from a severe nose infection. He was taken to the hospital on Monday after he suffered several dizzy spells while working in his office.

Hospital Notes and Bulletins

Some newspapers in the West regularly carry a hospital column. It may be merely a list of "Admitted" and "Discharged" with no details given. Some hospitals refuse to make such lists available; others have a more liberal policy on publicity. It is common practice at many hospitals to ask a patient or the family if there is any objection to being listed as a patient in the daily report to the press.

Some hospitals in India—both government and private—have the practice of issuing a health bulletin wherever an important person is being treated. This bulletin is read by the Medical Superintendent or any other hospital authority or by the Spokesperson of the hospital at the pre-announced scheduled time before the reporters. This helps the hospital to avoid repeated inquiries about the health of the prominent person admitted in its ward. Here is an example:

- The condition of Mr. Narasimha Rao is stable. All his important tests have been conducted. A team of specialists is monitoring his condition. They expect an improvement by tomorrow evening.

Deaths

Death is an important item of news. Regardless of news value, death is reported as a public record. No person ever becomes so unimportant that he or she is not valuable as a vital statistic. Even the nameless beggar found frozen to death on the pavement is not overlooked. The beggar fits somewhere in a chain of persons and events. Although practice will vary from paper to paper in the treatment of death stories, all newspapers report deaths.

One of the best descriptions of an obituary has been given by Arthur Gelb, deputy managing editor of *The New York Times.*

According to him—"An obit is the summing up of a person's life, the last statement about him for the record. It has to have fairness, balance, accuracy, and substantiation of fact. We see obits as short biographies, an analysis of the man and his time. What did his life mean? What was his impact on civilization? What was his paper? .... We try to put him in the context of history and of his field and what he meant to the people in that field."

Obituaries

Just as the practice of reporting deaths varies, so the terms used to describe this type of news story will also vary. At some newspapers, the word "obituary" means a news story written about the death of a person that is published with an individual headline. At others the obituary is the black, agate-type alphabetical listing of everyone who has died and has not yet been cremated. This list is also called "Death Notices" at some newspapers.

All newspapers publish stories of deaths free if they use them as separate stories. Many newspapers, however, make a per-word charge for death-column notices just as they do for classified advertisements, and such charges become part of the funeral costs. Whether the obituary is a paid item or not, the form used by the newspaper is standardized to get all essential information.

The amount of information in a death notice will vary. Because it is paid for by the family, it can include such information as the names of the family members and friends.

Death Stories

Reporters are called on to write death stories (or obituaries) that are handled in regular news style. Some newspapers publish these on the same page as the paid notices. Others have separate pages for them.

Other newspapers limit these stories to persons who are newsworthy enough to justify extra attention. In most large cities, the death of a person who has gained no prominence and who died of natural causes would be reported only in the paid notices column.

Although the information in the paid notice provides the basic facts for the news story, the reporter often must seek additional information by telephoning or visiting relatives or others mentioned in the notice. If the person is prominent, the reporter frequently checks the newspaper's library for additional information and calls friends, business associates and others for material on the deceased.

The news agencies and most large newspapers maintain rather complete files of hold-for-release obituaries on most big names—national and international leaders, for example. Many smaller newspapers maintain similar stories, ready for print, on the most prominent citizens in their communities. These usually are brought up to date at regular intervals.

Story Content

If a newspaper does carry individual stories on deaths, any reporter assigned to write them should keep in mind that the story must provide the following information:

1. Name and identification (address, occupation and affiliations) of the deceased.
2. Age.
3. Day and time of death.
4. Place of death.
5. Cause of death.
6. Duration of illness.
7. Names of members of the immediate family (survivors).
8. Effects of death on the person's public position (if applicable).

Although this information is routine, there should be nothing routine about the writing of the story. The reporter should use every journalistic device to show what manner of person the deceased was. This, of course, depends on details. The reporter should look for colourful incidents, anecdotes, personal traits, and personal remembrances of friends and family to convey exactly why this particular death is news.

The first paragraph should sum up the circumstances of the death with name, age, identification by position or profession, and time and place of death. The remainder of the story should be a carefully constructed biographical sketch of the person in an effort to picture for the reader what he or she really was like. It should not be a mere routine summarisation of the facts of his or her life and career. Although it should contain colourful highlights of the deceased's life history, it should not be light or frivolous.

Often newspapers will solicit comments from friends, co-workers and admirers when a prominent citizen or public figure dies. These comments are worked into a separate story that accompanies the story of the person's death. The more prominent the individual, the longer and more detailed the obituary. In some cases, several stories focussing on various aspects of the person's career also are used.

The reporter must write death stories objectively and with dignity. Every effort should be made to resist the temptation to make the reader weep. The language of the story should be simple and precise, avoiding saccharine words and phrases such as "He will be missed by all." The reporter should learn the practices of the various religions and refer to them properly in the story.

Occasionally, a reporter is faced with a problem in writing a death story about a person whose past was marred by a scandal—a prison term, disbarment or a messy divorce that had made the front pages. If the person was entirely private, many newspapers would elect to leave out such facts, especially if the person had lived down the incident. However, if the person who was once a convict later became a prominent public official, the story must mention the prison term. Because the deceased was a public person and the criminal case was a well-known fact, the newspaper cannot leave it out. Facts of that nature, no matter how unpleasant, are essential to an adequate story.

When a death is announced in the afternoon newspaper, the next day's morning newspaper in the same city generally does not repeat the same lead. It usually features a different angle—the announcement of the funeral, for example. Even if the funeral arrangements were carried in the original obit, they are the feature of the lead for the second-day story.

Funeral

The funeral announcement is the follow-up of a death story, except in the case of more prominent persons whose funerals might attract large numbers of mourners. As in any follow-up, a brief summary of the preceding story must be included, but the lead features the funeral.

Story Content

1. Time.
2. Place.
3. Whether public or private.
4. Place of cremation/burial.

The funeral story of a prominent person would be greatly expanded and reported in the same manner as any other news story of similar importance. It would include excerpts from the minister's eulogy, description of the service, and an account of relatives and prominent friends and members of associations who attended, in addition to any other information required to report the funeral adequately to readers.

Most newspapers prefer to list the cause of death. However, some families either refuse to give that information or request it be withheld. This is particularly true in the case of certain diseases such as cancer and Acquired Immune Deficiency Syndrome (AIDS). Newspapers generally defer to the family's wishes.

Fires and Accidents

Writing a fire or accident story can present a real challenge to a reporter because much of the information is collected after the event, and often the details of the accident or fire are quite similar to those of almost every fire or accident story.

Except for the most dramatic fires and accidents, facts for the story generally are obtained from records of the police and fire departments. To avoid writing a dull and routine story, an alert reporter will attempt to get additional information by telephone or in person from witnesses—policemen, firemen, spectators and the persons involved, if possible.

Although most stories of this type are picked up as routine on regular beats—police and hospitals—or from phone calls, the reporter has an obligation to the reader to make stories interesting as well as informative. Here's how a reporter began his story on a house fire that killed three children.

- By all accounts, Rahul was a good kid living in an area racked by poverty, drugs and violence.
  The boy helped his neighbours with chores, helped his friends, with their homework and gave the small bits of money he earned from odd jobs to just about anybody in need.
  On Saturday, Rahul celebrated his 11th birthday. He died at 1:50 a.m., Sunday, the victim of a house fire that also took the lives of his sister and niece, both 4.
  "I bought a motivating book to give him for his birthday, but I didn't get a chance," said Rakshit, 11, Rahul's best friend, who was standing Sunday outside the burned out two-storey row house in Shakarpur area, where Rahul lived. "He was generous and nice. He would always give me stuff when he had a little."
  Mr. Jagir Singh, Head of East Delhi Fire Department, said the cause of the fire that swept through the first-floor apartment about 12:45 a.m. remains unknown. Investigators suspect it was started by short circuit.

No matter how the information is gathered, certain facts are always required for a complete story. The newspaper reader is eager to know who was killed or injured; the extent and amount of property damage; and the disruption the event caused, such as blocked streets and traffic delays. If, in addition, the drama of major events can be effectively presented, so much the better. But the drama should be implicit in the facts. The reporter shouldn't overwrite for effect.

Here's a fire story lead with an unusual twist:

- New Delhi—One of the few items untouched by a fire that destroyed the 200-year-old mosque in the walled city yesterday was a Quran.
  "Allah had a hand in it. That's the only way I can explain

how the Quran was spared," said Maulvi Abbas Ali, Imam of the mosque that authorities believe was destroyed by arsonists.

"It was on the reading desk. The desk is not too badly ruined, but everything else is destroyed," said Ali, 78, who has been a Imam all his adult life.

The police, has taken, two persons in custody and interrogations are on to find out the cause of the arson.

Facts and Sources

Story and Contents

The following formula indicates the facts and sources usually available in a major fire or accident story. Minor stories use fewer details:

Facts	*Sources*
1. Casualties (*a*) Name and identification of every person killed and injured (*b*) Manner in which persons were injured (*c*) Nature of injuries (*d*) Disposition of dead and injured	1. Police, firemen, hospitals, funeral homes; friends and relatives of dead and injured; witness; neighbours
2. Damages (*a*) Damages to property (*b*) Description of property (*c*) Owner of property (*d*) Insurance (*e*) Other property threatened	2. Police, firemen and Property owners
3. Description (*a*) Cause (*b*) Time and duration (*c*) Chronological account of incidents (*d*) Relief work of firemen, police or others (*e*) Spectators	3. Police, firemen, persons involved, witnesses

(*Contd.*)

Facts	*Sources*
4. Escapes (*a*) Rescues (*b*) Experiences of those escaping	4. Police, firemen, persons involved, witnesses
5. Legal action (*a*) Investigations (*b*) Arrests (*c*) Suits	5. Police, firemen, property owners, lawyers
6. Sidelights (human interest, as part of main story or as separate story)	

In a major fire and accident story the number of persons dead or injured is usually featured. The amount of property damage is commonly featured if there are no injuries or deaths. But involvement of a prominent person, an unusual cause, a dramatic rescue or any one of the five Ws may sometimes be featured in the lead.

Story Forms

Fire and accident stories can range in form and size from a brief to a lengthy several-feature story. The multiple-casualty story form is often used when such treatment is justified. The following are examples of several fire story leads:

- A five-year-old boy was admitted to Lok Nayak Jayaprakash Hospital today suffering from smoke inhalation following a midday fire in his family's apartment.
  Haider was reported in critical but stable condition in the paediatrics intensive care unit, hospital officials said.
  The child was pulled by fire-fighters from the bedroom of a house located in a narrow lane behind Jama Masjid.
  Two other children, Nafeesa, 4 and Abbas, 3, fled the burning apartment and were uninjured.

Frequently a fire story will produce a follow-up that deals with the cause of the fire or the condition of the injured. Here is the lead on a follow-up to a story of a fire in which one child was killed and three were injured:

- The government has announced a compensation of Rs. 50,000 to the family of the child who was killed in the fire on Saturday. A help of Rs. 20,000 has been provided for the treatment of the three injured children.
  The police have not yet been able to find any foul play in the fire. The local residents have demanded a probe by a senior officer.

Sometimes fires can lead to criminal charges. Here is a short story about an arrest that grew out of an attempt to burn a house:

- A 59-year-old man was charged on Friday with trying to set his home on fire.
  Police said witnesses reported the man poured kerosene on his front door and porch and a side door on Thursday night, and then tried to light it. The witnesses said the man tried two matches, but they didn't work, so he went next door to borrow more.
  Police arrived, though, and caught him after a short chase. They charged Jimy, with attempted aggravated arson.

Accidents often involve injury and death. The leads on stories about them should focus on the human element as in this example:

- One person was killed and at least 14 were injured this morning in the fireball that erupted after a tractor-trailer rammed a stranded truck into a bus on the crossing of National Highway No. 12.
  Names of the victims were not immediately available, pending notification of families, a Highway Patrol official said.
  The truck was loaded with inflammable material, which burst into flames…

Vocabulary and Fact Reporting

In reporting accidents—notably automobile accidents, because of their frequency—the reporter must use words carefully, with an eye to precise meaning. Only moving objects collide, strictly speaking. Therefore, "struck a parked car" is better than "collided with a parked car." "The accident occurred when the car in which they were riding" is awkward, yet "their car" is usually inaccurate. A number of newspapers, however, have come to accept the latter.

Libel actions grow out of inaccurate phrasing, and shortcuts of language should be used with care. Except in reports of storms, earthquakes and other "acts of God," colourful language should always yield to fact reporting. The phrase 'completely demolished' (or destroyed) is redundant. To demolish or destroy means completely, so the word completely is unnecessary. A statement that, 'a person is not expected to live,' should be reported as critically injured unless a direct quote is available from a physician using those exact words.

Factual reporting and careful language will also help the reporter write without expressing an opinion on the person responsible for a fire or accident. The reporter does not attempt to fix that responsibility. Who the guilty person is may seem apparent from the facts, the arrests and the statements of officials as reported in the case; but the reporter makes no effort to point out the guilty party, for that is the job of the courts.

If the facts of a story tend to point the finger of guilt at a person, the ethics of fair play require that the reporter make an effort to get that person's side of the story and report it at the same time. If the reporter is unable to reach the person, then the story should indicate that fact.

Complete Reporting

Most disasters are treated adequately when presented as straight news, with little interpretation. However, if such events accumulate into a daily threat to the security of life and property, the newspaper may feel compelled to develop a story or series of stories dealing with the problem.

Many cities face the serious continuing problem of road accidents. New Delhi is one such city. Occasionally there may be a series of fires, and there are epidemics of disease and crime. What causes those disasters? How do they occur? How could they be avoided? Before the community can protect itself or take the proper remedial steps, it must know the facts. That is where the reporter and the newspaper come in.

In such cases, it is the reporter's job to report not merely the surface events but the underlying causes as well. Often it is the reporter and the newspaper who force reluctant or foot-dragging public officials to undertake programmes to correct potentially dangerous situations.

Almost every newspaper, at sometime during the year, will print a story or series of stories touched off by a single news event such as an accident or fire. Three school bus accidents in less than a month caused a newspaper in Delhi to do a series on how rash the drivers are. The stories forced the school board to institute rigid rules for the recruitment of drivers. Fires in three apartment complexes in the city sent reporters checking building codes and fire safety norms that turned out to be virtually non-existent. DDA officials quickly promised a new enforcement programme.

Some newspapers have used news events to bring about improved traffic enforcement and better sanitary conditions at public housing and sewage treatment plants, for example. In each case, the reporter and the newspaper saw a need to reach the heart of a civic problem. Rather than stopping with the initial report, the newspaper assigned the reporter to go beneath the surface of the initial event and through investigation and interpretative analysis present the problem to the public and public officials.

Seasons, Weather and Natural Disasters

- A tornado rips through a Mumbai suburb, killing 26 people and injuring 350. Damage to homes and property runs into thousands of rupees.
- A cyclone devastates the coastal areas of Andhra Pradesh, causing more than a crore rupees damage and leaving 35 dead; 26,000 are left homeless and 224,000 are temporarily out of work.
- A 7.1 point earthquake in the Himalayan region in Uttaranchal spreads death and destruction for more than 100 kilometers in Uttarkashi district. Sixty-seven die, 3,000 are injured and 14,000 are left homeless.

Major national disasters of this nature challenge and strain the strengths and talents of a newspaper's staff. But they also often bring out the best in the writers and editors. The impressive results of their individual and team efforts can and do result in national recognition.

But there is an equal challenge in having to write about the weather on a daily basis, especially when the forecast changes little from day-to-day. Until recently the daily weather story in many newspapers was dumped on the newest or weakest reporter in the newsroom. But not any longer. The continuing popularity of television weather forecasts changed all of that.

Newspapers pay attention to the weather story everyday now, not just when there is a thunderstorm or flood. And many newspapers send their reporters to seminars and short courses in meteorology and climatology to help them improve their ability to write about the weather accurately and authoritatively.

Weathers Stories

Newspaper editors know that the weather story is consistently one of the best read items in the paper everyday. Many newspapers carry a regular front-page news story about the forecast. Some newspapers carry a detailed weather map, frequently in colour, and complete local, regional and national forecasts that are provided by the meteorological department. A listing of high and low temperatures in major cities across the nation generally is included.

A reporter assigned to write the weather story is often faced with making the same or nearly the same forecast sound fresh and interesting day after day during extended hot or cold, wet or dry, spells. It's not easy.

To avoid a routine story based on the day's forecast only, many editors insist that the reporter look for a human-interest approach. But reporters should avoid trying to be overly cute or clever. Adding imaginary elements or stretching the facts could change or misrepresent the forecast and lead to angry readers.

Frequently the weather figures into other stories. Here is an example:

- A big-rig truck loaded with a cargo of new automobiles crashed into two cars stopped alongside a big crossing during a violent thunderstorm on Thursday.
  Seven people in the stopped cars were killed, the police said.

The carrier, hauling eight vehicles, came around a curve on Highway 5, sideswiped a concrete divider and careened into the cars.

And here's the lead on an animal story with a weather angle.

- The three normally snow-white polar bears at the Zoo have taken on a distinct green tinge—evidence they have been spending lots of time submerged during the searing summer heat.
  "We bleach the pools and we do everything we can to avoid it," Brady, the zoo's curator for animals, said on Thursday.
  "But once they start turning green, it's almost impossible to stop." The culprit is algae.

Special Weather Stories

Often the weather may become the lead story or one of the major stories of the day. A special story is demanded if:

1. The weather results in disasters—floods, hurricanes, tornadoes, droughts, dust storms, blizzards, lightning and other weather quirks that cause deaths or serious damages.
2. There are sudden changes—cold waves, early snows, heavy rains or other out-of-the ordinary conditions.
3. Records are approached or broken—highs and lows in monthly and annual temperatures or rainfall.
4. A special event is affected by the weather—football and baseball games or other major sports events, parades, other outdoor events and even some indoor events.

Readers are interested not merely in data but also in the social and economic effects of unusual weather. The effects of weather on crops in farming areas can be of major local interest and perhaps even have national and international implications.

Such news is obtained from a variety of sources: the hospitals for deaths, injuries, and illnesses; the police for accidents and traffic problems; the fire department for fires and rescues; the charity agencies for suffering of the poor; government offices for relief work; transportation and utility companies for interruptions in service. There is also a variety of reports that come into the newspaper office from eyewitnesses. All are usually bound together in one weather story.

The multiple-casualty story is a popular form to use for weather stories concerning a number of deaths and injuries. Even if there are no casualties, this same form may be used as a convenient method of presenting reports on a wide variety of property damages and other effects, the list of damages in this instance taking the place of the list of dead or injured.

Story Contents

The facts and sources of various weather stories include:

Facts	*Sources*
1. Statistics (*a*) Temperature (high and low) (*b*) Precipitation (*c*) Visibility (*d*) Humidity (*e*) Wind velocity (f) Flood stage (if any)	1. Weather Service
2. Forecast warnings (*a*) Crop warnings (*b*) Sea or lake warnings	2. Weather Service, police, fire department, relief workers, agriculture extension agents
3. Casualties (*a*) Names and identification of dead and injured (*b*) Cause of deaths and injuries (*c*) Nature of injuries (*d*) Disposition of dead and injured	3. Police, fire department, hospitals, friends and relatives, witnesses
4. Damages (*a*) Damages to property (*b*) Description of property (*c*) Cause of damage (*d*) Property threatened	4. Police, fire department, rescue workers, owners, witnesses
5. Relief (*a*) Relief provided (*b*) Relief needed	5. Police, fire department, charitable agencies, city officials, relief workers

(*Contd.*)

Facts	*Sources*
6. Escapes (*a*) Experiences of those who escaped (*b*) Rescues	6. Police, fire department, relief workers, witnesses
7. Legal action (*a*) Arrests (*b*) Investigations	7. Police
8. Tie-in or tie-back	8. Newspaper files, reference books

Natural Disasters

Some natural disasters are so monumental that they dominate the news for weeks and occasionally much longer because of their devastating impacts. Tsunami in Andamans Nicobar and Tamil Nadu, earthquakes in Latur and Uttarkashi and cyclones in Andhra Pradesh and Orissa in recent years are such examples.

Some newspapers in the West are prepared to continue their operation whenever a natural disaster strikes. They have disaster plans that encompass all aspects of their operation, from gathering the news to printing and delivering it. Newspapers in India unfortunately, do not.

On October 17, 1989, an earthquake hit the northern California in the United States causing devastation from Watsonville and Santa Cruz to Oakland and San Francisco. The newspaper *San Jose Mercury* News was ready with a plan that permitted it to publish a complete 104-page newspaper with a 12-page ad free earthquake wraparound the next morning and to distribute 175,000 extra copies of it. Although the earthquake knocked out power throughout the area, including *San Jose*, the *Mercury News*' backup generators provided the power for the editorial and production staff to work through the night. The *Mercury News* was on the streets by 6:30 a.m.

On succeeding days the paper contained a 16-page earthquake section on October 18; a 12-page section on October 19; and a 16-page commemorative section, "We will never forget," on October 21. For its distinguished coverage of one of the worst natural disasters to hit the United States that year, the *Mercury News* won a Pulitzer Prize.

The lead of a disaster story should describe the extent of the disaster, focusing on the human element—casualties in particular. Here is the lead on the *Mercury News'* main earthquake story, written by David Schrieberg:

- The biggest earthquake since 1906-07 on the Richter scale and possibly higher—hit the Bay Area at 5:04 p.m., Tuesday, killing at least 76 people, injuring more than 460, setting off fires in San Francisco and sending buildings, highways and bridges crashing down on people and cars across the region.
  The quake, centered in the Santa Cruz Mountains, lasted from 20 to 40 seconds and frightened millions from Ukiah to San Diego. It was as strong as the quake that ravaged much of Soviet Armenia in December.
  Damage throughout the Bay Area was staggering, as death and injury reports poured in to disaster centers and rose by the hour. Lt. Gov. Leo McCarthy said the damage could reach $1 billion.
  In Oakland, officials feared that up to 200 people may have died when an elevated section of Interstate 880 toppled onto another part of the road. And the Alameda County Coronor said the toll was expected to grow.

Writing the first story of a major disaster such as an earthquake or tornado presents a particular challenge because of conflicting reports of the casualties and damages. Officials often are unsure and can only guess, as those in Oakland did, about the total number of people who might have died when the interstate collapsed, and as the Lieutenant Governor did when he underestimated the total damage by about $9 billion. But they are the most reliable sources at the time and it is important to give the readers those figures. The readers know that they will be adjusted in subsequent stories.

The *Mercury News* editors just like their counterparts in other papers know that the real story of a natural disaster is in the human element—the people who are killed, those who are rescued, those who rescue them, the homeless, the displaced. That is why one of the prime elements of disaster coverage is the feature or human interest story focussing on the individuals whose lives were dramatically impacted by the disaster.

Here is the lead on the *Mercury News'* story of one of the most startling of all the rescues of the quake victims. It was written by Laura Kurtzman, Dan Stober and Phillip J. Trounstine.

- OAKLAND—They were dirty, drained and demoralised after a fruitless search for life in the rubble that once was the Cypress Street Viaduct.
  Then unbelievably, a Caltrans engineer in a cherry picker saw a movement—a faint promise—in a 3-1/2 foot high concrete tomb.
  And from the flattest and most hopeless section of I-880, rescue workers on Saturday pulled 220 pound dockworker Buck Helm form his squashed silver Chevrolet Sprint—89 hours after he was buried.
  "Thank God, I'm alive, "said the 57-year-old Weaverville man according to one of the rescue workers who cheered and wept as Helm waved weakly from his gurney.

Seasons

Seasonal stories are a staple in most newspapers. They also can become a problem for a reporter. How can he or she make this year's New Year's Day story different from last year's? Is there a new angle to Baisakhi, Basant Panchmi and the dozens of other holidays and anniversaries newspapers dutifully write about each year? Fortunately, most newspapers handle seasonal stories as features. If a reporter has an active imagination and a flair for words, what might have been a routine story can be turned into a clever, original and highly readable feature.

A Calendar of Annual Events and List of Holidays can be good guides to seasonal and other special events. The accompanying chart points out some of the events and dates that may receive attention by newspapers. Not all of them are reported by any one newspaper, although all are potential stories. Local interest and available space in the newspaper may be the deciding factors.

January

Date	*Occasion*
1.	New Year Day
10.	Lal Bahadur Shastri's death anniversary

12. Swami Vivekananda's birth anniversary
13. Lohri
14. Makar Sankranti
23. Subash Chandra Bose's birth anniversary
26. Republic Day
30. Shaheed Diwas—Mahatma Gandhi's death anniversary

February

Date varies....Basant Panchmi
14. St. Valentine's Day
Date varies...:Maha Shivratri

March

Date varies....Holi

April

1. Fool's Day
Date Varies.... Ram Navami
Mahavir Jayanti
13. Baisakhi
Date varies....Good Friday

May

1. May Day
....
Date varies.... Second Sunday is Mother's Day
13. Bhudha Poornima
27. Pt. Jawaharlal Nehru's death anniversary

June

Date varies....Third Sunday—Father's Day

August

15 Independence Day
20 Rajiv Gandhi's birthday
Date varies....Raksha Bandhan
Date varies....Janamashtmi

September

14 Hindi Diwas

October

2. Gandhi Jayanti....Mahatma Gandhi's birthday
2. Lal Bahadur Shastri's birthday
   Date varies....Dussehra

November

Date varies....Diwali
14 Bal Diwas....Pt. Jawharlal Nehru's birthday

December

25 Christmas Day
31 New Year-eve

Weaving the Story

The key to writing all seasonal or holiday stories is to combine the present and the past—to tell not only how the holiday will be observed but also why it is being observed—and to make the story sound fresh. Something is lacking if a feature on Gandhi Jayanti fails to recall the contribution of Mahatma Gandhi. In addition, the story is really incomplete if it mentions nothing of local residents' plans to observe the holiday.

For instance, in November 2004, Diwali was on November 12. Then November 13 was second Saturday and November 14 Sunday. November 15 was declared holiday because of Id. There were stories in newspapers as to how happy the people are by getting holidays for four days and how they are planning to enjoy it.

The source for seasonal stories is evident. In developing a feature, the reporter has to go to reference books or other sources to obtain facts of the past. But reporters also have to interview informed persons for facts of the present. This information has to be woven into a coherent and interesting story. To give the story timeliness, the reporter often puts emphasis on the present in the lead.

Research is the key. A reporter should not settle for the quickest, easiest reference work—an encyclopaedia. Much historical, and sometimes scientific research is done annually in many areas that might give a reporter a new approach to a holiday.

As we know that Ganesh Utsav is celebrated in Maharashtra and other parts of the country with fun and fair. While doing a report on the festival, the reporter might add some input from a study revealing as to why and how Lokmanya Tilak laid the foundation of Ganesh Utsav and whether the objective was achieved. There might even be a study tracing Ganesh Utsav to some ancient time.

Sometimes the cause of the celebration does not date back to a historical event—the vernal equinox, for example—and the reporter must develop a scientific rather than a historical background. The reporter may assume that many persons will approach a certain day with interest, and it is permissible to predict what will be done as an unplanned observance of that day.

Depending on the tenor of the story, the reporter sometimes may make his predictions imaginative as well as factual. However, this approach requires imagination similar to that of an Associated Press reporter who wrote a personality sketch on a turkey as a Thanks giving feature. Often an offbeat feature can be developed on one of the lesser known "days," such as Bachelor's Day on February 28.

Seeking information on local celebrations, the reporter naturally will question leaders of clubs and organisations. Information has to be collected from religious leaders in case of some religions gathering or congregation. Take for instance bathing taking place on Makar Sankranti. No doubt, administrative authorities making arrangements for the bath shall be an important source.

Similarly the labour unions should provide information for a May Day story. Schools observe most anniversaries by class programme. Most other organisations will announce such special programmes in advance.

Story Contents

The formula for a seasonal story is:

Facts	*Sources*
1. Explanation of seasonal event (*a*) History (*b*) Past observances	1. Reference books or reliable persons
2. Observance (*a*) Formally by organisations (*b*) Informally by whole city	2. Officials of orgnisations, reasonable predictions of reporter

10

Crime Reporting

Crime stories have universal appeal and attract wide attention regardless of the status of persons involved and their situation in life.

In our country evening newspapers are more specialised in crime reporting than of morning newspapers. Most of the crime cases take place in large cities and reports about them in evening newspapers is a matter of importance to the city readers. The morning papers also publish crime stories, but do not normally give any special treatment. Depending upon the importance of crime material, the papers may give prominence by placing it on the front page or inside page.

A crime involving persons of prominence and social position is bound to receive attention. Assassinations like that of former Prime Ministers, Indira Gandhi and Rajiv Gandhi or killing of the Akali leader Longoval by terrorists and murder of Lalit Maken, Pramod Mahajan always get wide coverage. Besides, shootings, stabbing, fights, group killing, suicides or large monetary losses in robberies are all suitable content for page 1 display.

Normally, kidnapping of children, murder, search for missing girls, family feud, theft, property loss, robbery, cheating etc., are situations receiving daily coverage in most of the newspapers.

Crime reporting is as complicated as reporting a political event. Unfortunately, it is not taken seriously in our country. Senior and experienced reporters are not given this beat, freshers with little knowledge of the intricacies of crime reporting are often assigned to report crimes. Thus newspapers often miss the depth and full implications of the story.

After the advent of a number of TV channels in India, the responsibility of a crime reporter, now, is not confined to the objective reporting of crime cases, rather, he/she has to present greater interpretation of crime cases, very often, with a backgrounder and graphics.

Indian national dailies of English have started giving psycho-analysis of criminals and crime cases so as to saturate all possible questions arising in the mind of a reader of higher awareness. The socio-economic scene which compels a man to commit crime, is also analysed.

Graphical or pictorial presentation of the crime, with the support of figures and coloured line sketches reveals the answers of why and how a photograph of the crime committed cannot be given. Even, if somehow, the reporter acquires any photo of gruesome killing, it shall be inadequate for the mindset of the reader to present it with report, hence it is better to depict the mode and sequences in sketches drawn.

Journalist's Responsibility in Crime Reporting

The broad coverage of law enforcement is something more than routine news gathering. It is a public service and perhaps even a deterrent for certain types of crime in an era when the incidents of crime are constantly on the rise.

Today both print and electronic media concentrate on crime stories. But the newspaper retains the primary public reliance for the detailed examination of the work of police, prosecutors and the courts.

The objective of the press is to report crime news, not to philosophise over it. Since local news remains the bread and butter of the average newspapers, thoughtful critics of the press frequently ask whether the excessive publication of crime news benefits the public or the publisher. Because of varying circumstances, there can be no categorical answer to this question. But it can and should be examined with care by every sensible journalist.

There are a lot of petty crime cases which are either ignored or summed up in a few lines, e.g. pick pocketing, petty theft, gambling and prostitution. But these seemingly small events can become major social evils if not checked in time and it is the job of the socially responsible crime reporter to collect details in depth and report the social and national implications of such small but spreading crime tendencies.

It should not be assumed that crime news is always easy to obtain. Many times, because of a proper concern for the results of an investigation, police secrecy is not only justifiable but mandatory. On other occasions, of course, secrecy is just a cover up to ward off too enthusiastic reporters. It is obvious, therefore, that a reporter on a crime story sometimes is placed in a difficult and unfair position because he cannot properly evaluate official motives. He/she must be guided in such cases by his/her own sense of responsibility and the judgments of his superiors.

Crime reporter must be imaginative, a person of vision, not for the sake of creating fictitious consequences and characters but for bringing out all possible aspects of criminal cases. He/she must have questions in his/her mind to be asked with IOs and witnesses, to be investigated through records and evidences. Sometimes a murder remains a mystery and for a long time the motive of the murder is not exposed. Even after the arrest of the accused and even after the court's decision, crime reporter may work out the motive behind crime without mentioning any name.

In August 2006, a murder was committed in Indralok in Delhi, in which, seven members of a family were brutally killed by an acquaintance who often visited the family earlier. Local newspapers of national repute highlighted the case, turned it to a burning issue and investigated all the aspects mentioning the possibilities and probabilities. Later police succeeded to work out the mystery and nabbed the accused who subsequently admitted his crime.

Sources of Crime News

The major sources of news for crime reporters is the police which is the prime law enforcing agency. They are the first official authority to get involved in the investigation of any crime. Depending upon the nature of crime, the police may arrest or detain or take in custody or let off the culprit.

It is always a shock to a young reporter when he/she discovers that he/she has no inherent right to examine police records at will or go through a police station to talk with prisoners. These images, fostered by script writers are shattered by a single day's experience on a police beat.

Success of a reporter is dependant on his/her influence and

access to the law enforcing authority. The police may or may not divulge the whole facts. It depends more on the nature of the crime and method of investigation.

The reporter, therefore, must act in accordance with the situation. To any veteran covering police stations or the courts, this is done through the judicious cultivation of relations with various police officials. It is only a rank amateur who barges into a station house and demands access to the police blotter, which is the surest way of being thrown out of the place. The only recourse for the beginner on the police beat is to work with the veterans, until he/she is sufficiently well-known to have his/her own sources; or, if his/her newspaper is sufficiently prominent.

Most police departments have a routine method for informing the press of incidents that are telephoned or telegraphed to headquarters from outlying precincts. These are usually called "police slips" written by hand in small organizations and distributed by teletype in metropolitan or inter-state organisations.

Police slips are made available to reporters in a central spot, but nobody informs them that something newsworthy is contained in them. However, the slips suggest the possibility of major stories.

The police radio or wireless system, the fire department's alarms, are valuable to the crime reporter who is constantly on the alert for the off-beat story. Few police departments officially welcome reporters to their communications or operations rooms, but as a practical matter they do have access in most places. A good reporter can be of great help to the police, but he/she can also be troublesome, if he/she wants to be. It is through the communications and operations bureaus or branches that the reporter gets his/her best initial results.

If he/she has friends in the police department, he/she can often persuade them to get information. On an investigation the reporter must get his/her news at the scene, no matter how long it may take him/her to arrive there. Naturally, he/she can leave his/her beat uncovered only with his/her desk's consent.

Dealing with the Police

The first thing any reporter must know about the police department is its organisation, its regulations, its relationship to other departments, and its contacts, with allied peace-keeping organisations in the State and at the Centre.

Whether the department is large or small, one official is usually designated to handle the news media. Such an official can be helpful, if he/she is permitted to be, but he/she also is likely by the nature of his/her office to withhold more news than he/she issues.

It is necessary for a reporter to protect himself/herself by maintaining good relationships with other officials who will, for a variety of motives, give him/her information or check facts. The more a reporter knows about a police organisation, the easier it will be for him/her to acquire such valuable sources.

A reporter may have to question several people other than the police to get all the answers to his/her questions. But without the required answers, one should not start writing a crime story. The police report will be a narration of events only and the job of the reporter is to make out a news story from the facts available in the police report and from other sources.

Apart from the civil police, investigating agencies like local investigation units, CBI, Criminal Investigation Departments, Intelligence Bureau and Crime Branch may also be of great help in getting the crime story if the reporter cherishes a rapport with the officials of these departments. Often they provide off-the-record background information and the perspective which may or may not be useful immediately, yet can be unitised later on at the opportune moment.

Other Sources

Additional facts about the cases have to be collected through interviews with the eyewitnesses or the persons involved in the case, thus giving a more accurate picture of the crime. Reporters should not depend fully on information provided by the police but try to gather information from different people present at the venue of the incident.

In Vasant Kunj area of Delhi, a milkman was killed while a speeding car, driven by a minor ran over him. The details of the incident were narrated by the driver of a following vehicle, who revealed that the car was racing with another car with a speed of about 200 kmph. The reader could understand the extent of callousness and negligence.

A reporter can also talk to the persons who know the victim or the accused as well as their family members. Crime reporters should also try to develop their personal contacts or hidden sources.

Areas Covered under Crime Reporting

A crime reporter or anyone assigned the beat of crime reporting should have reasonable knowledge of various kinds of acts which come within the purview of crime. Areas coming under crime reporting:

1. Offences relating to the human body:
   (*a*) Murder, assassination
   (*b*) Culpable homicide—act done with knowledge that it is likely to cause death, with or without intention of doing so.
   (*c*) Causing death by rash or negligent act.
   (*d*) Abetment of suicide committed by child, insaner, idiot, delirious or intoxicated person.
   (*e*) Attempt to murder.
   (*f*) Attempt to commit suicide.
   (*g*) Being a thug.
   (*h*) Wrongful restraint or confinement.
   (*i*) Criminal force and assault such as to deter a public servant from his duties, to commit theft, assault on a woman to outrage her modesty, to dishonour a person or to wrongfully confine.
   (*j*) Kidnapping, abduction, slavery and forced labour.
   (*k*) Rape.
2. Offences against property:
   (*a*) Theft.
   (*b*) Extortion—blackmail, obtaining illegal compensation.
   (*c*) Robbery and dacoity.
   (*d*) Criminal misappropriation of property.
   (*e*) Criminal breach of trust.
   (*f*) Receiving stolen property, or assisting in its concealment or disposal. Cheating by impersonation.
   (*g*) Criminal trespass.
   (*h*) Arson/fire.

3. Offences relating to documents and trade property:
   (*a*) Criminal breach of contracts of service.
   (*b*) Defamation or printed matter known to be defamatory.
   (*c*) Criminal intimidation, insult and annoyance.

4. Obstructing Justice:
   (*a*) Interfering with an officer.
   (*b*) Perjury.
   (*c*) Bribery.
   (*d*) Contempt of court.

5. Conspiracy in Crime:
   (*a*) Accessory before act.
   (*b*) Accessory after act.

6. Others:
   (*a*) Terrorist violence.
   (*b*) Genocide.
   (*c*) Manufacture, possession or sale of illegal beverages and drugs.
   (*d*) Disturbing peace, group fighting, riots.
   (*e*) Sexual crimes.
   (*f*) Criminal rebel.
   (*g*) Accidents.
   (*h*) Police encounters.

A reporter must use extreme care when copying information from a police blotter and especially in the use of complaint sheets. Both of these records frequently contain misspellings of names and incorrect addresses. In addition, complaint sheets often contain misinformation, exaggerations and from time to time, outright lies. They usually are a form of interoffice correspondence between the complaint desk and the investigating officers. Reporters should verify everything in the complaint sheet with the investigating officers before making use of complaint sheet information. The reporter also is expected to use good judgment in handling information from police sources if publication would aid a suspect in escaping, prevent a fair trial or cause other difficulties.

In a village of Uttar Pradesh, adjacent to Jharkhand, the police claimed to have shot dead a hard-core Naxalite in an encounter.

Reporter's personal investigation revealed that the dead was neither a Naxalite, nor was it an encounter. In the report, he did not follow blindly the FIR or the police version, though he also did not add up his own viewpoint as the further investigation was to be done and the news lead narrated, "A villager was shot dead by the police in Khoradih village of Sonbhadra district. As it was claimed by the police, the deceased was a Naxalite and he opened fire first. But according to the neighbours of the dead, he worked in Delhi and was on a visit to home in Dussehra holidays."

In another case, the police claimed to have killed a notorious criminal Dhananjay Singh in an encounter in Bhadohi district of U.P. The reporter came to know that the killed person was not Dhananjay Singh as it was revealed by people who saw Dhananjay earlier. There, a precaution on the part of reporter was essential, else, police would have closed the criminal file of the notorious criminal and he would have continued his spree of crime.

Story Contents

The usual information and sources for a crime story might be outlined as follows:

Facts	*Sources*
1. Casualties (*a*) Names and identification of persons (*b*) How persons were killed or injured (*c*) Nature of injuries (*d*) Disposition of dead and injured	1. Police, hospitals, friends and relatives of dead and injured, witnesses
2. Damages (*a*) Value, property stolen or destroyed (*b*) Description of property (*c*) Owner (*d*) Insurance (*e*) Other threatened property (*f*) Mode of destruction, theft or lost	2. Police, property owner

(*Contd.*)

Facts	*Sources*
3. Description (*a*) Chronological account (*b*) Description of involved persons	3. Police, involved persons, witnesses
4. Escapes (*a*) Rescues (*b*) Experiences of those escaping	4. Police, involved persons
5. Legal action (*a*) Investigation, clues, evidence (*b*) Arrests	5. Police
6. Tie-backs	6. Library-morgue

The length of a crime story is usually determined by the seriousness of the crime. Other factors that add paragraphs and increase the size of the headline are the prominence of the persons involved, the place of the crime, unusual circumstances and incidents of human interest. Often one of those factors leads a reporter to write a feature lead, or an entire feature story, about the incident instead of a straight news story.

In selecting facts to go into the story and in the treatment of those facts, the reporter must be careful to observe the ethics of the newspaper. How much gory description should be included in the story of a particularly gruesome murder, for example?

Here are some examples of leads on crime stories:

- A man who stole glass tabletops from an unoccupied apartment was killed by the police on Thursday, investigators said.
  The victim, about 19, died in Max Hospital three hours after the 8:30 p.m. shooting. The police would not release the victim's name.
- A woman was burnt to death in a three-alarm fire set after she was locked inside a steel-enclosed room in the headquarters of a major Brooklyn crack operations, the police said yesterday.

Precautions Required for Crime Reporters

Today, when organised crime is strong enough to challenge the business community in some cities and reckless hoodlums are able to touch off rioting in many cities, the news media can scarcely serve the public by merely printing the news. Today's crime reporter often has to go behind the news to investigate, to explain, and sometimes even to recommend.

The following safeguards often are helpful to reporters covering crime:

1. *Arrests*: It is a serious matter to report that a person has been placed under arrest. When such a report is made, the exact charge against the arrested person should be given and it should be documented by either a record or attribution to a responsible official. If such documentation cannot be obtained, the reporter should better check his facts.
   The person in question may not have been under arrest at all. Sometimes police resort to holding someone for questioning, asking witnesses to appear voluntarily to cooperate with an investigation, which indicate the person is being detained, but may or may not be subject to arrest. An arrest is not formally accomplished until a prisoner is booked. The news, in any case, must be handled with care.
2. *Accusations*: It is commonly written that someone is being sought for robbery, suspected of arson, or tried for murder. This is journalistic shorthand, which has gained acceptance through usage, but it is neither precise nor correct.
   Persons are sought in connection with a robbery, unless a charge has actually been made, in which case they are charged with robbery. When a person is under suspicion, he is not necessarily going to be charged with a crime, and it is generally not privileged matter to indicate that suspicion is attached to any individual by name. Where the police suspect someone, but lack proof, that person may be held as a material witness—which is far different from being accused of a crime.
   Therefore, cases of suspicion are not usually given too extensive and detailed news treatment if no privileged material is available for use. The practice of reporting that a defendant is being tried for murder, while widely used is obviously prejudicial and could be more accurately, if

less dramatically, stated, as "being tried on a charge of murder."

3. *Confessions*: The use of the word confession to describe statements made by a person to the police or to prosecuting authorities is dangerous when it is not a matter of public record. The fact that a police chief or a prosecutor has claimed to have a confession, except in open court, may be used only at the risk of the reporter. The records are full of supposed confessions that backfired later for a variety of reasons and of persons who admitted crimes they could not possibly have committed.

   Unless and until it is established in fact that a person has confessed, approved procedure for reporters is to use such terms as "statement," "admission", "description", or "explanation". They convey the shade of meaning that is warranted by circumstances and do not subject the reporter or his organisation to unnecessary risk.

   The reporter must always remember that under the law, a person is presumed to be innocent until he has been found guilty.

4. *Investigations*: Certain stages of police investigations require secrecy in public interest. This also pertains to some of the aspects of prosecutions and trails. The secrecy of the courtroom and of a trial jury's deliberations are soundly based on public policy. Expect under the most extraordinary circumstances, no reporter and no news organisation have any right to interfere.

   Often, during the course of investigations, reporters are confined to listing the identities of witnesses who have entered or left a police station or courtroom, if the names can be obtained. They have every right to try to interview such witnesses, if the circumstances are favourable, before and after appearances of this kind. But it is the business of the prosecution, defense lawyers, and the witnesses themselves to decide whether or not they should talk.

5. *Cases of Violent Death*: Nowhere is there a greater tendency to jump to conclusions in the field of crime reporting than in the initial reporting of a violent death. The amateur reporter is invariably in a hurry to characterise the event as a suicide or murder when it may be an accidental death.

It is advisable, therefore, to report only what is known and avoid speculation in the absence of an official verdict by a medical examiner, or some other competent authority.

An apparent suicide is one of the most difficult crime stories to handle. If the police report that a man was found shot to death with a bullet in his right temple and a revolver in or near his right hand, the story should be written in exactly that way.

In the case of a police finding that someone "jumped or fell" to his death, the reporter should not go beyond the facts but use that phrase in his copy. If a woman is found dead in bed with an empty bottle labelled sleeping tablets beside her, no conclusions should be drawn.

Bollywood actress Divya Bharti's death remained a mystery for a long time. Apparently it was a suicide by jumping from an apartment of the higher floor but investigations disclosed that she was pushed forcibly out of the apartment, hence, it was a murder.

In all such cases, it is proper to note any other circumstances that have a bearing on the story, particularly as to whether notes were left. It may not always be proper to publish such notes, even if the text is made available by the police, unless the material is privileged.

Moreover, unless there is a formal announcement of suicide by a responsible authority, the news account can do no more than to note that an investigation is being made to determine whether the death was a suicide.

When violent deaths occur without any indication as to whether they may be accidents, suicides, murders, or combination of all three, the story should report the identities of the victims and the manner of their deaths. It is usually fruitless, to try to unravel such a mystery in a newsroom. That is the job of the police and the prosecuting authorities. In the absence of any word from them a factual account of the event must suffice.

There are a few fundamentals of which every reporter must take account.

The first is that police and prosecutors rarely will give him information on a silver platter. That means a tremendous amount of interviewing and research must be done in a very short time so that a coherent story may be written.

The second is that there can be no guarantee of police accuracy. So, police versions of names, addresses, and other facts must be checked.

The third is that police and journalistic terminology are not necessarily identical. The legal term for a slaying is a homicide, but many newspapers loosely and incorrectly refer to such crimes automatically as murder. In a grand jury indictment the homicide eventually may be defined as first or second degree murder, depending on whether there was premeditation; or first—or second—degree manslaughter, depending on whether there was provocation or negligence. Manslaughter is not murder so that care must be used in defining a homicide. Indictments charging murder have been found to be deficient in the past, so that a writer should be precise in his statements whenever he refers to the legal basis of any charge.

6. *Assessment of Blame*: Whenever there is a fight, shooting, or collision involving police action, it is only human to wonder what happened and who was at fault. Often only a trial can determine this; therefore, most reporters use as many versions of the incident as there are witnesses if such extensive treatment is warranted.

Such accounts begin with a statement that two men had a fight in a night club, or that there was a shooting, or that two automobiles collided. The body of the story then documents the non-committal lead, giving such versions of the event as are necessary. The attribution of documentation of this type always presents a problem for writers who want to avoid using "he said," or "she said," or "the police said" in every sentence.

There are several ways of doing this. One is to quote the various versions, if they are brief enough. Another is to write; "The police version of the incident follows," and then report it without further attribution. In any case, unless there is some official assessment of blame, it is usually not necessary for the reporter to try to act in such matters.

7. *Identification*: The identification of persons in crime stories sometimes leads to trouble, no matter how carefully they are checked. Confusion of persons with identical last names, mistakes in middle initials, mix-ups in addresses, misspellings of names, and police errors all conspire against the reporter. There is no real safety in the familiar formula, "The suspect gave his name as.....," or, "The prisoner was identified as...." If the identification is incorrect, the reporter and his organisation are in trouble. It is usually a good rule, in stories that warrant it, to include material showing how the identification was made—by papers in the person's possession, by friends or relatives, or by other means. If there is any doubt, the reporter will find it does no harm to add a clause or even a sentence indicating that the identification was partial and remained to be checked.

Civil Disorder

The coverage of civil disorder imposes enormous responsibilities on the journalist. On the one hand, he must exercise the greatest care not to spread rumours. On the other, he must expose himself to danger if necessary to determine the magnitude of any street incident. But whatever he does, he must always be conscious that careless reporting or the provocative appearance of still or television cameras can cause untold harm in a tense situation, particularly in the crowded inner cores of many cities.

The conduct of the journalist at the scene of action must be circumspect. A hard hated, swaggering White reporter in the centre of an angry Negro community can provoke trouble. A television cameraman, training his instrument on a floodlighted crowd, is likely to get more action than he bargains for when fighting has broken out all around him. Nor is there any great sense in sending an armored truck bearing the name of a news organisation into a trouble area. These are the things that cause the news media to be blamed for spreading disorder. Complete coverage is desirable at all times, but no one is thereby justified to put on a circus like performance.

In both written and oral reports of any incident, every effort should be made to arrive at accurate evaluations. An isolated act of vandalism, or a street fight between two boys in the midst of a crowd, must not be called a race riot. And if shooting is heard in a crowded neighbourhood at night, it is not automatically "sniper fire" until an investigation determines that snipers are at work. Nor are all fires the work of arsonists. Looting, too, should be carefully defined. Great damage can be done if radio, television, and published wire service and newspaper reports exaggerate a few small incidents. Consequently, in the early stages of any civil disorder, the basic rule is to work and report with the greatest restraint.

At the moment of Babri Masjid demolition, most of the Hindi newspapers of UP published highly sensitive news items with bold banner frontpage headlines containing exaggerated figures of the persons killed in police shoot-out. Imaginatively, the figure was raised up to 200 and they also narrated that the water of river Saryu turned red by bloodshed. In fact, accidentally, only one person was killed in the entire incident.

Necessarily, once a news organisation's editors have evidence to show that they are dealing with a riot of major proportions, there is no justification for not making a complete report available to the community at large. When reporters see arsonists setting fires and looters carrying merchandise from wrecked stores, these things must be communicated. Yet, the need for restraint and patient inquiry cannot be abandoned even in such circumstances. For when shooting breaks out, the reporter is never justified to leap to conclusions that all the damage is being done by demonstrators or that race is aligned against race.

These precautions, which are the product of experience in the coverage of civil disorders, have been incorporated into a number of informal arrangements between the press and the authorities. The oldest is the Chicago plan, which seeks to keep a lid on news of a disorder until it is under control, something that is not always practical. Another procedure, followed in St. Louis, makes a police information centre responsible for the clearance of all factual information before it is used by the news media.

Rapes

Traditionally newspapers do not print the names for rape victims, even during the course of a trial. However, the issue became a topic of considerable discussion among journalists, lawyers and women's rights advocates in the early 1990s after one victim permitted her name to be used by The *Des Monies Register* in a five-part series that detailed the emotional pain she experienced after the rape.

A newspaper should shield the identities of complainants in sex crimes, while awaiting the courts' judgment about the truth of their accusation.

The *Times* pointed out that it used her name finally because "NBC's nationwide broadcast took the matter of her privacy out of the hands" of its editors.

The practice of withholding names has become almost unanimous in India since women argued that it would make rape victims more likely to come forward. Many editors said that using names would increase the pain of a traumatic experience. But some editors now believe that failing to identify rape victims perpetuates the idea that rape is a crime that permanently damages a woman's reputation.

Generally speaking, rape stories are relatively brief. They may include:

Facts	*Sources*
Statement of alleged victim	Police
Hospital treatment	Hospital officials, police
Arrest of suspect	Police
Possible statement of suspect	Suspect, suspect's lawyer
Possible court action	Police, district court

It should be noted, however, that in many rape cases the victim is unable to identify her attacker or the attacker is never caught.

Suicides

In covering a suicide, the reporter must be extremely careful. The official police report, not the reporter's judgment, determines whether a death is a suicide. Even if a man plunges from a 14-storey window in front of a large crowd, it may not be a suicide. Even if a woman is found dead on a lonely road with a pistol in her hand and a bullet in her head, there may be no definite evidence that she fired the bullet. Until police completes the investigation, the reporter should only say only that the person was "found dead".

If police report they found a suicide note or say that the wound was self inflicted, the reporter should quote them. But the reporter should not say the case was a suicide without quoting an authority.

It may be possible to discover a motive, after suicide has been clearly established, but the reporter must be careful. Reporters should not piece together certain facts about the person's ill-health, financial difficulties or love affairs and then conclude that what were the motives. If there is a definite, authentic statement of motive from a suicide note or a close relative, it is generally safe to use that information in the story. However, if no motive is found, the reporter should say so in the story by quoting an authoritative source.

Even more caution is necessary in reporting attempted suicides. Unless the suicide attempt is evident and backed up by statements of authorities, or unless the person admits the suicide attempt, the reporter must give only the facts. It is wise to be cautious even in cases in which the person admits the attempted suicide. It could be a grandstand play for attention or a fabrication for some other reason.

The method of suicide is usually described only in general terms. Newspapers never give details of methods because that might show others how to commit suicide. For example, the name of a poison or drug is not used in suicide stories. The means of suicide is simply called "a poison" or "a drug". Gory details are nearly always omitted in suicide stories.

The following is a formula for the usual suicide story:

Facts

1. Name and identification:
   (*a*) Disposition of body.
2. Method:
   (*a*) Cause of death.
   (*b*) Circumstances surrounding death (when and how found).
3. Motive
   (*a*) Suicide note.
   (*b*) Statement from relatives, physician, friends, and business associates.

Any of the three principal facts named above may be the feature of the suicide story. An unusual method or motive is usually the feature, unless the person's prominence overshadows that feature. Under no circumstances should the reporter attempt to treat a suicide story in a light-hearted or humorous manner.

Crime Reporters

Crime reporters are men of action. Yet most of them spend their days—or nights—covering the patient and unspectacular routine of police work. Heroics are not for them. Nor are they singled out for special attention.

They do the job to which they are assigned—asking questions, checking and investigating stories. Of all reporters assigned to particular beats, those covering the police news and the courts are most likely to stick together. Unlike the political and diplomatic reporters on the national and international levels. The local crime reporter often tries to make life easier for the beginner.

Although some police and court reporters of today are better educated than the old ones. It is a mistake to think of them as a particular type. They are of all ages and come from every walk of life. However, crime reporters are often looked upon as representatives of the lower orders.

A crime reporter should be a daring person because covering crimes is not a work for weak hearted. He should be ready to risk anything for an adventurous job. Reporting a crime often leads reporter into trouble. But a cool-minded reporter will get away with anything.

Taking sides of branding one group or party whenever there is a fight between two individuals or groups or between police and groups should be avoided. An objective reporter should only give the views of witnesses or parties involved from both camps.

Apart from having a sound knowledge of the law and legal procedure prevailing in our land, a crime reporter should be well connected and have hidden sources that can confirm the facts.

Above all a crime reporter should have a feeling of being socially responsible. He should not try to emotionalise and work for the benefit of society.

Follow-Ups

Follow-up is the soul of crime reporting. No reporter can outshine with byelines if he/she neglects follow-up and becomes oblivious of the case once reported. Sometimes apparently trivial criminal incidents have grave reasons and if proper notice of crime is taken by reporter, police are also compelled to go ahead, particularly in Indian perspective.

Example 1: A Jeweller dealing in gold and precious stones was shot dead by an unidentified assailant, who fled from the venue but was immediately held captive by neighbours and handed over to the police.

Notably, the killer did not escape with any valuables. Then what was the motive behind murder?

After the arrest, the police ended their efforts, a petty criminal was sent to jail after conviction.

Reporter's investigation revealed that the liberal trade policy of the deceased damaged the interest of a politician, who was said to be indulging in illegal trade of gold and precious stones. Hence, he hired the petty criminal to murder.

Further, police investigations unravelled the entire sequence and the kingpin. The politician who conspired the murder, was arrested.

Example 2: It was only the follow-up of media because of which Priyadarshini Mattoo case could be reopened.

Priyadarshini, a 23-year-old Delhi University law student, was allegedly raped and murdered by Santosh Kumar Singh at her south Delhi apartment on January 23, 1996. The investigation into the case was transferred to the CBI as Santosh was the son of J.P. Singh, then a serving IPS officer with the Delhi Police.

In a 449-page judgment delivered on December 3, 1999, the Additional Session Judge G.P. Thareja had acquitted Santosh. In the year 2000, the CBI had filed a review petition with the Delhi High Court. It took six years for the petition to the listed, that too after pressure was put on by nationwide protests following the acquittal of the main accused in the Jessica Lal murder case, which was listed a couple of months back.

Following the filing of a PIL, the Delhi High Court ordered on August 31, 2006, a day-today hearing in the case. On October 17, the court convicted Santosh on the charge of rape and murder and on October 30, he was given a death sentence.

The conviction of Santosh was a victory for the media. The lawyer friends of Santosh even attacked media persons outside the courtroom on the day of conviction alleging that it was because of media that Santosh had suffered.

Example 3: What crime reporting can do for the delivery of justice and bringing the culprits to book is proved by the coverage given to the Jessica Lall case.

Jessica Lall, a model, was shot dead on April 29/30, 1999, at Tamarind Court in South Delhi. Since all the witnesses turned hostile in the court, all the nine accused were acquitted by the trial judge Bhayana in his judgment on February 21, 2006.

This was reported in the media in a manner that resulted in public outcry. The Delhi High Court took cognisance of media reports and decided to take suo motto action. This compelled the Delhi police to file an appeal in the High Court against the judgment of trial court.

Hearing began in the High Court on October 3, 2006, and it was completed in a record time on November 29. This became possible with the day-today hearing of the case by the court. On December 18, High Court bench of Justice R.S. Sodhi and P.K. Bhasin convicted Manu Sharma, Vikas Yadav and Amardeep Singh Gill. On December 20, High Court sentenced Manu Sharma to life imprisonment. Two other convicts Vikas and Amardeep were sentenced to four years' rigorous imprisonment.

Tools of Reporters

A crime reporter should take help of the following so as to gather information more quickly and accurately. These will help him/her in working more efficiently.

These are:

1. Tape recorder
2. Camera
3. Copies of IPC and Cr PC
4. Copy of Police Manual
5. Telephone directory
6. Reference Note-book.

General Terms used in Crime Reporting

Knowledge of legal terms is necessary for a reporter particularly one who is assigned the beat of crime. This knowledge not only helps a reporter to understand the things better but also saves him from wrong usages.

Following are some such terms:

1. *Homicide*: The legal term for slaying is homicide. It is killing of a human being by a human being. It is defined as first or second degree murder committed in a planned manner.
2. *Manslaughter*: It is not murder but killing of a man in the wake of provocation or negligence. It may be referred to the killing of people in Salman Khan road accidents. Slaughter is mainly used for the killing of animals and is normally not used for the killing of man.
3. *Culpable Homicide*: Whoever causes death by doing an act with the intention of causing death or with the intention of causing such bodily injury as is likely to cause death, commits the offence of culpable homicide.
4. *Bail*: A sum of money demanded by a law court and paid by or for an accused as security that he will appear for his trial until which time he is allowed to go free.
5. *Acquittal*: If a magistrate, in view of the evidence produced before him finds that the accused is not guilty, he issues an order of acquittal.
6. *Accomplice*: It means the helper or companion in a wrong doing. So, if somebody accompanies a person or helps him in the commitment of crime, he becomes an accomplice in the eyes of the law.
7. *Misdemeanor*: Means a petty crime. It refers to all those crimes and offences for which the law has not provided a particular name and which are punishable by fine or imprisonment.
8. *Abduction*: Carrying away a man unlawfully.
9. *Abetment*: Instigation of a person to do a thing and involvement of one or more persons in any conspiracy for doing that thing.
10. *Abscond*: To hide oneself in order to escape arrest for a crime. It is immaterial whether the person is hiding in his residence or has fled away to some distant place. As long as he remains in hiding, he is treated as absconding.
11. *Interim*: During the interim period, temporarily, till the time the court finally decides something.

12. *Adjourn*: Postponement of the hearing of a case to some later date as fixed by the court.
13. *Adjourn Sine Die*: Postponement of the hearing of a case for an indefinite period, meaning thereby not finalising the next date of hearing at the time of adjournment.

11

Reporting Beats

Introduction

A news organisation's major thrust is to gather news and it deploy competent reporters to execute this task efficiently. Gathering news is a continuous process. News comes from all the directions--North, East, West and South. If we see the spatial relationship in between geographical territory and media organisation, we would find that covering news in a vast country like India is a difficult task, so news organisations usually form bureaus/reporting rooms and different reporting beats. This segmentation is quite essential and inevitable for the smooth and systematic functioning of the press.

What is Reporting Beats?

The answer to that question is just for every newspaper reporter in the land. Certainly it is one of the elementary things every young newsman dips into almost immediately and he/she is more or less in touch with it throughout his/her career. Basically, 'reporting beats are nothing but a reporter's regular territory for news coverage.' Every beginner as per his/her interest selects a particular beat like civil/local bodies beat, crime beat, education beat, legal beat, cultural beat, health beat, religion/festival beat etc.

Merely, covering a beat does not amount to success. To excel in this field reporters have to establish their separate identity and one can do it by considering following *mantras*:

- A reporter should have the ability to spell bound his/her readers through his/her words.
- A reporter should develop a unique style of writing;

- A reporter should have new thoughts always coming into his/her mind;
- A reporter should acquire the dexterity in the usage of language and grammar;

In order to be adept at the art and science of beat reporting, a person has to undergo training for nearly four to five years. With training and regular practice, reporters do acquire the reporting skills. However, the fire must be within the heart of the reporter as well.

After the discussion about reporting beats, lets us look at various reporting beats:

Civic/Local Bodies Beat

We begin with civic/local bodies beat. Here, we will learn the main features of local bodies and see how reporting takes a shape step-wise from locating sources to writing news reports. Also, we will study the important items of information that any civic reporter must know.

Scope of Civic Beat

Let us now see the scope of civic beat. Local self-government bodies like—Municipal Corporation, Municipal Council, Nagar Mahapalika, Town Area Committee, District Board and Panchayat Committee etc., come under purview of civic/local bodies beat. Apart from these, there is some more scope like—the departments responsible for the supply of drinking water, electricity, etc.

Thus, a reporter covering this beat must have a very good understanding of municipalities and panchayats. He/she should be aware of each and every constitutional provisions and Acts related to local bodies.

Sources of Local Bodies News

This is for every reporter that if he/she wants to reach at the apex of this field, he/she should have a variety of reliable and high contacts. These contacts may become a source of reporters. Sometimes even an ordinary person such as the driver of a minister's car, even a *Subziwala*, or any other person could provide valuable information.

Here in local bodies beat following are the main sources and a reporter functioning in this beat should develop his/her good relations at various levels.

- Mayor (elected by the elected members of Municipal Corporation).
- Chairman of a District Board or District Panchayat Office.
- Corporators-Councillors (elected representatives of different wards of a local body).
- Session of elected house of a local body and the deliberations taking place therein.
- Bureaucrats posted at local bodies like Administrator, Mukhya Nagar Adhikari and Chief Executive Officer.
- Sanitation officers and subordinate staff working at a local body.
- Personnel working at water works department.
- Officers and other staff responsible for distribution of power within Municipal limits.
- Workers' unions, their representations/demands.
- Political leaders involved in politics of local bodies.

Qualities of a Civic Reporter

However, besides these main sources a reporter covering local bodies should try to develop his/her relations with every prominent and even common man of the society. A reporter should know the trick to utilise his/her sources. Let us now examine the traits a reporter must possess.

- He/she must be aware of the concept of local self-governance like 'Municipality' which means an institution of self-government. He/she must know the composition of municipalities, constitution and composition of ward committees, reservation of seats, tenure of municipalities, disqualification of membership, power, authority and responsibilities of municipalities, etc.
  (Article 243 P to 244 A of Part IX A which was included in the Indian Constitution by the Seventy-third Amendment

Act, 1994 describes each and every detail of 'The Municipalities'.)

- A reporter must also be aware of the related constitutional provisions.
- He/she must understand the formation and functions of local bodies.
- He/she must understand the panchayati raj system. (Article 242-243 (O) of Part IX of the Constitution describes all the legal provisions and constituents of the panchayats.)

Thus, a reporter covering a local beat must possess the above mentioned qualities to do his/her job competently. Moreover, every reporter should have inquisitive mind. Inquisitiveness is the only thing which leads every reporter to dig out the hidden facts.

Precautions Required in Coverage

While covering an event, a reporter must take some precautions like:

- Meetings of Elected House of a Municipal Corporation should be regularly attended whenever it is in session. Otherwise, a reporter may miss some important announcements or decisions taken by the Municipal Corporation.
- During municipal elections, the reporter concerned should make ward-wise surveys and try to analyse the situation on the basis of first-hand information. Local elections make interesting copies and readers show more concern for the local elections. Thus, the survey should be free from any bias.
- Complaints of improper sanitation in different localities should be given due consideration by the reporter.
- The reporter should personally keep a watch on the basic issues like water and power supply. Whenever, there are disruptions or major breakdowns, it is his/her responsibility to give expression to people's anguish.
- Adequate space should be provided to whatever is said by the elected office-bearers or senior bureaucrats of local

bodies by holding press conferences, issuing press statements or revealing something informally.

- If roads are in bad shape, it is the responsibility of a civic reporter to project this problem. 'Roads' is a subject which falls under the jurisdiction of local bodies.
- Again, health is also a subject to be taken care of by civic authorities within municipal limits.
- The problems faced by the sanitation staff or employees of the electricity and water works departments should be properly highlighted.

Cultural Beat

Introduction

Before submerging into the topic we need to understand media-culture interrelationship. The international working group on "Training of Personnel Engaged in the Production and Dissemination of Cultural Goods and Services" co-sponsored by UNESCO in Vienna in 1986 agreed that "Culture is not to be interpreted in the restricted sense of artistic alone." It encompasses the whole gamut of phenomena ranging from sports to educational programmes, from the motivation of creative articles to the habits of audiences, from the simple consumption of cultural activities. The notion of culture attends to the lifestyle of the population concerned and thus comprises all sections of social life.

Culture is to a considerable extent preserved and promoted by tradition. And tradition is the handling down beliefs, experiences and customs from generation to generation especially by oral form or by a process of traditional performance and communication. All over the world, the vehicle that has carried the tradition and customs which comprises oral folklore such as folk songs, folk dances, dramas etc., and material folklore such as crafts, arts, costumes etc.

Folk media have been traditionally used in India as a means of dissemination of information or the spreading of heritage, history, value, social values, faiths and philosophy of the community. Story, action, music, dance, instruments, colour are so combined in the traditional media that they become the best means of instruction through entertainment without making the people conscious what they are learning.

This is enough to understand how important reporting beat is (cultural beat). It requires a different kind of skill, different bend of mind. A cultural story sounds different and is a very efficient tool to promote cultural heritage of the country.

Scope of Cultural Beat

Let us now have a brief look at the scope of the cultural beat. Following areas are covered under the cultural beat:

1. *Visual Arts*: It includes all kind of usual display materials which depict culture e.g:
   - Painting Exhibition
   - Cartoon Exhibition
   - Sculpture Exhibition
2. *Performing Arts*: Sometimes ministries, organisations and even NGOs also organise programmes to promote or to create awareness about the culture. We can see this (performing arts) on the Republic Day where many groups represent different states by staging cultural programmes of a particular state like—Garba Dance, Kutchipuri Dance, Kathak, Bharat Natyam, etc. Performing arts include;
   - Dance performance
   - Music performance
   - Drama performance
   - Fashion parade
3. *Eminent Artists*: Cultural reporters always look for interviews of eminent artists like—Ustad Zakir Hussain, Pd. Ravi Shanker as these interviews make good copies. Sometimes personality sketches of eminent artists can also make interesting news copies like—personality sketch of Ustad Bismillah Khan, a meastro of Shehnai who has elevated Shehnai from a pipe played at weddings to a concert instrument.
4. *Arts Institutions*: Activities of all Government as well as non-government art institutions like:
   - Sangeet Natak Akademi
   - Lalit Kala Akademi

- Sahitya Akademi
- National School of Drama
- Shri Ram Centre of Art and Culture
- Sahitya Kala Parishad
- ICCR

5. *Special Occasions*: Some special occasions can also provide raw material to a reporter covering cultural beats like:
   - Independence Day golden-jubilee programme at Rajpath.
   - Independence Day golden-jubilee programme at Central Hall, Parliament House.
   - Republic Day Parade.
   - Programmes organised by Gandhi Smriti and Darshan Samiti in the loving memory of the Father of the Nation–Mahatma Gandhi.

Sources of Cultural News

After having an understanding of the scope of cultural beat, let us now see what are the sources of cultural news:

1. *Seminar on any art subject*—From time to time many organisations and the ministry of cultural affairs organise seminars related to the culture or art of the nation like—art seminar on 'evolution of Vedic civilisation. These seminars can provide many valuable tips to reporters so they should not miss such seminars.
2. *Workshop on any discipline*—Many institutes and organisations now-a-days organise workshops on various disciplines for the benefit of their students or their employees. Such workshops may provide some interesting information to cultural reporters.
3. *Special Lectures*—Many institutes or even corporate offices occasionally organise lectures on special topics like—environment, water scarcity, pollution, ethical use of new technology etc., such lecture may be a good source of news.
4. *Research work*—Research work provides authentic, even interesting data. Reporters can use the research to present interesting facts but he/she should be cautious about the findings. First, they should cross-check the

facts from authentic sources before using them as a reference otherwise stories based on wrong facts may create chaos.

5. *Published literature on an art subject*—It may also become a good source of information for e.g., book published by heritage department, 'INDIA' of HRD Ministry give extensive details of culture and other development issues.
6. *Audience oriented programme*—Audience is an important source in programmes targeted at them, reporters can use the feedback from the audience while writing their reports.
7. *Press conference*—organised by institutions/personalities, press conference provides a major source to reporters.
8. *Press release*—issued by the competent authority programme officer/PRO etc., press conference is an important source to a cultural reporter.

Every reporter covering cultural beat should be well versed in the 'language of culture' means he/she should have a fair understanding of culture only then he/she can write interpretative articles which could ultimately give the piece a distinct identity. Moreover, a cultural reporter should have an interest as well as an inclination towards various art form. He/she should be knowledgeable with a deep understanding of art.

Reporting Cultural Programmes

Coverage of cultural programme by a reporter may be classified as:

(*i*) *Review*: It includes an analysis of positive and negative points of a programme with balanced remarks. It requires deep understanding and thorough knowledge of subject.

(*ii*) *Critique/Criticism*: It includes comparatively a tough analysis with critical, even personal remarks. The reporter enjoys liberty of expressing his/her opinion and making judgments while writing criticism.

Precautions Required in Cultural Reporting

The following is the list of points to remember while reporting for cultural beat:

- A cultural reporter should not allow his/her prejudices and bias to come in the way of his/her writings.
- He/she should be unfavourable and non-partisan in his/her attitude.
- His/her approach should be balanced and his/her writings should be objective.
- A cultural report should not be written in a half-hearted manner and all necessary information be made available to the readers.
- Instead of imposing his/her own views on the audience in an arbitrary manner, the reporter should try to take into consideration their likings/dislikings.
- Cultural programmes should not be reviewed on the basis of information revealed by secondary sources. Reviewing should be done only after viewing.
- Publications of cultural reports should not be delayed otherwise they may appear uninteresting to readers.

Health Beat

Now-a-days health issues are given utmost importance be many broadsheets. People show more concern about their health and environment. A reporter covering health beat must have a very good understanding of existing health related problems. He/she should always keep an eye on the recent developments which help to overcome outrageous diseases.

A disease is a condition that impairs the proper function of the body or of one of its parts. Every living thing, both plants and animals, can succumb to disease. Hundreds of different diseases exist. Each has its own particular set of symptoms, signs, clues that enable a physician to diagnose the problem. A symptom is something a patient can detect, such as fever, bleeding, or pain.

A sign is something a doctor can detect such as swollen blood vessel or an enlarged internal body organ. A reporter working on health beat must have basic understanding of diseases and medico-legal issues. He/she must be knowledgeable enough about the various types of diseases so that he/she can inform the public about Dos & Don'ts during an illness.

Scope of Health Beat

Following areas are covered under this beat:

1. *Government Hospitals*: These hospitals occupy an important place not only in health reporting but crime reporting, too.
   - In medico-legal cases (cases related to medical treatment of persons injured in accidents or criminal incidents), First Information Reports are essentially lodged with the police. Such cases are accepted in government hospitals only.
   - Post-mortems of those who suffer unnatural deaths are also performed at government hospitals. Thus, crime reporters get vital information for their reports from government hospitals.
   - The subjects which are/should be chased by a health reporter include:
     - Important operations conducted by doctors and their success/failure.
     - Care or neglect of the patients and their responses/ reactions.
     - Lack of facilities or availability of modern facilities and latest equipments.
     - Availability/unavailability of life saving drugs and other important medicines.
     - Corruption in administration of government hospitals.
2. *Private Hospitals/Nursing Homes*: These days the number of private hospitals, nursing homes and maternity homes is constantly increasing. This is apparently for three reasons:
   - The existing government hospitals are not well-equipped to take the load of increasing number of patients.
   - There is growing health consciousness among the people.
   - A large section of the population demands sophisticated treatment of the diseases and is capable to avail costly medical facilities.

Private hospitals and nursing homes have contributed a lot to the field of health care and medical treatment. These hospitals have merits as well as demerits. To mention a few merits:

- These hospitals extend a great help to people in case of emergency.
- They provide modern health facilities normally unavailable at government hospitals.
- They provide best care facilities to the patients.

However, they have some demerits also, such as:

- These hospitals are not meant for poor people; as they tax patients by asking them to pay exorbitant fee for the medical care.
- They also create legal problems; cases like illegal abortions, female foeticide, gender identification etc., are some of the social problems which have their origin with the mushrooming of these homes. Take for instance the case of female foeticide in Punjab where a doctor was doing this ghastly act in his nursing home.

3. *Health Facilities in Rural Areas*: A health reporter should also take into account health facilities in rural areas. In villages and remote areas, inadequate health facilities are available. Primary health centres have been set up by the government in some rural areas, but the condition of these centres is not so good that they can tackle any emergency case:
    - The doctors posted at these centres are rarely seen as many of them indulge in private practice.
    - These centres are basically ill-equipped and cannot provide other than first-aid facilities.
    - Though some private doctors practice in rural areas, they don't possess the required qualification. Thus, they are always dangerous to the health of villagers.
4. *Public Health*: Many public health schemes are launched at the national and international level, and massive campaigning is done for the success of these schemes. These schemes are aimed at the following:
    - Creating social awareness for public health like—polio vaccination campaign.

- Motivating people to take remedial steps for the eradication of epidemics as was done during the spread of dengue, plague, cholera etc.

All such schemes whether run by the government or international agencies like the World Health Organisation (WHO) provide enough material for coverage.

5. *Activities of Medical Institutes*: The academic activities of medical institutes like ICMR, AIIMS should be properly covered by a health reporter. The findings of research done at these institutes make big news but reporter should take precaution while taking reference from research works. In medical research many jargons are used, while writing any news these jargons should be translated properly. Otherwise, it could be misinterpreted. Sources for health reporter include; doctors, researchers, directors of medical institutes, medical superintendents of hospitals, paramedical staff, patients and their attendants, health related literature like magazines, posters, folders etc., seminars, workshops, meet of medical practitioners at IMA (Indian Medical Association), CMO (Chief Medical Officer) of government and local hospitals.
   Even a driver of CMO's car, persons who dispose the medical garbage and even medical stores nearby hospitals could be a good source. On occasions even a less important person may provide some important clue to a health reporter. However, the reporter needs to know how to utilise his/her source.

Qualities of a Health Reporter

1. A health reporter should have a basic understanding of medical science and different branches like:
   - Physiology (Science of the normal functions of living things).
   - Anatomy (Science of the structure of animal bodies).
   - Neurology (Branch of medical science concerned with nerves).
   - Cardiology (Study of heart related problems) etc.

- ➢ Medical terms and names of equipment like; ICU, ECG, Pace-maker, etc.

2. A reporter should have a knowledge of the symptoms and remedies of diseases people normally suffer from, like:
   - ➢ Asthma (chronic chest disease marked by difficulty in breathing),
   - ➢ Appendicitis (Diseased condition of the vermiform—a worm like appendage of large intestine) and epidemics, communicable and infectious diseases like Malaria, Dengue, AIDS (Acquired Immuno Deficiency Syndrome), Plague (Disease spread by rats).
3. He/she should know the basic facts about the health of the countrymen like the birth rate and the morality rate.
4. He/she should be aware of different health schemes and campaigns launched by the government or international organisations.
5. He/she should be conscious for public health and be sensitive to sick people.

Precautions Required for a Health Reporter

- ■ He/she should be cautious white reporting medico-legal cases. The facts should be ascertained from the hospital authorities before writing such reports.
- ■ He/she should not hesitate in exposing the corruption rampant in government hospitals but before doing so, he must collect necessary evidence.
- ■ He/she should be ready to take up the people's cause by narrating the plight of patients in hospital but he/she should not adopt a partisan attitude while doing so.
- ■ He/she should also give due coverage to the version of the hospital authorities with regard to a particular situation.
- ■ He/she should ascertain the status and the administrative set up of a hospital while making a reference to it in a news report.
- ■ He/she should take pains to promote the cause of public health by highlighting the activities of voluntary organisations like Red Cross, or holding an eye check up camps and health melas by social service organisations.

- He/she should take care of the rural health by physically examining the medical facilities available at the primary health centres and government dispensaries.
- He/she should always be eager to know about the innovations in the field of medical science. The successful operations performed by expert doctors should be projected.

Civil Administration Beat

The work of modern government has two closely integrated aspects. One is formulation of a blueprint for the operation of the government, and the other is conduct of administration within its framework. Civil administration is all about the implementation of these drafted rules by the administration at the grassroot level or lower level of society.

Individual plus many individuals form a group and groups plus many groups form a society. For the smooth functioning of this small unit of any state we need some rules, some laws. Civil administration provides framed guidelines of law and order for a particular administrative unit. We can trace its origin in the theory of separation of powers.

Historical Background

In every modern state there are three well defined organs of the government—legislature, executive and judiciary. Aristotle was the first writer to note distinction among the three functions of the government. He called them deliberative, magistrative and judicial. Roman writers like Cicero and Palybius praised the Republican constitution of Rome because in it they found balance between the Senate (Legislature), Councils (executive) and Tribunes (judiciary). But in practice the senate was the supreme authority to which the other functionaries bowed down. Bodin, the French publicist of the 16th century was the first modern writer to demand a separation of powers. He argued that, if the king were both the law-maker and judge, then a cruel king might give cruel punishments. During the Commonwealth-period in England, Cromwell separated the executive and legislative functions. However, as the head of the executive, he dismissed the judges.

The theory of separation of powers, however, emerged finally in the writings of Montesquieu—(a liberal political philosopher).

After this brief introduction let us now examine the scope of the civil administration beat.

Scope of Civil Administration Beat

1. All kinds of administrative actions taken at sub-divisional, district and divisional level.
2. Issues related to law and order in any particular administrative unit.
3. The measures taken by the administrative officers for the people's cause, mainly for development purposes and relief during natural calamities.
4. The actions taken by administrative officers in their magisterial capacity.

Sources of Civil Administration News

1. Sub-Divisional Magistrate/Sub-Divisional Officer, City Magistrate, Additional District Magistrate, District Magistrate, Assistant Divisional Commissioner and Commissioner.
2. The subordinate staff posted at the offices of these administrative officers.
3. The associations/unions of IPS officers, PCS officers and ministerial staff.
4. Information officer and Deputy Director (Information) posted at the district level.

Qualities of a Civil Administration Reporter

1. A civil administration reporter should be well aware of the administrative set-up at different levels.
2. The administrative authority and the responsibilities of civil officers must be known to him/her.
3. He/she should also have a knowledge of the magisterial powers of these civil officers.
4. He/she should have an understanding of the constitution and nature of the administrative unit he/she is covering.

Precautions Required for a Civil Administration Reporter

1. The reporter covering civil administration must be in constant touch with the administrative officers posted in his/her area of operation. This will help him/her to get news from administrative circles.
2. He/she must be aware of the administrative structure in the concerned administrative unit. This will help him/her to understand administrative activities and get something newsworthy.
3. He/she must maintain contacts with the Dy. Director (Information) or the District Information Officer so as to get the latest information. The press releases and other literature issued by this office provide vital information to him/her.
4. He/she should also take care of the developmental tasks undertaken by the government. The details of the developmental schemes and the stage of their implementation make sufficient material available for writing good news stories.
5. He/she should be watchful of the administrative actions during the hour of crisis particularly when some natural calamity occurs or a big accident takes place. The communication of information regarding relief measures undertaken by the administration may be of great help to the people. And whenever these measures are inadequate, the reporter has every right to hit the administrative in action.
6. The reporter should always try to cross check the facts he/she has received through some responsible administrative officer. This will naturally make his/her report authentic.

Legal Beat/Court Reporting

There are only a few big newspapers in India who have full-time correspondents exclusively for their court beat. These few correspondents generally have adequate legal background. Other newspapers mostly hire stingers to cover court stories. Many of stingers are professional advocates, who are mostly part-timers, cover court stories in their respective areas.

Many newspaper do not have the resources to cover all the courts of their main circulation area, reason behind it is that there are too many courts. Newspapers neither have the time nor the space to cover everything that happens in the courts. Papers cover only those stories in which their readers are interested. The emphasis of media is on criminal courts, high courts and the Supreme Court.

Here, we are discussing legal beat as a local beat which means coverage from lower judiciary. This further means reporting of cases in the trial courts or the district courts—civil as well as criminal.

Must for a Law Reporter

One would expect the law reporter to be knowledgeable about law. Let us now discuss the range and nature of information one must have at-one's finger tips. A trainee Journalist aiming to be a future court reporter must have some understanding of the court-jurisdiction, its procedures and hierarchy.

At the apex, we have the Supreme Court of India. Then there are high courts, sessions courts, magistrate courts etc. Also there are tribunals, for e.g., the Tribunal of Central Govt. employee known as CAT. If a reporter is acquainted with the jurisdiction of different courts, then one can easily locate the specific court for a particular matter. Similarly if one is familiar with the hierarchy in the courts, one can easily guess where appeal would be filed.

Sources of Legal News

1. FIR.
2. Inquiry by investigating agencies.
3. Charges framed by a court.
4. Legal documents such as affidavits, counter-affidavits, bail papers etc.
5. Hearing of a case in any court.
6. Statement of witnesses.
7. Pleading by advocates in a court of law.
8. Judgments delivered by a judge or jury.
9. Statements of the accused.
10. Statements of the aggrieved parties.

Equipment with a Legal Reporter

1. Constitution of India.
2. Details of the amendments made in the Constitution.
3. Book on judicial system of India.
4. Copy of IPC, Cr.P.C.
5. Copies of other important laws.
6. Details of important judgments.

Stages of Legal Reporting

Legal reporting is done at three stages:

A. *Before the Hearing of a Case*

A legal reporter comes into action as soon as:

1. A crime or otherwise important incident happens.
2. First information report is lodged with the Police.
3. Raids are conducted.
4. Arrests are made.
5. Accused persons are produced before the Magistrate.
6. Remanded to police custody or judicial custody.
7. Charge-sheets are filed.

B. *During the Hearing of a Case*

Hearings of important cases are covered by a legal reporter which in any case is the most important in legal reporting.

C. *After completion of the hearing*

After the hearing is over, the court delivers its judgment which may make a big hews.

Precautions to be Taken by a Legal Reporter

First Stage

1. The person named in the FIR should be referred as an accused and not as a criminal in the news report. Nobody is treated a criminal until penalised by a court of law.
2. It should be ensured whether somebody has been arrested, or only taken into custody for preliminary interrogations.

Nobody can be arrested unless warrants have been issued and served on him.

3. It should be checked if somebody is detained illegally.
4. Nothing should be written about the accused or his involvement in some illegal act on the basis of unconfirmed reports.
5. It should be ensured that the background of the accused, the details of the offence committed by him and the action taken by the police are mentioned in the news report.
6. In civil cases, the background of the dispute as well as the names and other details of the plaintiff and the defendant should be mentioned in the news report.

Second Stage

1. Proceedings in a court should be reported by a legal reporter without making any additions or modifications.
2. No attempt should be made to sensationalise the news report based on the hearing of a case.
3. Reporter's tilt towards either plaintiff or defendant should not bear reflections on the news report. He/she should make an objective writing.
4. The important points raised and the witnesses appeared on any particular day of hearing should be clearly mentioned in the news report. The next day of the hearing and the expected course of the proceedings on that day should also be pointed out.
5. The stage of the hearing and the expected time of its completion should also be pointed out.
6. The background of the case and the gist of the past hearings should be mentioned while writing report on the hearing on any particular day.
7. Comments made by the judges, arguments put forth by the advocates and statements given by the witnesses should be quoted exactly in the words uttered by them.
8. Complicated legal terminology should be replaced by easily communicable words for the understanding of a large number of readers.
9. The legal reporter should not express his or her opinion/ views while reporting the hearing of a case since it may be regarded by the court an interference in the judicial process.

Third Stage

1. The highlights of the judgment should be made the base of a news report, picking up the most important point as the lead.
2. The details of the charges framed and the punitive action taken by the court should be mentioned clearly.
3. The arguments made by the public prosecutor or the advocates of the plaintiff to prove the commitment of the crime and the counter arguments of the defence lawyers should be pointed out.
4. The names of the judges and the lawyers may be mentioned in a legal report.

Details for Legal Reporting

A legal reporter must possess a thorough knowledge of the important laws and the judicial system of India. He/she must have a clear understanding of the following:

A. *Nature of Cases*

1. *Criminal:* Serious law-breaking, disturbing order in the society. The state is duty-bound to nab the offender and fight the case on behalf of the aggrieved.
2. *Civil:* Law dealing with private rights of citizens, not with crime.

B. *Criminal Jurisdiction*

1. *IPC:* It deals with the provisions detailing the crime and the extent of penalties for various offences.
2. *Cr PC:* It deals with the provisions related to trial proceedings.

C. *Original Jurisdiction*

Lower courts possess the authority for original jurisdiction.

1. *Criminal Cases:* Magistrates, Additional session judges and session judges hear such cases.
2. *Civil Cases:* Sub-judges (Munsifs) and senior sub-judges (District Judges) hear such cases.

D. *Higher Jurisdiction*

High Courts and the Supreme Court have the following jurisdiction:

1. *Appellate Jurisdiction:* Appeals against the judgments of the lower courts.
2. *Constitutional Matters:* Whenever validity of some constitutional provision or law is questioned, or some action of a constitutional authority is challenged.

E. *Contempt of Court*

If a reporter doesn't possess required knowledge of various laws and the judicial process and doesn't show restraint while reporting legal matters, he/she may invite the annoyance of a court anytime and any such court may initiate contempt proceedings against him/her.

Subordinate or lower courts don't have the power of declaring 'contempt' but these courts can recommend to the High Courts for initiating contempt proceedings. High Courts and the Supreme Court are empowered to declare 'Contempt'.

Important Legal Terms

1. *Affidavit* A sworn statement in writing made especially under oath or on affirmation before an authorised magistrate or officer.
2. *Caveat*: A legal warning to a judicial officer to suspend a proceeding until the opposition has a hearing.
3. *Cognizable Offence*: An offence in which a police officer may, in accordance with the first schedule of the code of Criminal Procedure, or under any law for the time being in force, arrest without warrant.
4. *Criminal Breach of Trust:* It a person entrusted with property dishonestly misappropriates or converts that property to his own use, he is guilty of criminal breach of trust.
5. *Ex-Gratia:* As a matter of favour or grace.
6. *Injunction:* A judicial process whereby a party is ordered to refrain from doing a particular act.
7. *Libel:* A false and defamatory statement made or conveyed by written or printed words without lawful justification or excuse. Libel is a criminal offence.
8. *Plaintiff:* One who commences a law suit, the complaining party in any litigation.

9. *Prima Facie Case*: When it is clear that a case can be made out on the evidence available.
10. *Protem:* For the time being.
11. *Respondent*: The defendant in an appeal.
12. *Seduction*: The inducing of a girl or woman to part with her virtue for the first time.
13. *Subjudice*: In course of trial, pending decision of a competent court.

Religion and Festival Beat

Introduction

"I try to cover life as it is, not as we would wish it to be. There is a tendency among White liberal editors and reporters to revert to what I call gee-whiz stories about minorities, stories that have a message, hidden or blatant, that says, 'They are real people, just like us.' Conversely, there is sometimes a tendency among minority journalist to do advocacy types of stories, stories that paint a particular under-represented group in a purely positive light ... I simply try to do what I think is honest journalism—truth-telling."

— *Alisa Valdes, reporter, The Boston Globe, quoted in "Reporting and Writing: Basics for the 21st Century." by Christopher Scanlan.*

A newspaper is a mirror for a community, reflecting both its good and bad points. But if the paper does a poor job covering certain segments of that community, those readers may feel ignored or rejected.

Large newspaper group uses a technique called "mainstreaming." It means including a variety of voices in all news stories—not just those dealing with diversity issues. This tactic can be taken to an extreme—reporters choosing sources strictly on the basis of their caste or colour rather than their expertise, in order to meet a corporate quota. But used sensibly and with knowledge of your community's makeup, mainstreaming can help the newspaper be a truer reflection of its readers.

Example: A reporter and a photographer cover football tailgating. Knowing that this event involves a wide cross-section of, they find a variety of people to talk to and photograph—people of different races, ethnicities, Greeks and non-Greeks, people of different ages.

Religion/Festival News

Many newspapers do a terrible job of covering religion/festival in their communities. A high percentage of readers say religion news is important to them. College students' interest in religion has increased in recent years, too.

How Newspapers have Failed at Religion Reporting?

1. Doing just the predictable holiday stories—usually assigned at the last minute. These stories generally read like a National Geographic article about a foreign culture, simply explaining what the holiday means and how people observe it.
2. Presenting a story as if there are only two sides. Religion stories often have far more. *Example*: A church may have an official position on gay marriage, but its members may be divided into several distinct opinions.
3. Presenting religious people as fanatics. Sometimes the loudest voices are the only ones the press pays attention to. Generally, there are far-more intelligent voices on just about any issue if you look for them.
4. Failure to realise that faith often shapes people's actions, not just terrorists, but regular, everyday people of any religion. Many stories from just about any beat have religious angles that reporters often miss.

How Can a Newspaper Improve Its Religion Coverage?

1. As with other beats, look for trends and look for stories about people.
2. Background yourself, especially on religions other than your own.
3. Build a table of smart sources.
4. Don't rely strictly on clergy for quotes. Talk to regular people, too.

Can a Reporter who is Religious Cover Religion News?

Can a sports fan cover sports? Of course. A reporter with deep religious faith will understand issues far better than a reporter who isn't religious at all.

Reporters on any beat do need to recognise their biases and make every effort to write a fair and balanced story. Example: A reporter who is a devout Hindu is assigned to do a story about a new Muslim group on campus. The reporter simply writes a fair story and lets readers draw their own conclusions.

A true conflict of interest would occur, say, if a reporter who is part of Inter Varsity Christian Fellowship was assigned to cover an event sponsored by that group. Those situations should be avoided, just as with any other beat.

Scope of Religion/Festival Beat

Following areas are covered under this beat:

1. Important festivals of different religions like Holi, Deepawali, Id, Christmas, etc.
2. Congregations (gathering of people for some religious purpose) like—
   Preachings (*Pravachan*), discourses (*Satsang*) and Story-telling (*Kathavachan*) from mythological or religious books by *Gurus, sadhus* etc.
   Performances of *Yajna, Havan,* and *Ganga-Snan* on different occasions, Assembly of Churches, gathering of monks normally addressed by the Dalai Lama.
3. Religious fairs held periodically at a particular place like Kumbha, Ardhkumbha, Ramlila etc.
4. Religious houses/institutions/trusts (*Ashram, Math, Akhara*) like R.K. Mission, Vivekanand Mission, Arya Samaj, Nirankari Akhara, etc.
5. Worship places like—temple, gurdwara, mosque and church.
6. Religious organisations like the Vishwa Hindu Parishad.
7. Religious conferences like Virat Hindu Sammelan, Hajis' Conference.
8. Religious journeys, like—Vaishno Devi Yatra, Haj Yatra.

Sources of Religion/Festive News

1. Religious gurus, saints, mahatmas, mahantas, sadhus, maulvis etc.

2. People managing religious houses/institutions or religious organisations.
3. Pujaris, Imams and Fathers.
4. Organisers of religious meets, conferences etc.
5. Government agencies and officers deputed for administering religious fairs.
6. Participants of religious gatherings, fairs, conferences or journeys.
7. Devouts.

Qualities of a Reporter Covering Religion/Festival Beat

1. The reporter covering this beat must have an understanding and appreciation of spiritual and religious matters.
2. He/she must have a knowledge of the origin and development of different religions; also about the Gurus and Lords worshipped by the followers of a particular religion.
3. He/she must honour all religions, faiths and beliefs and should not show disregard to any particular religion.
4. The tenets of all important religions must be known to him/her.
5. He/she must be aware of the religious customs and traditions; also the way rituals are performed in different religions.
6. He/she should adopt an unbiased approach while writing about religions. He should not be inclined towards any particular religion, whatsoever may be the reason.

Precautions Required for a Reporter

1. The reporter covering this beat should never write anything provocative and should take recourse to balanced writing.
2. He/she must take a first-hand account of the situation and should personally verify the things before reporting.
3. He/she must possess a detailed list of festivals, religious fairs, religious meets, religious institutions, religious organisations, religious journeys and prominent worship

places. He/she must also keep a calendar to record the dates important to different religions.

4. He/she must maintain contacts with important religious leaders and should try to seek their views whenever some controversy arises on any issue.
5. He/she must not hesitate in having clarifications from these religious leaders whenever some confusion arises on any point. He/she should also consult other sources, including books on such an occasion.
6. He/she must be in touch with the government agencies and bureaucrats dealing in religious matters.

Political Beat

Introduction

Political beat is full of happenings and requires a great analytical bend of mind to analyse various decisions and policies. Who covers politics? The answer to the questions is just every newspaper reporter! No this is not the case.

Political beat is covered by only those who are reasoned in interpretation. Certainly it is one of the subjects every young newsman clips into almost immediately and he/she is more or less in touch with it throughout his/her career. Because politics is something which has influence over almost entire things of a particular country such as; politics has influence over the market, economy, development, infrastructure, environment, wildlife, communal harmony etc.

We speak of politics here in the broad sense on the science or art of government. As such to ramifications, like the root of a tree, extend deep into the life of every community, large or small. It plays a part in public affairs from international diplomacy down to doing of the township treasurer and the village postmaster. In the more restricted sense politics consists of news that precedes and is climaxed by an election—local, state or national.

Elections are widely spaced and political news between them in thin. During the lull periods small papers pay scant attention to politics, and depute non-specialists to handle a campaign and the voting. Only the large newspaper can afford to employ purely political specialists, and in official election periods even these are subject to arrangements which carry them into allied and diversified field of public affairs and governmental operations.

Scope of Political Beat

Following areas may be covered under this beat:

1. Activities of political parties at different levels—national, state, district etc., like holding demonstrations, staging dharnas, taking out processions, organising rallies, arranging public meetings.
2. Internal affairs of a party as infighting, dissension, bickering, defection, formation of pressure groups, elections, tussle over leadership.
3. Important developments affecting the national/state politics like formation/breaking of alliances, extension/ withdrawal of support to a party/alliance by some other party/group/individuals.
4. General elections/mid-term polls for Vidhan Sabhas and Lok Sabha. Also elections for Upper Houses.
5. Activities of prominent political leaders, particularly related to national and social cause; also their efforts to promote/damage their parties.

Sources of Political News

1. Statements of political leaders/MPs/MLAs/Ministers.
2. Press conferences organised by political leaders/MPs/ MLAs/Ministers.
3. Informal chats with prominent leaders/Ministers/MPs/ MLAs.
4. Visits of prominent leaders/ministers.
5. Public meetings addressed by prominent leaders/ ministers.
6. Press releases issued by offices of the political parties.

Qualities of a Political Reporter

1. A political reporter must have a thorough understanding of the political system.

2. He/she must be aware of the set-up and functioning of the political institutions.
3. The organisational set-up and the status of different political parties must be known to a political reporter.
4. He/she must be well-acquainted with the prevailing political atmosphere in the country.

Precautions Required for a Political Reporter

1. He/she should keep a watch on the activities of political parties and their leaders, and write a report after proper verification of the political developments.
2. He/she should be in touch with prominent leaders/ministers either physically or telephonically. He/she should also keep the record of residential addresses and telephone numbers of these leaders.
3. He/she must possess a knowledge of the political equations and the factors influencing politics at different levels.
4. He/she should never miss or avoid attending the press conferences of prominent leaders since these conferences may reveal something important and newsworthy.
5. A political reporter should try to get formal interviews recorded so that the concerned political leader cannot dare to disown what was said by him during the course of the interview.
6. He/she should memorise whatever is said by a political leader during informal interview and maintain accuracy while writing report of such an interview.
7. He/she should keep the background material ready for reference. It is better not to depend on the memory but to prepare a file of press clippings on important subjects. He/she may also put the relevant information in the memory of his/her computer.
8. He/she should not make election analysis sitting on his/her chair but after touring the constituency and taking stock of the situation.
9. He/she should conduct the survey of the electorate, interview the contesting candidates, take note of the past results and the present trend in any particular constituency while writing election reports.

10. He/she should be patient while covering counting after the polling. He/she can use his discretion while reporting counting trends but never report a final result unless it is ratified by the Election Commission and officially announced by the concerned election officer.

Since we are studying political beat in this chapter as a local beat, it should be clear enough that the reporter in the local reporting room should concentrate on the coverage of politics and political happenings at the district or city level.

Education Beat

Introduction

In India, education has become a major beat in newspapers. The little red house has been replaced by a massive concentration of buildings. The growth in the field of education has brought enormous problems in funding, educational philosophy, religious integration, campus safety, prayers in schools and many more. Education reporters can no longer fulfill their functions by covering schools, board meetings and writing about best students of the year.

There is an awareness in the media that education cannot be separated from mainstream of society. Issues such as school prayer, crime, lunch-programme funding etc., are interlinked with society. While writing a standard news article, the education reporter must present a complex subject in a very simple manner. One headache for such reporters is the tendency for educating professionals to talk in the kind of jargon they use among themselves and in the never-ending stream of articles they write for journals in their field. In writing the story, care must be taken to convert tough words or phrases into lucid English.

The education beat includes all school levels from KG to standard 12th and colleges, universities and other higher bodies such as UGC, NCERT, etc. Sources of education beat include teachers, principals, school boards officials, college departments, chairpersons, university president, deans, teachers, students, unions etc. Sometimes events like teachers' strike for higher pay and strikes by students' union to oppose fee hike could be a good source for education beat.

Scope of Education Beat

Following educational institutions are covered under the educational beat:

1. Universities
2. Deemed Universities
3. Autonomous Colleges
4. Institutes of higher studies
5. Research/Professional Institutes
6. Technical Institutes
7. Schools and Colleges
8. Education Departments
9. University Grants Commission
10. All-India Council for Technical Education.

Sources of Education News

1. Academic discussions held during seminars.
2. Trainings imparted during specially organised workshops.
3. Special lectures addressed by eminent scholars.
4. Papers/Souvenirs/other literature published during academic discourses.
5. Research work undertaken by scholars and students.
6. Extracurricular activities in educational institutions like debates or essay writing competitions.
7. Press releases issued by the Public Relation Officers/other competent authorities in universities/institutions.
8. Deliberations held in the meetings of high-level committees like Executive Council, Academic Council or Governing Body in universities/institutions.
9. Conduct of examinations—examination schedule, paper leakage, result announcement etc.
10. Press Conferences addressed by Vice-Chancellors/ Registrars of universities, Directors/Principals of institutions/colleges.
11. Non-academic activities of various groups/sections/unions formed by students, non-teaching staff and teachers.
12. Statements issued by union leaders.

Precautions Required in the Coverage of Education News

While covering seminars, workshops and lectures by eminent personalities, following precautions are required to be taken by a reporter:

1. List of the prominent speakers and distinguished personalities participating in a seminar/workshop should be obtained or prepared, so as to decide initially who are the persons to be covered.
2. A reporter should never miss the press kit normally made available to the scribes at the inaugural function of a seminar/workshop. This kit contains all relevant informations, including the subject of the discussion; points to be raised; names of the persons delivering inaugural speech, making keynote address or valedictory address, presiding over the sessions; and printed speeches or papers; and photographs besides pen, paper and file cover.
3. A reporter should not solely depend on the printed speech. Sometimes distinguished speakers deviate from the printed speech and start making spontaneous expressions. So, a reporter should make a patient hearing to the speech because extempore portions may at times expose something big.
4. A reporter should avoid writing reports of purely academic nature. He/she should try to pick up such points during the discourses that may be useful and interesting to common man and attract a large number of readers.
5. The most important point raised by the most distinguished speaker should form the lead/intro of the news report. A departure from this practice is acceptable if somebody from among the speakers says something really very important.
6. If a programme is inaugurated by some VVIP, it becomes obligatory for the reporter to give prominence to his/her speech.
   For example, the convocation address delivered by the President or the Vice-President of India.
7. If something ambiguous is said by a speaker, the reporter

may seek a clarification during the question-answer session if that follows the speech, or he/she may meet the speaker personally to have the correct version.

8. Normally, resolutions are adopted or recommendations are made to the concerned agencies at the conclusion of seminars. For instance, a seminar on rural communication may forward its recommendations to the Agriculture Ministry, Indian Council for Agricultural Research (ICAR), All India Radio, Doordarshan, Ministry of Information and Broadcasting and media institutions. A reporter should give due weightage to such recommendations and resolutions.

Film/Entertainment Beat

Scope of Film/Entertainment Beat

Media coverage of television, movies and music dominate arts news at the expense of dance, architecture and the visual arts, and newspapers have come to rely on listings-heavy weekend sections as they struggle to keep pace with India's thriving arts scene. In many newsrooms, arts journalism or film and entertainment journalism continues to be a lower priority than other fields such as business and sports. The study also describes battles being waged in many editorial offices as editors and journalists try to define the very nature of arts journalism.

"Assessments of arts journalism tend to be based on vague impressions and hyperbole," says Andras Szanto, NAJP's associate director and one of the authors of the study. "To have an informed conversation around what the press is doing"—or not doing—about communicating arts and culture to the public. To understand the nature of film and entertainment beat one need to go through the following things:

- The film/entertainment beat is larger and more heterogeneous than anticipated. Newspapers frequently mix the high arts with mass culture and lifestyle coverage such as fashion and design.
- Major expanded weekend supplements showcase arts and entertainment. Features and reviews are more common

than arts news. The daily section frequently contains little more than television-plus.

- Event listings occupy close to 50 per cent of the space devoted to arts and entertainment in the print media.
- In-house staffing and resources have not been increased to match a nationwide explosion of arts activity.
- The daily arts and living section lags behind both business and sports as a priority at almost every newspaper, both in its allotment of pages and staff.
- The visual arts, architecture, dance and radio receive only cursory attention. The visual arts are rarely handled by full-time staffer. By contrast, television, movies, music and books are usually heavily covered.
- Newspapers adopt desperate policies for supplementing their staffers, work with local freelancers and national wire syndicates.
- Big city newspapers cover the arts in more detail and in greater diversity than those in smaller cities. Significant differences also exist in national newspapers' approaches to arts and cultural news.
- Network television arts journalism is concentrated in the morning programmes, not nightly newscasts or prime time magazine. Publishing is the most frequently covered medium, and the book-tour interview with the author is the dominant format.

Reporting the arts chronicles internal struggles as editors and writers try to balance high art and popular culture, critical and celebrity journalism. An accompanying section includes background on the ten metropolitan areas major papers and interviews with the publications' editors and critics about their coverage, resources, staff, budgets and space. In the interviews, the journalists candidly reveal the tensions they have dealing with competition, attracting younger readers, interacting with the entertainment industry and arts advocacy groups, among other topics.

Scope of Entertainment Beat

Following areas are covered under this beat:

1. Feature films, documentaries, short films, animation films.

2. TV channels like—Doordarshan, STAR, Zee, Sony etc.
3. Radio channels like—AIR's primary channel, Private and AIR, FM channels, Vividh Bharti & BBC, Voice of America, etc.
4. Film/TV production units/banners like R.K., AVM, Cinevista, Creative Eye, Shadow and Light Production etc.
5. Film studios used for sound recording, editing and dubbing like— Filmistan, Mehboob, Natraj, Sahara, etc.
6. Government agencies involved in the promotion and development of films like—National Film Development Corporation (NFDC), Films Division of India, National Council for Children and Young People (NCYP), Directorate of Film Festival.
7. Film/TV training institutes like Film and Television Institute of India (FTII) at Pune and Kolkata.
8. Audio cassettes and video albums.

Sources of Film/Entertainment News

1. Persons involved in the film/TV serials production like producer, financer, distributor, director, music director, singer, art director, costume designer, story writer, script writer, cinematographer, actor, actress etc.
2. Anchor persons, programme presenters, comperes.
3. Bureaucrats/Managers administering TV/Radio Channels.
4. Persons managing the affairs of film/TV production units and studios.
5. Public Relation Officers of production units and secretaries of actors/actresses.

Film/Entertainment Reporting

Besides doing routine job of covering *muhurats* of films, get-together of film persons, launching of audio/video albums, activities at film production units and studios and achievements of film-related government establishments, a film reporter basically do two kinds of writings: (*a*) Reviews and (*b*) Interviews.

Review

Film journalists are invited to view the premiere or any other show on the first day of the public screening of the film. They are also provided photos, cassettes and other literature of the film. Following this, reviews are written:

Following aspects should be analysed while reviewing a film/ TV serial/tele film or any other entertainment programme:

1. Objective of the film/serial
2. Story
3. Script
4. Dialogues
5. Music
6. Lyrics
7. Acting
8. Direction
9. Dance Direction
10. Art Direction
11. Cinematography
12. Editing
13. Make-up
14. Costumes

Film reviews are done at two levels: (A) Pre-view (B) Re-view.

Pre-view

Pre-view show is organised before the formal launch of the film. Only a selective audience which include journalists and other distinguished persons is invited to view this screening. The purpose of the pre-view is to get the film publicised just before the release.

Interviews

Keep the following points in mind while taking interviews of film/ TV personalities:

1. Collect information regarding achievements of the interviewee and his/her contribution to the area he/she has been operating in.
2. Fix up the time for a formal interview. However, an informal interview can be taken at any time and at any place, be it a party or a location of shooting.

There are two ways of writing an interview:

1. One, in which a brief intro is written and then the text is given verbatim.
2. The other is like an interview article. In this, the interviewer has a freedom to describe the person, the place and the atmosphere. Third person narrative is used with direct quotes.

The second style is preferred while writing interviews of film personalities.

Essentials for a Film/Entertainment Reporter

1. The reporter covering films, radio and TV channels must have a sound knowledge of audio-visual media, their reach and effectiveness.
2. The evolution of cinema, and the history of world cinema as well as that of Indian cinema must be known to him/her.
3. He/she must have a deep understanding of the film craft, the process of film-making and its different aspects, and the production techniques.
4. He/she must have technical knowledge, including the details of the apparatus and equipment used in film-making.
5. He/she must also have an understanding and knowledge of the functions and production techniques of radio and television.

Precautions Required for a Film/Entertainment Reporter

1. Facts regarding a film or TV entertainment programme should be ascertained before making a review or doing any film based writing. It is always good to view first and review then.
2. The reporter covering this beat should develop a habit of regular listening to radio and viewing TV programmes so as to remain in touch with the quality of varied programmes.

3. The organisational structure and functioning of various government agencies like NFDC, FDI, NCYP and FTII should be well understood before writing anything related to them.
4. Relevant information regarding the managerial and production set-up of different radio and TV channels like All India Radio, Doordarshan, BBC, Zee TV, STAR and Sony, and film/TV production units and studios like RK, AVM, Cinevista, Filmistan and Sahara Studio should be gathered before attempting to write anything concerned to them.
5. With an intention to get first-hand information, the film/entertainment reporter should have wide-spread contacts in the film/TV world, and be in good relations with film/TV personalities.
6. With a view to avoiding any factual mistake, the reporter concerned should keep an up-date knowledge of different laws, rules and regulations applicable to film/TV world, like Prasar Bharti Act, Broadcast Bill, film censorship rules (as framed by the Film Certification Board of India).
7. He/she should have full knowledge of film awards given at the national and international levels, like—Dada Saheb Phalke Award, National Awards, Filmfare Awards and Oscar Awards.
8. He/she should also have a knowledge of various national and international film festivals like—Film Festival of India, International Film Festival of India, Cannes International Film Festival, Chicago Film Festival, Tokyo Film Festival. This knowledge will be of great help in covering these festivals.

Examples: Following are given some newspaper reports as examples under various beats.

Example: Cultural Beat.

Don't Mess with Humayun's Tomb

Global flak is following local criticism. The International Council on Monuments and Sites (ICOMOS) has given the thumbs down to the PWD's plan to connect the Commonwealth Games Village and the Jawaharlal Nehru Stadium viz. Nizamuddin.

The ICOMOS said the six-lane road passing by the Humayun's tomb would affect the 'visual integrity' of the World Heritage Site. ICOMOS president Michael Petzel wrote to Sports Minister Mani Shankar Aiyar, "The outstanding artistic quality of the Humayun's tomb ... should not be sacrificed for short-term considerations such as improvement of traffic route."

Asking the minister to find an alternative plan, Petzel said he would take the matter up with the UNESCO World Hertiage Centre. But the other proposal doing the rounds—constructing an underground road till Subz Burj—does not get the consent of conservationsists. Conservation architect Ratish Nanda, consultant with the Agha Khan Trust that restored the Humayun tomb gardens (in a joint venture with the Culture and Tourism Ministry) said an underground road would kill the access to the World Heritage Site. The Ring Road, he said, was meant to take the load off central Delhi, not vice versa, and the proposed road would save just 3 km at the cost of the most valuable heritage zone in the city.

Earlier, the Delhi Urban Art Commission had rejected the PWD's proposal.

Example: Civic Beat.

MCD's Makes Magic: Areas Redefined

The MCD has cleared a list of roads in residential areas on which commercial activities will be permitted. On Monday, the municipal body put its stamp of approval on 1,979 roads and said more such stretches would be included in the list soon.

The move sets in motion the process of bringing relief to traders facing sealing action for operating in residential areas. The Urban Development Ministry had recently made changes to the Delhi Master Plan and had asked the MCD to identify stretches that can be given the commercial area status.

Several major residential stretches—like Lala Lajpat Rai Marg (from Nirula's to Defence Colony), New Daryaganj Road (from Subhash Marg to Ring Road), Ajmal Khan Road (from New Rohtak Road to Tank Road) and Shanker Road (Upper Ridge Road to

Sidhhartha roundabout) have been declared commercial roads. Many blocks in Shastri Nagar are also included.

MCD Standing Committee chairman, J.K. Sharma said the list would expand in the next fews days. "We have only taken up roads in colony categories E, F and G, and the Master Plan roads," said Sharma. He said the MCD would next concentrate on posh colonies. "Roads in colony categories, A, B, C and D are yet to be taken up. We are hopeful of completing the process on these stretches by September 16," Sharma Said.

On the directions of the Supreme Court, sealing squads were supposed to start work from September 16 and if the process is completed before that if is expected to bring relief to an estimated 90 per cent of traders in residential areas.

"For the past six months, there has been uncertainty about the fate of lakhs of traders operating in residential areas. We will be able to save nearly 90 per cent of them," MCD Leader of House Jitender Kochhar said.

MCD Commissioner A.K. Nigam said the process could be completed quickly now as the Centre has given the municipal body the power to identify and declare roads as commercial/mixed land.

Former Urban Development Minister Jagmohan, opposed to regularisation of unauthorised shops and constructions, said the move to declare the roads commercial will damage the city's planning. "The Ring Road and Master Plan roads that are supposed to ensure smooth flow of traffic will get choked and properties of law-abiding citizens will be taken over to create parking lots," Jagmohan said.

As many as 682 stretches in residential areas have been declared fully commercial. Also getting the status were another 125 roads, which were earlier under mixed-land-use areas where shops are permitted on the ground floor only. Commercial-area status—that allows commercial activity on any floor—has been granted to those stretches that have already been commercialised more than 70 per cent.

Also, mixed-land-use has been allowed on another 573 roads, as they have been commercialised more than 50 per cent. Another 599 stretches have been declared pedestrian shopping streets—a concept introduced under the amended Master Plan 2001—in which shops will be allowed on the ground floor.

After the MCD Standing Committee cleared the names of the stretches, Mayor Farhad Suri granted his approval and the list was sent to the Delhi Government. The Government will soon publish the road stretches in the form of a gazette notification.

Example: Legal Beat

Order Staggered, One of Guilty Shouts at Judge

Thirteen years after serial blasts killed 257 people in Mumbai, a Tada court on Tuesday pronounced its first verdict, convicting three brothers and a sister-in-law of prime accused Tiger Memon, who is absconding.

Three other members of the Memon family—Tiger Memon's mother, another brother and another sister-in-law were let off by Judge P.D. Kode, who gave them the benefit of doubt. The court will hear arguments on the quantum of sentence on Wednesday.

Tiger Memon's brothers Yakub, Essa, Yusuf and sister-in-law Rubina were found guilty of conspiracy for the 13 serial blasts—including one at the Bombay Stock Exchange building and the Air-India headquarters—in Mumbai on March 12, 1993.

Tiger Memon's brother Suleiman, mother Hanifa and sister-in-law Rahin were acquitted by the judge, who will deliver the verdict in batches of eight as a larger number—123—of people, including actor Sanjay Dutt, are accused in the case. Legal experts said it would take the court over two months to pronounce the final judgment. Special public prosecutor Ujjwal Nikam told HT: "The method adopted by the court is unique and it is happening for the first time. It won't take less than two months for the court to hand over the judgment."

Tiger Memon's father Abdual Razzak was also an accused but the case against him was closed after he died during the course of the trial.

After the judge announced the verdict, an angry Yakub Memon, a chartered accountant, shouted expletives and said his family did not want any lawyer to argue on its behalf for the quantum of sentence. "We have seen that for the last 13 years innocent people have been labelled terrorists. We do not need anyone to protect us," Yakub said.

In its charge-sheet, the CBI had claimed the blasts were masterminded by underworld don Dawood Ibrahim with the help of his lieutenants Tiger Memon and Mohammed Dossa, at the instance of Pakistan's intelligence agency, the ISI, to avenge the demolition of the Babri Masjid. Dawood, Memon and Dossa are absconding. While Dawood was already abroad when the blasts occurred, Memon and Dossa fled a day before.

The trial, held in a court inside a prison complex for security reasons, began in June 1995 and concluded in 2003.

Example: Education Beat.

College Denies Dyslexic Student Disability Quota

Dyslexic students seeking admission under the disability quota better prepare themselves for a rude shock. For, the Delhi University is not sure if dyslexia, a learning disability affecting reading ability, falls in the ambit of disability quota for educational institutions.

Sonum Malhorta, a student of DPS Mathura Road, scored 84 per cent in Class XII and applied for Bachelors in Fine Arts at the Delhi College of Arts, Delhi Government College. She was seeking admission under the disability quota because she was detected to be dyslexic when she was in the sixth standard.

To her surprise she was refused admission by the college, while St. Stephen's and LSR accepted her for History Hons. and Psychology Hons. courses respectively under the disability quota.

"We know it will be difficult for her to cope with the academic pressure. She is interested in Arts so we thought Fine Arts would be a better course for her," says her mother Vijay Laxmi. The student's parents claim that they approached the Delhi University and the Education Ministry only to get tangled in the bureaucratic set-up. However, S.K. Vij, Dean Students Welfare, Delhi University, said, "We have not got any such complaint. But if we do we will study the particulars of the case and see if the candidate is eligible for admission."

"In the Disability Act of 1995 there are seven types of disabilities, learning disabilities being one of them," says Javed Abidi, executive director, Disabled Rights Group.

Example: Entertainment Beat.

Ordinary Superstar

All right, so Shah Rukh Khan has a "naughty sense of humour" and no, the superstar has no interest in politics— national, professional or personal. "Why is it that everytime I show my films to Sonia Gandhi and her family, people think that I'm entering politics? Why doesn't it occur to people that they may be entering Bollywood?" For now, Shah Rukh Khan is just an entertainer—be it as the grey Dev in KANK or as a dancer at private parties.

"*Entertainment is my Job*: I've no qualms singing and dancing at weddings, on the streets or on a stage. If you are running a business you can pay me and I will do the *Chhaiya Chhaiya* for you, for charity, I will do it for free," says the star who is often accused of being too commercial. "M.F. Husain once told me that he and I have corrupted art and films by being too commercial. Since I'm not the highest paid star in the country, why shouldn't I make money using my star status? After all, how many people can dance at a wedding and get paid for it?"

So, is Shah Rukh really the biggest star? "That is the positive side of the population explosion in our country. Every fourth face is Indian and by default, every fourth face in the world recognises me because I'm the face of Indian movies."

Ask his friend Karan Johar about Shah Rukh's super stardom and he says, "At the end of the day, Shah Rukh and Gauri are normal, middle-class Delhiites. He is too ordinary to be a superstar. He is a guy who is uncomfortable in a typical "society" atmosphere. He lives an ordinary life. He is a guy who spends four hours in the loo. "Can you imagine that the biggest star in India takes all his important decisions sitting on the pot?"

"Considering the kind of films that Indian filmmakers make, I think that is really the best place to read the scripts," quips Shah Rukh. But four hours? "I need moments of solitude when I'm at home and it is not really possible with kids running around in the house. What I really do is keep the seat down, sit on it and read a book." Probably, the reason why the star is never on time anywhere. The average grace period is two hours!

"*That's because I believe I can make it*: One day I will be able to make it on time too. When I wake up in the morning, I believe that I will be the best father, husband, entertainer." Which is why, Shah Rukh finds rumours of his supposed rivalry with the Bachchans amusing. "I'm not competing. In fact, I am learning to maintain a stubble and I thought of taking lessons from Abhishek. When I say I don't want any politics, I mean all kinds of politics—personal and professional."

Example: Religion/Festival Beat.

Buddhism Makes a Comeback in China

Piety and a knowledge of Buddhist scriptures used to qualify one to be a Chinese monk. Now, add computer skills, foreign language ability and a degree in financial management.

Three decades after temples were destroyed and scriptures burnt during the Cultural Revolution, Buddhism is making a comeback in China. And like most things in the super-competitive, rapidly developing country, it's become both big business and field in which people are eager to get ahead.

That's creating a new breed of multi-tasking, tech-savvy, upwardly mobile monks. "Our recruiting process is highly competitive," said Hui Jue, deputy general manager of the 120-year-old Jade Buddha Temple in downtown Shanghai. With his head shaven and dressed in long, orange-brown monk's robes, he recently completed a master of business administration degree at prestigious Jiaotong University.

Fifteen monks from the temple have been sent to take foreign language courses at the Shanghai International Studies University and a second batch has started MBA studies in the business school of Jiaotong University.

Such skills are necessary, Hui Jue believes, for the temple to both spread Buddhist teachings in the modern world and manage its growing business interests.

In addition to the temple grounds, Jade Buddha owns a vegetarian restaurant, a four-star hotel with uniformed security guards to protect VIP guests, a seven-floor office building and a food factory.

Many of China's temples have been little touched by time, especially in remote areas of the country. But Jade Buddha Temple's modern approach is no longer unusual.

Buddhism, introduced in China around the first century, is the biggest religion in China with as many as 100 million adherents, over 8 per cent of the Chinese population, according to some estimates.

The persecution of the Cultural Revolution is long gone and while the government is not very enthusiastic about any religion, in recent decades it has given more support to Buddhism than other faiths.

That has permitted the rise of a string of highly outward-looking and ambitious temples in recent years. China now has 13,000—some Buddhist temples and about 200,000 Buddhist monks and nuns, according to the State Administration for Religious Affairs. The number is believed to be rising.

Lucrative, fast-growing temples have also sprung up elsewhere in Asia, such as in Taiwan and Thailand. But China's size and entrepreneurial flair may be unmatched.

The ancient Shaolin Temple in Henan Province, for example, has capitalised on its reputation as a birthplace of the martial arts to host glamorous international guests and stage performances around the world.

The Internet is key to many temples' expansion plans. Guangdong Province's Guangziao Temple, which claims to be the oldest and biggest temple in south China, has launched an online worshipping system at www.gzgxs.org., through which users offer virtual incense, fruit and flowers to a variety of electronic Buddhas.

12

Editorial Department

A daily newspaper is a big organisation comprising many departments like editorial, advertising, circulation, production and personnel. These departments are knit together in their working so as to make the newspaper organisation a composite unit. Each of these departments is headed by a manager who works in close co-ordination with his/her counterparts and thus, they all ensure the achievement of objectives of the organisation.

However, we are not going to discuss here the management functions or the principles of management which fall under the spectrum of media management. We are also not going to elaborate the functions of the circulation and advertising departments which is part of the marketing activities. In this chapter, our focus is on the editorial department but before proceeding further, we would certainly like to have a look at the organisational structure of a daily.

Organisational Structure of a Daily

On the top, the organisational structure of a daily depends to a great extent on the kind of ownership the newspaper has. The hierarchical positions and set-up of departments also vary from newspaper to newspaper. However, the broad structure remains the same in almost all the newspapers. Let us have a look at the organisational structure in given diagram.

The diagram will precisely give you a clear idea about the basic functions of different departments in a newspaper organisation. Undoubtedly, the most important among all these departments is the editorial department as it provides contents—the new stories and other news based material.

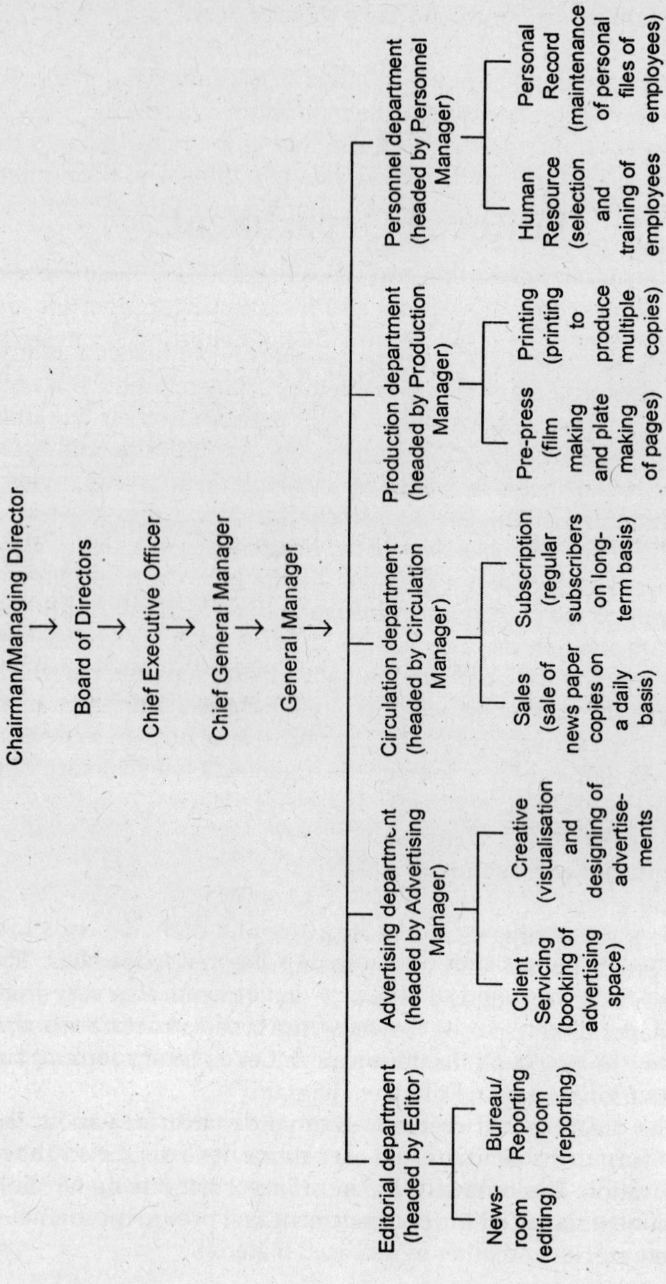

Chairman/Managing Director
Board of Directors
Chief Executive Officer
Chief General Manager
General Manager
Editorial department (headed by Editor)
News-room (editing)
Bureau/ Reporting room (reporting)
Advertising department (headed by Advertising Manager)
Client Servicing (booking of advertising space)
Creative (visualisation and designing of advertise-ments
Circulation department (headed by Circulation Manager)
Sales (sale of news paper copies on a daily basis)
Subscription (regular subscribers on long-term basis)
Production department (headed by Production Manager)
Pre-press (film making and plate making of pages)
Printing (printing to produce multiple copies)
Personnel department (headed by Personnel Manager)
Human Resource (selection and training of employees
Personal Record (maintenance of personal files of employees)

Editorial Department in Today's Newspapers

Broadly two functions are performed in the editorial department of a newspaper—one is reporting and another is editing. The size of the editorial department as also that of the reporting and the editing sections depends basically on two things, (*a*) the number of pages the daily carries, (*b*) the number of editions published from that very place.

The number of editing and reporting staff i.e., the number of copy editors in the newsroom and the number of reporters and correspondents in the bureau and the city Reporting Room is also decided on the basis of the above mentioned two factors. The hierarchical positions too are decided depending on the size of the editorial department. For example, a big newspaper can have two News Editors, also a Deputy News Editor or even a Chief News Editor, unlike a small newspaper.

Newspapers fall into three categories depending on their circulation. The categorisation is likewise—Small Newspapers—less than 25 thousand, Medium Size Newspapers—more than 25,000 and up to 75,000 and Big Newspapers—more than 75,000.

Many big newspapers have now started taking out many editions from different places. This is basically done for two reasons (*a*) to increase circulation by covering more cities and towns and (*b*) to increase the volume of advertising in extended areas. The examples of such multi-edition newspapers in English are *The Times of India, The Hindustan Times, The Indian Express* and in Hindi, *Hindustan, Amar Ujala, Dainik Jagran,* etc.

The editorial set-up in multi-edition newspapers is slightly different as compared to single-edition newspapers. In multi-edition newspapers, the Editor might be designated as Chief Editor or Editor-in-Chief, and each edition will be headed by a Resident Editor. Also, many such newspapers prefer to have a news pool for an exchange of important stories among different editions and so there will be a Pool Editor.

The structure or set-up of editorial department varies from one newspaper to another, the reasons we have discussed above. Despite this the broad structure of the editorial department remains the same. For a better understanding refer to the following diagram:

Set-up of Editorial Department

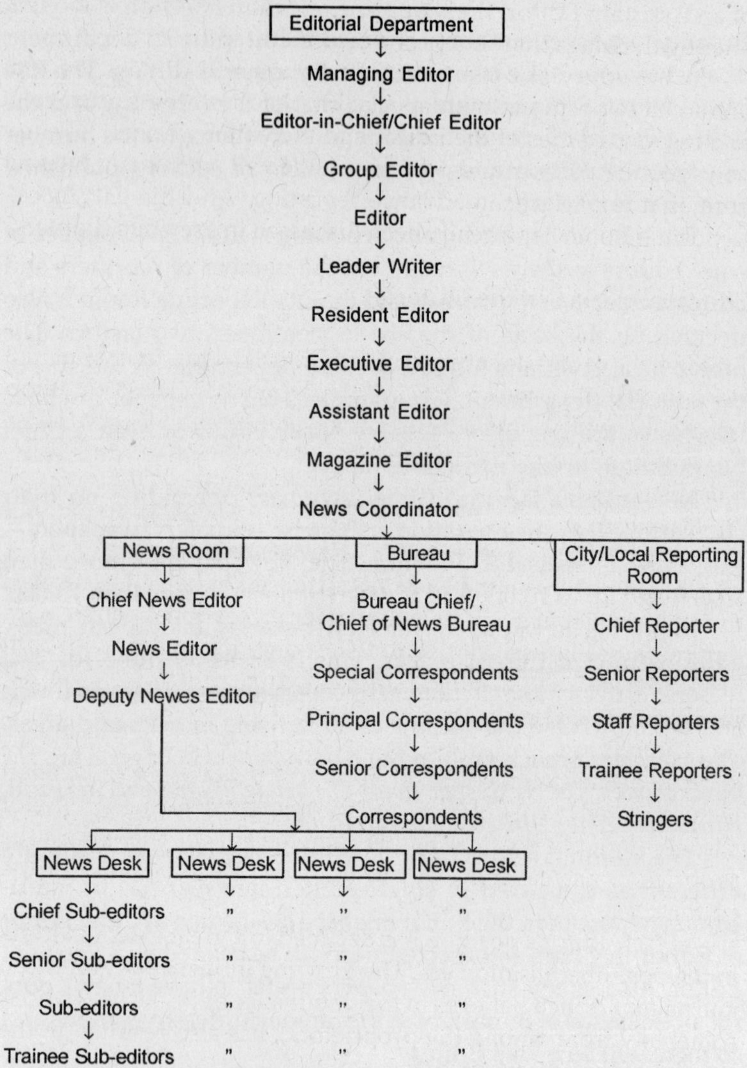

In addition to the above-mentioned News Room, Bureau and City Reporting Room, the editorial department also has two other important sections, Editorial Page and Magazine or Feature Section. While the Editorial page remains under the supervision of an Assistant Editor, the Magazine or Feature Section is looked after by the Magazine Editor or Feature Editor.

In the editorial department, firstly we will discuss the top hierarchical positions with special emphasis on the status, role and responsibilities of the Editor and thereafter we shall take up news room, its set-up and operations. We will not take up bureau here as it is part of the advance reporting. And the City/Local Reporting Room has already been discussed in previous chapters.

Editor's Position in the Editorial

Editor is the professional head of the editorial department but his/her position is not confined to this department alone. Editor is too big a person in the newspaper set-up and he/she is regarded as the representative of the newspaper in the outside world. Thus, he/she becomes the first person in the organisation.

There are two kinds of persons around the editor, one the proprietor with the position of Chairman or Managing Director who might be having the wish to see himself or herself as head of the editorial department, two the senior professional people with designations like assistant editor. The editor has to deal with both of them as any or both could be too ambitious creating disruption in smooth functioning.

The hierarchy in the editorial department is also affected because of the same reason. Despite editor's prominent position in the editorial set-up, we find many instances where the proprietor tries to acquire a position higher than the editor. These days the proprietors use several ways to undermine the position of the editor.

In fact, editor's position has declined to a great extent in India in the post-liberalisation era. The growing influence of American journalism, which believes in the dominance of publisher (who is somebody from among the proprietors), has also resulted in the erosion of the editor's status.

Going by the provisions of the Press and Registration of Books Act, there are three persons important in the newspaper set-up—editor, publisher and printer. When the proprietor decides to take out a newspaper, he/she has to file a declaration in which the names of all three editor, publisher and printer have to be mentioned. Normally, the proprietor puts his/her name as publisher and some professional journalist's name as editor. The Printer could be somebody from among the proprietors or a professional person.

However, there are exceptions to the practices we have already discussed. There are even examples of newspapers where editor's institution appears strong. Take for instance *The Hindu* in which the printer, publisher and the editor, all three positions are held by Mr. N. Ram. The same happens in *The Tribune,* where Mr. H.K. Dua is holding all three positions. But we must remember that this could happen only in the case of legendary editors.

Editor's Team

Before proceeding to discuss the role and responsibilities of the editor, it will be appropriate to have a look at his/her team—the top level people above and below him/her.

Managing Editor

In any newspaper, the ambition of the proprietor can lead him/her to acquire a position higher than the editor in the editorial set-up. But the problem occurs how to find a designation which is more loaded and catchy. In some newspapers, the proprietors have found a solution to this problem, as they decide to designate themselves as managing editors.

However, the position of the managing editor has no legal or official sanctity if we go by the PRB Act. But it certainly gives the proprietor the satisfaction of heading the editorial department. This satisfaction reflects only the mental state of the proprietor as he/she is either incapable or unwilling of performing the professional duties of the editor. Obviously the editor, who happens to be a professional journalist, continues to be the real working head of the editorial department.

Many newspapers, including *The Times of India,* have been having the post of the Managing Editor. There are newspapers like *The Indian Express* where the proprietor's name is mentioned as Chairman of the Board: Viveck Goenka in the print line.

Editor-in-chief

The editor of a chained publication or multi-edition newspaper is normally designated as *Editor-in-Chief or Chief Editor*. Take for instances the example of *The Indian Express* which is published from Ahmedabad, Chandigarh, Delhi, Jammu, Kolkata, Lucknow, Mumbai, Nagpur, Pune and Varodara and the name of the editorial head is mentioned as *Editor-in-Chief*: Shekhar Gupta in the print line. The same is the case with *The Hindustan Times* (Editor-in-Chief, Chinmaya Kalbag) and *The Times of India* (Editor-in-Chief, Arindam Sengupta).

Editor-in-Chief is responsible for all the editorial matter published in various editions of the newspaper. He/she takes decisions on policy matters and issues necessary guidelines for the editorial working. In all multi-edition newspapers, each edition is headed by a resident editor who works directly under the Editor-in-Chief.

There are exceptions to the above rule. We can find editorial head designated as Chief Editor even in newspapers which are published from one place only. We even have the example of weekly INDIA TODAY which is published from one place Delhi, yet the editorial head is designated as Editor-in-Chief. Incidentally this post is held by Aroon Purie who is the proprietor of the magazine.

Group Editor

Group editor is a designation which we rarely find in newspapers and magazines. There are media houses which have more than one publications—news-interest as well as non-news from one or more than one places and they decide to make an eminent journalist editorial head of all the publications. This editorial head can be designated as Group Editor.

Take for instance the example of *The Hindustan Times* group which has designated Mrinal Pandey, Group Editor of all its Hindi publications.

Editor

Still there are many newspapers which prefer to designate their editorial head as editor whether the newspaper is single-edition or multi-edition publication. We have seen the examples of multi-editions *The Indian Express, The Times of India* and *The Hindustan Times* where the editorial head is designated as Editor-in-Chief. Now, we can look at the examples of *The Hindu* and *The Statesman. The Hindu* published from Chennai and New Delhi is headed by Mr. N. Ram as editor and *The Statesman* published from Kolkata and New Delhi is headed by Mr. Ravindra Kumar as editor. Similarly, Mrinal Pandey's name goes as editor in the print line of Hindi daily HINDUSTAN which is published from many places.

In Hindi and language newspapers, editor is the most used designation for the editorial head. We shall discuss the editor in detail in the following pages in this chapter.

Leader Writer

Leader Writer is a person who regularly writes leaders (editorials). Besides, he/she may also write other kind of articles, reviews, analysis and comments for use on the editorial page as per requirements. In the editorial department of a newspaper, Leader Writer enjoys the position of an Assistant Editor. He/she is, however, not involved in the main working of the department and remains confined to the editorial page.

We don't find leader writers in small and medium-size newspapers, but most of the big newspapers engage leader writers. These leader writers seem to be able to turn their hands to almost any subject in any part of the world. They are treated as experts who are capable of writing an editorial piece within the shortest possible time.

Normally editorial writing is considered the responsibility of the editor. But in big newspapers editor does not have enough time to sit and write editorial pieces, and so the job is handed over to the leader writer. No doubt, the topics on which editorial pieces are being written on a particular day have to be decided by the editor in consultation with the leader writer and other senior colleagues.

In India, not many newspapers have leader writers. In such a case, the editor is responsible for writing editorial pieces. Most of the newspapers today have two editorial pieces and as the practice goes, the first piece is written by the editor and the second one by an assistant editor who would have been delegated that responsibility by the editor.

Resident Editor

Resident Editor is a senior editorial person who heads the editorial department in a particular unit of the newspaper. Take for example, *The Hindustan Times*, which has Editor-in-Chief: Chaitanya Kalbag sitting in the head office at New Delhi and resident editors in each of its units, including Delhi unit. The name of Arun Roy Chowdhury is mentioned as Resident Editor in the Delhi edition of *The Hindustan Times*.

We can also take the example of *The Statesman* in which each unit is headed by a resident editor. The name of Usha Mahadevan is mentioned as Resident Editor of the Delhi edition in the print line of the newspaper. In Hindi daily HINDUSTAN, the name of Pramod Joshi appears as Resident Editor in the print line.

The post of the Resident Editor is almost equivalent to an assistant editor. For instance, if *The Hindustan Times* decides to take out a new edition from Agartala, it might transfer any of its assistant editors from New Delhi to Agartala to take over that unit as Resident Editor.

Any newspaper can decide to further elevate the post of the resident editor. Take for example *The Indian Express* which gives the designation of editor to all its resident editors heading different units. We can find the name of Coomi Kapoor mentioned as Editor (Delhi) in the print line in Delhi edition of the newspaper.

In such a case it can also be mentioned as to who will be legally or officially responsible for the editorial contents published in the newspaper. As we have already discussed, the editor has to owe responsibility for this under the PRB Act. If the resident editor is being designated as editor of a particular unit/edition, he/she has to accept responsibility for the editorial content. If you look at the print line in Delhi edition of *The Indian Express*, you can find a mention that Coomi Kapoor is "Responsible for selection of News under the PRB Act."

The resident editor is bound by the editorial policy of the newspaper as decided by the editor. He/she has to follow and seek instructions from the editor. No doubt, for the news selection in that particular edition he/she is the final authority.

Executive Editor

In newspapers where the proprietor decides to become the editor himself or herself, a professional journalist has to be employed to discharge the functions of editor. This professional journalist is normally designated as Executive Editor.

As we have already discussed, the proprietor would be interested only in projecting himself/herself as editor but he/she is not willing to perform day-to-day functions. Or he/she might not be professionally competent to function as editor. In either of the case, he/she needs a professional person to take over his/her responsibility.

There can be an exception to the above practice which we find in *The Indian Express*. In this newspaper, the person posted next to the Editor-in-Chief (Shekhar Gupta) is designated as Executive Editor (Raj Kamal Jha). And both Mr. Gupta and Mr. Jha are professional journalists.

Assistant Editor

A newspaper can have one or more than one assistant editor. An assistant editor is next to the editor in the hierarchy of the editorial department. He/she is a very senior person who is always ready to take up an assignment given by the editor or the management.

An assistant editor can be elevated to the post of executive editor or can even be sent to one of the units of the newspaper as resident editor. Under normal circumstances, he/she enjoys delegated powers of the editor, for example, he might be asked to write an editorial piece everyday which is primarily the duty of the editor.

An assistant editor does multi-farious jobs depending on what he/she has been assigned. He/she may be asked to look after the editorial page, also the OPED page, Sunday magazine, also the Saturday supplement, Week-day pull-outs, other feature pages, or any special section like West Delhi Plus, East Delhi Plus or South Delhi Plus.

Magazine Editor

As we have discussed above, magazine editor's basic job is to take out Sunday magazine of the newspaper. He/she decides about the cover story or the main story and either writes it himself/herself or gets it written by some expert or freelance writer. He/she takes decision about other articles and features and gets all the material produced by the deadline.

Magazine Editor performs a specialised job and his/her calibre and competence is reflected in the quality of Sunday magazine. And the quality of Sunday magazine determines to a great extent the quality of the newspaper which finally affects its circulation.

Some Other Designations

In the editorial department of a newspaper, there could be too many hierarchies depending on the size and the nature of the organisation. Most of the top positions we have discussed above, yet we can find some more positions like deputy editor, senior editor, joint editor, associate editor and so on.

Take for example, Hindi daily *Navbharat Times* in which we find a mention of the name of Madhusudan Anand as Senior Editor in the print line.

A few of the above mentioned designations can be found in this or that newspaper. However, these designations are more common in news magazines.

News Coordinator

The post of the news coordinator is mostly found in big newspapers—one the newspapers which take out many editions from one place, two the newspapers which publish independent editions from different places.

If a newspaper takes out four or five editions from the same place, it should have two to three news editors and one chief news editor. Whether or not the newspaper has a chief news editor, it can always have a news coordinator who will be coordinating among different editions of the newspaper.

We must understand that all big newspapers take out many editions from the same place. For example, a newspaper like *The Times of India* or *The Hindustan Times* can take out Ghaziabad edition, NOIDA edition, Faridabad edition, Gurgaon edition, City edition, late city edition, South Delhi edition, East Delhi edition, West Delhi edition and so on from Delhi office itself.

Since the release timings of all these editions differ, the news coverage also varies. News particularly national and international items have to be updated in each issue. Local news coverage will depend on which area the newspaper copies are going to be distributed. This demands coordination on the news front and that is why newspapers need a news coordinator.

The newspapers, which are published from different places, develop a system of exchange of important news stories. This helps in better coverage of news in all the editions which become possible with the optimum use of existing resources. The exchange of news items has to take place under supervision of a senior person like news coordinator.

For the purpose mentioned above, newspapers create a pool which is looked after by the pool editor in the head office. The pool editor is a person equivalent to the position of news coordinator. We shall not go into the detail of news pool here as it has already been discussed in one of the previous chapters.

Role and Responsibilities of Editor

To be the editor of a daily newspaper with a nation-wide circulation is an ambition which very few journalists can attain. There are, however, occasions when many intelligent reporters and correspondents are satisfied with the excitement and thrill of their job and do not relish to have the ambition of a more ordered routine of an indoor job of the editor, even though it may bring them greater name and fame.

The role and responsibilities of editor can be discussed with the help of following points:

(1) *Decision on Editorial Policy*

Like the newspaper itself, the functions and responsibilities of the editor keep on changing. When there were few newspapers, the editor was regarded as a ruler who ruled by the force of his/her personality. The editor of a big newspaper enjoyed more power than he/she does now. Present day newspapers are more led by the public opinion than editors.

Today, a newspaper has become a commercial organisation rather than a political institution as it used to be in the pre-independence days. The editor, in order to maintain and increase the circulation constantly has to calculate the public mind and express opinions in the light of popular trends prevailing at different points of time.

If a newspaper takes an elitist approach, it can be classified as an anti-people newspaper and many of its readers may not only stop buying it but also build public opinion against it. For this reason, most of the editors give out their ideas and opinions on current issues after reading the public mind.

Besides, the individual opinion of an editor is subject to all the views of his/her colleagues, correspondents and the editorial staff. No newspaper allows one-man control, however intelligent the editor may be. But the editor's views always dominate while editorial policy is being finalised.

The editorial policy is an important document in a newspaper though lot many newspapers might not be having a written document. The policy includes guidelines and instructions with regard to news coverage, and presentation besides so many other things. In news coverage, the thrust area needs to be decided—whether crime news shall be given more coverage or the development news. Also whether the news will be more interpretative (See *The Hindu*) or investigative (See *The Indian Express*).

Even this could be decided whether the newspaper will follow a pro-establishment approach (See *The Hindustan Times*), anti-establishment approach (See *The Indian Express*) or a middle-path (See *The Times of India*). Sometimes the political leanings could also be decided at the insistence of the proprietors but a professional editor will never permit any such tilt. Newspapers with open political leanings can never grow (See *Vir Arjun*) or survive (See *National Herald*).

A professionally sound editor will always prefer a pro-people editorial policy where the aspirations, needs and opinions of the people are given utmost importance. No doubt, a socially inclined editor will try to refine the people's opinions so as to be sure that the contents of the newspaper are genuinely serving the interests of the society.

(2) *Control Over Editorial Working*

The editor of a newspaper must have patience, human sympathy, a working knowledge of the latest technology, the faculty of being able to distinguish between public right and public wrong as well as private right and private wrong. He/she must possess a courageous heart which enables him/her to say 'yes' or 'no' at the right time.

He/she should be able to inspire confidence in his/her staff whom he/she can presumably trust. He/she should not build an iron curtain around himself/herself through which he/she emerges only on rare occasions. A good editor is one who is familiar with his/her staff and does not make himself/herself inaccessible.

Unless the spirit of good companionship prevails in a newspaper, the workers cannot show good results. If a grave issue of any kind arises, it is the editor's duty to take the final decision without fear or fervour irrespective of the difference of opinion expressed by some staff members. He/she should not even get influenced by the management or proprietors while taking decision on a vital issue.

A competent and successful editor enjoys confidence of and has tremendous faith in his/her staff particularly the senior people like assistant editors and news editors. Monitoring of the subordinate staff is possible only when his/her core team members are ready to rub shoulders with him/her.

The editor is always loaded with the work whether he/she is in his/her office or outside. He/she remains ready to get disturbed even at odd hours if something unusual happens in the office or his/her instructions are sought with regard to any vital news or article. No doubt, he/she can always delegate responsibility to any of the assistant editors.

The opinions are divided whether the editor himself/herself should write leading articles or whether he/she should confine himself/herself to briefing other members of his/her staff. Many feel that the editor should not write regularly. An editorial piece from his pen should be an event of special importance and should be reserved for very importance occasions. Most leader writers are able to assimilate very quickly the ideas which the editor has passed on to them before they begin to write, and it is always the editor's privilege to revise the article and, if he/she is really dissatisfied, to re-write it.

(3) *Performance of Managerial Responsibility*

The editor performs twin responsibilities—as a journalist and also as a manager. He/she directs and monitors editorial working as editor and regulates the functions of the editorial department as an administrator. This makes his/her position not only important but also sensitive in the newspaper set-up.

Editorial is the only department which is not headed by a manager, all other departments—circulation, advertising, production and personnel are headed by managers. This can lead us to the conclusion that an editor is not a manager. But this is mistaking and is not absolutely true. As head, the editor is managing the affairs of the editorial department and thus performs the functions of a manager.

The managerial responsibilities of the editor include selection of editorial staff, their training on job and through refresher courses, promotions and transfers, incentives to competent persons, regulation of working in the department and disciplinary action against erring staff members. His/her job will also include doing forward planning, setting objectives, achieving targets, providing necessary help and assistance, offering guidance and motivation and patronising the subordinate staff.

The editor is also responsible for the well-being of his/her staff. He/she is supposed to ensure that the editorial people are being provided healthy working conditions and wages. He/she should even be ready to fight with the proprietors for the genuine cause of his/her subordinates.

But in view of his/her senior position, the editor is treated a member of the core group of managers. And as a manager, his/her responsibility is to ensure that all the orders and instructions of the top management (particularly those applicable to the editorial department) are carried out. This makes him/her harsh and tough to his/her colleagues on occasions.

In fact, the editor functions as a bridge between the editorial staff and the management. He/she is expected to watch the interests of both and needs to be balanced in this exercise. This is not an easy task keeping in view the delicate position of the editor. In some newspapers the editor rises so big that he/she becomes all in all in the newspaper. We have examples of *The Hindu* and *The Tribune* where the editors—Mr. N. Ram and Mr. H.K. Dua respectively—have also acquired the positions of printer and publisher. But even a big person has to be responsive to his/her editorial colleagues.

(4) *Representative of the Newspaper*

A newspaper is known by the name of its editor. Think of *The Indian Express*, Shekhar Gupta's name will come to your mind.

Think of *The Hindu*, N. Ram's name will strike your mind. The office of the editor is so big that it overshadows all circulation managers, advertisement managers, production managers, even the general managers and the managing directors of the newspaper.

The editor is the face of a newspaper. He/she represents the newspaper in the outside world, at all forums whether it is a seminar, workshop, lecture or meeting with a senior bureaucrat or minister. Even the government may consult editors on vital issues related to media.

Conventionally editor is considered to be a highly intellectual person. But in today's time an editor is also one who is professionally sound and capable of performing multifarious jobs. Two examples can be given in support on this contention. Shekhar Gupta, the editor-in-chief of *The Indian Express*, is involved in the production of many news-based programmes on TV. Also Vir Sanghvi, former editor of *The Hindustan Times*, has also been involved in a number of TV shows anchored and produced by him.

Editor is active in a lot of professional activities outside the four walls of his/her newspaper. He/she is represented in the Press Council of India. He/she can also be made a member of the Wage Board being set-up for journalist and non-journalist employees of newspapers and news agencies. He/she can choose to be represented on any journalists' body like IFWJ or NUJ. With the purpose of raising the standard of the profession, the editors have even formed an organisation 'Editors Guild of India'.

For all official and legal purposes, editor is the representative of the newspaper. In government organisations and agencies like Registrar of Newspapers for India (RNI), Directorate of Advertising and Visual Publicity (DAVP), Press Information Bureau (PIB), the newspaper is represented by the editor. In industrial organisations like Audit Bureau of Circulation (ABC) or National Readership Survey (NRS), the editor represents his/her newspaper.

13

News Room Operations

News Room

News Room is the most important section or unit in the editorial department of a newspaper. It is, in fact, a place essential to all news organisations be it a newspaper, radio news channel or TV news channel. It is the central point of all news related activities, reporting as well as editing.

News Room is a place where news reports pour in from different sources—newspapers own reporters and correspondents, news agencies and other sources. These reports are sorted, compiled, selected, edited and prepared or produced for end use. The end use differs in different media. In newspapers news reports are prepared for placement on different pages, in radio and TV reports are produced as per requirement of various news bulletins.

News Room is regarded as the custodian of the newspaper policy. It is here that the news items are screened and processed on the basis of their relevance to the paper's policy. News selection and news testing is a difficult job which demands lot of news sense on the part of the editing staff.

News Room Set-up

News Room is the backbone of a news organisation. It remains functional for most of the time in a day. In a newspaper, news room working starts at around 9 a.m. and it is over around 2 a.m. In radio and T.V. news channels, news room remains functional round-the-clock as lights are never switched off.

The head of the News Room is the News Editor and under him/her are Deputy News Editors. Below them are the Chief Sub-editors, called Slot Men in the USA, and at the bottom of the News Room hierarchy are the Sub-editors, known as Copy Editors or Rim Men.

News Room comprises several separate desks for general news, local news, sports news, business news etc. Every newspaper differs in the number and the functioning of its desks. Generally, sports and commerce desks are separate. Some newspapers also have separate local and district desks. English newspapers even have international desk.

News Room Set-up

News Desk

The size of a desk depends on the size of the newspaper in general and the number of pages in that particular section. In a newspaper that carries four pages on sports, there should be five to six persons on the sports desk—one chief sub, two senior subs and two to three sub-editors. If the number of sports pages is only two, there is no need of having more than three persons on the sports desk.

A desk is responsible for the selection of news items from the bulk of stories received from news agencies and own correspondents. The selected items are then edited, headlined and placed on the page as per the layout. The editorial staff on the desk is responsible for the layout and makeup of the pages under them.

It must be noted that work on a desk does not actually start with the selection of stories. The chief sub-editor in-charge of the desk has also to think from where and how to acquire news stories. News agencies, no doubt, are the major supplier of news to a newspaper but that might not serve the purpose on a particular desk. For this reason, every newspaper tries to develop its own network of reporting.

It may be reminded that a newspaper gets news reports from the following:

(*a*) News Bureau in the national capital.
(*b*) News Bureau in the State capital.
(*c*) City Reporting Room at the place of publication.
(*d*) Reporting Offices/Bureaus at the district headquarters.
(*e*) Stringers at cities/towns.
(*f*) Correspondents abroad.

While the general news desk depends on all the above sources, international desk depends on the correspondents abroad in addition to the national news bureau. District news desk solely depends on the reporting offices/bureaus in the district or on the stringers. Local news desk solely depends on the city reporting room for getting stories to be placed on the local pages.

Sports and business news desks hardly depend on the above mentioned sources. In most of the newspapers correspondents with relevant specialisation (sports or business) are posted on the desk itself. Thus, correspondents form a team with chief sub-editor, senior sub and sub on a desk. While local sports events or business activities are covered by the correspondents, other national or international stories are taken from the news agencies.

For photo coverage, all the desks depend on the staff photographers at the newspaper. Some photographs can also be sent by bureaus or district offices. However, one major source of photographs is the photo service of news agencies.

News Room Functions

News Room is the centre of activities in a newspaper organisation. News Room activities are determined by the activities outside (happenings in the country or abroad) as well as inside (the pressure of work and that of deadlines). All the time news reports are received or acquired, received reports are collected and compiled, sorted and distributed, tested and valued, selected or rejected, selected reports are edited and headlined to be finally placed on the page.

News room functions are diverse and their handling demands lot of foresight and efficiency on the part of the editorial staff. News room operations have changed a lot over the years mainly due to advancement in technology. In the conventional news room, many manual functions have been involved whereas in a modern news room the working is totally computerised.

Here, we shall firstly discuss the functions of a conventional news room and thereafter try to understand the changes brought about by technological innovations in the modern news room.

Conventional News Room

News room functions can be broadly divided under six heads:

(*a*) Receiving/acquiring news reports
(*b*) Selection of news reports
(*c*) Editing and headlining of selected items
(*d*) Composing of edited news items
(*e*) Proof-reading of composed matter
(*f*) Layouting and page-making/pasting.

Receiving/Acquiring News Reports

News reports are received in a newspaper through two sources—news agencies and newspaper's own correspondents. Normally, a daily subscribes to the services of both the domestic news agencies—Press Trust of India (PTI) and the United News of India (UNI) so as to get an extensive coverage and reduce the risk of missing the stories. Hindi newspapers can subscribe to Hindi services of these agencies—BHASHA (PTI) and VARTA (UNI), and language newspapers subscribe to language services of these agencies subject to availability.

Newspapers in India are not allowed to subscribe to the services of foreign news agencies directly and so they have to depend on PTI and UNI. These domestic agencies collaborate with foreign news agencies—Reuters, Associated Press (AP), United Press International (UPI), AFP etc., for the exchange of important newsworthy news items. Most of the newspapers are satisfied with

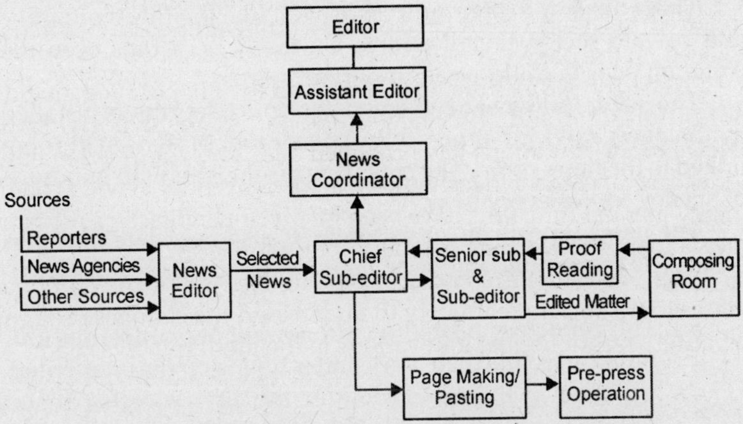

Conventional News Room

the international news reports provided by PTI and UNI with the help of their collaboration with foreign agencies. However, big newspapers depute their correspondents at important locations in the world for getting some exclusive coverage.

PTI and UNI have their special services as well and newspapers are free to avail those services. For instances, UNI has a financial service UNIFIN which is of great use to newspapers giving more importance to business coverage. Agency services are also categorised depending on the area (national, international, sports, business etc.) covered and the extent or quality of coverage. For instance, Hindi newspaper with no page on international news can choose a category where less number of international items are supplied, and a English newspaper having two pages on international news can opt for a category where more and varied news items are supplied. It may be noted that news agencies quote different rates for different category of services.

Besides news agencies, newspaper's own correspondents are also a big source of news. A newspaper needs to have its own fleet of correspondents for two reasons, one to ensure originality and exclusivity in its reporting, two to make sure an extensive coverage of areas where the newspaper is largely circulated. The correspondent, reporters and stringers are posted in bureau, city reporting room, and all such cities, towns, villages which fall under the circulation area of the newspaper.

There are some other sources as well like the PROs of public and private sector organisations. On many occasions even the common people could be an important source.

The major inflow of news emanates from teleprinters installed by the news agencies either in the news room or in a small room linked to the news room. The news room is flooded with hundreds of agency copies every hour.

The news reports of correspondents also inundate the news room. The correspondents send their reports in three ways:

(*a*) The reporters posted at the newspaper office/place of publication file their stories after typing on the typewriters installed in the news room or the city reporting room. These stories are directly submitted in the news room by the reporters concerned.

(*b*) The teleprinters are installed at the bureaus and other reporting units of the newspaper at outside locations. The correspondents posted at bureaus/units send their copies through these teleprinters and the copies are received at the teleprinters installed at the newspaper headquarter/ place of publication.

(*c*) The outstation correspondents posted at locations where no teleprinters have been installed can send their stories through telegrams. The Post and Telegraph Department provides a special service for this purpose. The newspaper concerned has to apply to the Telegraph Department for availing this service following which the department will issue a telegraphic authority in favour of the correspondent.

A correspondent equipped with telegraphic authority can send a news item from any telegraph office on a priority basis without any payment. The payment is subsidised and is made by the newspaper to the Telegraph Department on an annual basis. Thus, the news item is received in the newspaper office in the form of a telegram. No doubt, the correspondents need to keep such stories short. These stories may take some time in reaching the news room.

All the news items land on the table of the news editor who is in-charge of the news room. Some newspapers have a system where the news items are first reaching the table of the Chief

Sub-editor in-charge of the general desk who will subsequently send the important news items to the news editor for his/her perusal and necessary instructions. In some other newspapers, the deputy news editor might be first handling the news items.

Though the news room is at the receiving end, it is not a passive section or unit. If the news editor or the chief sub-editor in-charge on a particular desk does not feel satisfied with whatever reports have been received, he/she can always give necessary instructions to the correspondents concerned for filing revised or new stories. The news editor is authorised and responsible for arranging or acquiring stories which he/she feels must be there.

Selection of News Reports

Hundreds of news stories are received in the news room of a newspaper everyday. The agency news items received through teleprinters are normally taken out from the machine and collected by some Class IV employee posted in the news room. He/she tears the pages/takes from the paper roll installed in the teleprinter and will submit all the copies to the chief sub-editor in-charge of the general desk. The chief sub-editor will arrange the copies by putting the related takes together and arranging or keeping all the copies in a proper order.

The chief sub-editor in-charge of the general desk also does the job of sorting. He/she has five or six baskets on his/her table and during sorting will keep the sports items in the sports basket, business item in the business basket and so on. The concerned news items sports, business, etc., are finally handed over to the respective desks. The most important news items of the day—national, international, sports, business etc., are submitted to the news editor who will then decide the treatment to be given to those items.

The news value of each and every news item needs to be ascertained. This job is performed by the chief sub-editor in-charges of different desks under the supervision and instructions of the news editor. The in-charge of the general desk will evaluate the national and international items particularly those which could be displayed on the front page and the continued page, the in-charge of the sports desk will decide the news value of the sports items and the in-charge of the business desk will weigh the news items on the business desk.

However, the news value must be ascertained in close coordination with the news editor. The chief subs must consult the news editor and seek his/her guidance at all levels. The news editor is also supposed to give necessary instructions to chief subs with regard to tasting the news value of news items. Based on their news value, the items are either selected or rejected.

The news editor plays a key role in the selection of news items. Besides news value, the other factors which play an important role in the selection of news items include the editorial policy of the newspaper and the space availability on the concerned page/pages.

Editing of Selected Items

Selected stories are edited on specific desks by the editorial staff posted there. The chief sub-editor in-charge either edits the copy himself/herself or assigns the editing job to his/her fellow senior sub-editor or sub-editor. Mostly editing is done in a coordinated manner where the chief sub is editing some copies and getting other copies edited by his/her junior colleagues.

In any case, the role of the chief sub-editor in-charge is very vital. On his/her desk, he/she is the final authority for the selection and editing of stories. At the stage of editing, he/she is supposed to decide the size and shape of the story, the size and shape of the headline as also the placement of the story on the page. He/she ensures that the work is being done as per his/her guidelines and instructions, and takes necessary steps for improvement.

We are not discussing in this chapter what all is included in the editing of stories. Editing is a difficult and complex exercise and we shall discuss it in detail in the following chapter.

Composing of Edited News Items

The edited stories are sent to the composing room for composing. Composing room is a place where news items are typeset by the compositors in the format used in that newspaper. A few decades ago, typesetting was being done manually with the help of metal types. The hand setting was replaced by mechanical devices of monotype and linotype. In huge monotype and linotype machines, the hot metal was being cast to give shape to letters.

The mono and line machines were replaced by Photo Typesetting (PTS) in 1980s and this brought transformation in printing technology from hot metal to cold metal. In 1990s, PTS was replaced by Desk Top Publishing (DTP) and this was regarded a revolution in printing technology.

In today's time, composing room is in fact the DTP room where number of computer terminals have been installed. The compositors here are the DTP operators who will type the matter written in the copy given to them. The edited matter is typed as per the instructions marked on the copy by the sub-editor. The instructions include the size and shape of the font, width of the typed matter depending on the column size in the newspaper, use of the light, bold or italic font, headline font and its size etc.

The matter is typed and set by using any of the DTP softwares available. After typesetting, the printout of the typed matter is taken with the help of a printer which is attached to the computer terminal. The print out and the edited copy is sent to the proof-reading section.

Proof-reading of Composed Matter

In the proof-reading section, the proof-readers read the typed matter on the printout and mark the desirable corrections. The main job of the proof-reader is to detect the mistakes committed by the DTP operator during typing, and for this he/she has to tally the typed matter with the original copy.

The proof-reader's extended job includes noticing any glaring mistakes committed by the reporter while writing the report and missed by the sub-editor while editing the copy. In the case of any such mistake, the proof-readers should be responsible enough to mark the corrections. Even if he/she is not sure of the commitment of the mistake, he/she must consult the sub-editor concerned for clearing his/her doubt.

Proof-reading as a job has been taken up in much detail in the following chapter and so we are not going into any further detail of proof-reading here in this chapter.

Layouting and Page-making/Pasting

The proof-read copy is sent back to the composing room/DTP room for corrections. After carrying out necessary corrections, the DTP operator will again take a printout which is then sent to the concerned desk.

If so warranted, the chief sub-editor in-charge of the desk will show the final printout to the news editor or the news coordinator who may further show it to the editor. However, for routine stories this is not done.

Having received all the final printouts of the news items scheduled for a page, the chief sub-editor will prepare the layout of the page. He/she can also get the layouting done by any of his/her junior colleagues on the desk.

The layout is sent to the makeup man/paster who prepares the page with the help of printouts as per the specification. The make-up man cuts the printouts with the help of a scissors and pastes them on the broadsheet page with the help of gum. The page is made in the supervision of the sub-editor concerned. The made-up page is sent to the production department for pre-press operations.

Teleprinters

There are so many equipments or tools required in a conventional news room but the most important among them is teleprinter. The teleprinter is a tele-communication device that helps in the transmission of news reports from one end to another. It is most prominently used by news agencies for transmitting their copies to newspaper organisations and other subscribers. It is also used by bureaus of newspapers for sending news reports to their head offices.

Teleprinter is a machine very similar to that of a typewriter. It makes the transmission of news possible without any delay. While for typing and despatching the copy an operator is required, the receiving of copy is an easy job. Transmission of copies through teleprinter is less expensive as compared to other devices used for the same purpose.

Technological advancement has affected the teleprinter too. Till 1980s, there used to be a big teleprinter machine but in 1990s it was replaced by an electronic machine, comparatively smaller in size. This new machine works at a high speed and gives good results.

The copies are printed on the paper coming out from the roll installed in the machine. In news room, the takes or copies are torn from the long sheet of paper. This is essential for compilation and editing of news reports.

The electronic teleprinter machine remains operative almost round-the-clock and mechanical faults erupt rarely. However, there are occasions when TP copies received in the news room are found mutilated due to technical faults. Also, the transmission may disrupt due to power failure.

The faults may be repaired either by the mechanic of the newspaper office or by the technician of the news agency. If the fault is somewhere in the underground cables, the telecom department has to be approached for repairing the line.

In case of mutilated or missed copies, the headquarter or the bureau of the concerned news agency may be requested to repeat the takes. For this, the number or slug of the copies/takes needs to be communicated to the news agency office.

Now-a-days, teleprinter is becoming more and more outdated. With the arrival of FAX, modern, computer, and internet the whole scenario of information technology has changed. Now, most of the bureaus and outstation offices of newspapers are equipped with FAX machines and internet. And most of the newspaper offices prefer computers over TP machines to get news agency services 'on-line'.

Modern News Room

The introduction of computer has changed the shape and working of news room. All manual operations have become mechanical which has brought substantial improvement in its functioning. The working has become smooth and fast and a quality change is noticed at every stage in the news room.

The modern news room is paperless as no hard copies are used. Right from receiving news reports to selection and editing of copies, everything is done on the computer. Since no hard copies are used, the question of composing of news items does not arise. No composing means no proof-reading. And when there are no hard copies, the pasting of page cannot take place. It is not even required as pages can be made on computer itself.

Computer with internet has brought 'on-line' working to the modern news room. Now, no teleprinters are required for sending or receiving news reports either between a bureau and the news room or between a news agency and the news room. Within the news room also, no copies are to be given or taken either between the news editor and the chief sub-editor or between the chief sub and the sub-editor.

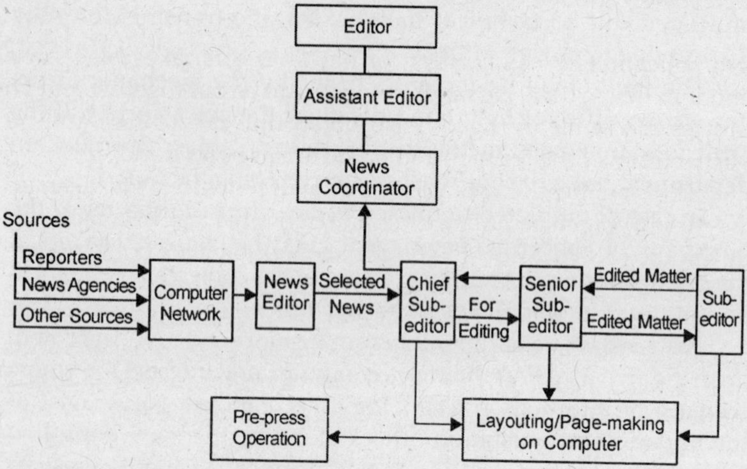

Modern News Room.

Here is an attempt to understand the working of modern news room in comparison to conventional news room.

Receiving News Reports

Today no underground cables are laid between the news agency office and the news room of a newspaper, since no teleprinters need to be installed. At present, news agencies make their services available directly on the internet and sitting in the news room you can always get an access to news reports if your newspaper has subscribed to the agency service.

The correspondents posted abroad or those in the bureau can send their reports to the news room with the help of the net. The reporters sitting in the city reporting room also file their reports directly on the computer terminal from where the reports can be picked by the local news desk for editing.

The offices of the newspaper in small cities and towns might not be equipped with computers. The reporters at such offices as also the stringers can use FAX for sending their reports. Today's news rooms are always equipped with FAX machines and receiving reports on FAX is not at all difficult.

Selection of News Reports

No collection or compilation of news reports takes place in a modern news room. No takes/copies are to be put together and no stories are to be arranged. Also no sorting takes place and no distribution of copies required on different news desks.

The classification or categorisation of news items is taken up by the news agencies themselves and hence the task becomes easy in the news room. The sub-editors on a desk need not bother where to find news of their requirement.

It is too easy to select the news items for the kitty of news agencies. The selected items are marked and downloaded to the file of the concerned desk. If this job is being done by the sub-editor, the chief-sub can easily monitor and supervise it.

Editing of Selected Items

Editing of selected items is done on-line in a modern news room. This means that editing takes place on the computer terminal itself and there is no need of taking a printout and thereafter editing the copy by pen. Editing is convenient on the computer as errors can easily be detected and spell check is available to the help of the sub-editor.

The edited copy is headlined by the sub-editor concerned. For headlining, the sub-editor has to type the matter himself/herself, has also to decide the font and the size and has to adjust the headline as per the size and projection of the story.

Composing and Proof-Reading of News Items

No composing of news items takes place in a modern news room as already a soft copy is available. This has made the composing room or the DTP section redundant in the news room.

Since, no composing is taking place, proof-reading becomes out of question. Thus, proof-reading section has been done away in a modern news room.

Layouting and Page-making

The computer terminals installed in the modern news room are equipped with DTP softwares which could help in layouting and page-making. Earlier, the newspapers were using the page-maker software but most of the newspapers now have switched over to quark express. Thus, the sub-editor today can easily manage not only with the layouting but page-making as well.

In a modern news room, there is no place for a make-up man or paster as all cutting and pasting take place on the computer terminal itself. With the help of software, the made-up pages today appear neat and sober. The design of pages has improved and even difficult things have become possible. This has resulted in enhancing the printing quality of today's newspapers.

Conclusively we can say that the modern news room has revolutionised the news room working. While the old institutions of composing room, proof-reading section and page-making section have vanished, too much load has been thrown on the sub-editors. But at the same time, the institution of sub-editors or copy editors has become too important. This also demands a lot of expertise, skill and efficiency on the part of sub-editors.

The networking of computers in the news room has made the working smooth and the job of the sub-editors convenient. The running away from one place to another in the news room has reduced and the activities appear more organised and streamlined. The coordination between the senior and junior editorial staff has also intensified and for everybody it has become a smooth sailing.

News Editor

The News Editor is one of the most important persons who plans a daily newspaper. His role in a newspaper office is supreme. In a daily newspaper, an active and enterprising news editor is always seen loaded. He/she is an intelligent person who knows how to give the newspaper a new look. He/she is responsible for a steady and continuous inflow of news in the news room.

Though most of the news supplied is a mechanical process covered by daily routine, but like all machinery of news gathering, the news editor is responsible for watching its smooth functioning. The news editor keeps a careful eye on the routine side of his/her news collection as also on the other side of his/her work on the news desks which calls for more imaginative approach.

The functions and responsibilities of a news editor can be discussed with the help of the following points:

(1) *Selection of News Stories*: An ideal news editor manages to get all the obvious stories into his paper with a good proportion of them as exclusives. While the selection of obvious stories is important, greater importance is attached to the original ones produced by his/her team of correspondents. His/her motivation and direction can result in the generation of many exclusive stories.

There are some such hard stories which no newspaper can afford to miss as these appear in a daily newspaper without exception. While these stories are important and have to be included, there are others called exclusive stories. Only an alert news editor can discover them from the large ocean of copies pouring in the news room during the day.

The scoops and investigative stories need to be given weightage by the news editor if he/she want to give a distinct identity to his/her newspaper and enhance its credibility and reputation. In this context, we can take the example of *The Indian Express* which is seen standing alone in the crowd of newspapers with its investigative stories.

The number of words received on the teleprinters or computers in the news room is so large that if each word is to be printed, the newspaper will have to run into hundreds of pages each morning. The news editor uses his/her discretion and imagination in reading the public mind and select the stories which have real news value and can be called important by his/her readers.

The news editor is also responsible for final scrutiny of important news stories submitted by different correspondents, stringers and outstation correspondents. He/she gives special attention to the facts and figures included in the write-ups and wherever he/she is in doubt, he/she takes pains to check-up their accuracy from the authentic source. Any slip on his/her part can land the newspaper in trouble.

(2) *Managing Affairs in News Room*: The hurry of daily routine makes heavy demands upon the managerial skills of the news editor and his/her decisions, specially when time is short, yet there has to be accuracy.

There are certain qualities that the news editor must possess. He/she must have an infinite amount of patience and a keen interest in varied kind of news. He/she must have a good general educational background with a fair amount of historical, political and economic knowledge. He/she must try to keep himself/herself informed on every important development in the world. He/she must enjoy reading the newspapers, the weeklies, and the magazines.

The news editor maintains a complete hold on the news room. He/she issues necessary instructions to the chief sub-editors and sub-editors and ensures that his/her decisions are carried. Besides professional working, he is also responsible for the administrative functioning of the news room. This includes making weekly duty chart, organising and channelising the work force, pulling up the errant staff and taking disciplinary action against them in case of need.

The responsibility of enforcing the rules and regulations in the news room lies on the news editor. The instructions normally come from the editor, sometimes might be directly from the management, and the news editor has to ensure that these instructions are honoured.

(3) *Monitoring the Reporting*: Usually there is an editorial meeting every morning which is presided over by the editor and is attended by the news editor, chief of bureau, chief reporter, photo editor and sometimes chief sub-editors. It begins with a post-mortem of the day's paper, discussing gains and losses, credit and blame. Then follow up action is decided on stories missed which are then assigned for the day. An examination of any creditable editing or blunders in headlines is also done. Then the participants of the editorial room return to their assigned tasks. The editor cautions a few sub-editors and tells the news editor to be on the look out for a major outbreak and to make preparations for it. Budget, train accidents, elections, police firing etc., need special instructions for the news room. Though the activity of the news room is editing, it also has to organise news collection.

During the first hour of the morning, the news editor sends appropriate instructions to state capitals or other cities if he/she needs special stories or photographs. He/she has a meeting with the chief photographer for commissioning pictures, he/she briefs individual special correspondents or their chiefs if he/she needs a special story, he/she speaks to the sports editor and sends messengers to bring reports and other documents for use in the news room. The most important and constant guideline for the newspaper is the paper's policy. When in doubt in a new situation, the news editor must get it cleared or make arrangements to tackle it.

The news editor has a direct hold on the city or local reporting. He/she must mark the diary and assign the reporters the coverage which need to be specially done and not to be left to news agencies. He/she must allot reporters the news stories which have cropped up and the enquiries which may not produce immediate results but which may be the preliminary step towards a first class report a few days later.

The news editor also asks the reporters to do follow-up stories wherever he/she finds a possibility. Going by Lord Northcliffe's dictum that a first class news will always stand up to one or two follow-up stories, he/she puts his/her reporters to the task for doing some good follow-ups.

Big stories often lead to several sub-stories which must be organised in a matter of minutes. The sole aim is to reach the reader before any other newspaper is out. Its display must be better, its coverage extensive and photos eloquent. This is not an easy task, but if well done the credit goes to the editor and his entire team.

(4) *Coordination with Other Departments*: The news editor maintains close cooperation with other departments particularly circulation, advertising and production. As head of the news room, he/she is considered representative of the editorial department for in-house coordination. For better coordination, he/she holds regular meetings with circulation manager, advertising manager and production manager.

The circulation people are always concerned for the number of pages in a newspaper, the contents and the thrust of the coverage, the target audience and the circulation figures. The circulation manager seeks the help of the news editor since an improved coverage of any particular segment of audience or a geographical region can help him in showing a better report as reflected in increased circulation.

There is always a tug of war between editorial and the advertising department as both try to grab more space on the pages of a newspaper. The advertising department has an upper hand in space allocation and the editorial department is virtually left to fill the vacant space on different pages. But the news editor can always protest against advertising overloading, can ask the advertising manager to shift some ad from one page to another, or can even ask him/her to increase the number of pages on a particular day so as to accommodate increased advertising and more rational distribution of advertisements on different pages.

Coordination with the production department is all the more necessary as the efficiency/inefficiency of the editorial staff has a direct bearing on the production activity. The production deadlines solely depend on the release timings of different pages in the news room. Any lapse in the news room is bound to disturb the production activity. The news editor has to make sure of the observance of deadlines in the news room and in case of any delay has to request the production people for necessary adjustments.

Chief Sub-editor

Chief sub-editor is in-charge of a news desk. He/she is considered a senior person on the copy desk and occupies an important position in the news room. The news editor relies the most on his/her chief sub-editors as they are the people who give the coverage and presentation of the newspaper the final shape.

The functions of the chief sub-editor can be discussed likewise.

(1) *Gate-keeping*: The primary and most important task of a chief sub-editor is gate-keeping. He/she is a person who examines every bit of information and decides what is really news. This calls for great skill and what we all say a sixth sense. It is also known as having nose for news.

Though the news editor or the editor may step in to suggest or recommend different treatment of news, chief sub's point of view is always taken seriously. He/she may suggest greater importance to some news items and ask that some other items be played down.

(2) *Selection of News Items*: Primarily, it is the chief sub-editor who is responsible for the selection of news on a particular desk. All the copies that go to the press pass through the chief sub-editor, who holds back a lot of material that is received, because to print all that pours into the news room is impossible.

Depending on the set-up of desks, the chief sub-editor in-charge of general desk distributes copies to different desks or individual sub-editors. Foreign items go to international desk, local stories go to the local desk, sports items to the sports desk and so on. No doubt, he/she is required to consult the news editor, while selecting the main stories of the day on the concerned desk.

(3) *Assigning Work to Subordinates*: Chief sub-editor performs the job of editing of main stories. He/she is assisted in the editing job by the sub-editors working on his/her desk. He/she marks the size of the heading, indicates if the story has to be cut or if some matter has to be added, shows if the news is independent, or it is a story related to a major story. He/she remembers who has handled what stories and distributes copies in a manner that certain stories go to a person who would have handled parent stories earlier. This helps in improving the quality of editing.

For example, a sub-editor who has been editing NITHARI village stories for quite some time will be given stories on that incident everyday for editing. Similarly, if the US has attacked Iraq and war is on, that sub-editor will be given Iraq related stories for editing who would have been handling Iraq related stories for some time. The sub-editor having done the stories earlier has a thorough background of the situation and treats the stories not as a fresh development but as continuation of a process already reported.

(4) *Monitoring and Page-making*: The chief sub-editor monitors and supervises the work on his/her desk. He/she is not only responsible for the selection and editing of stories but layouting and page-making as well. He/she may take up the job himself/herself or instruct any of the senior subs or sub-editors to do the same.

Senior Sub-editor

Senior sub-editor performs the basic function of editing the copy on his/her news desk. He/she is no different than a sub-editor except he/she is considered a more responsible person and comparatively senior in the editorial hierarchy. Normally a sub-editor rises to the position of senior sub-editor after investing four or five years in the profession.

In view of his/her seniority, the senior sub-editor can even be made in-charge of a news desk if no chief sub-editor is available to head that particular desk under normal circumstances also, the senior sub-editor acts as in-charge of a desk whenever, the chief sub-editor is enjoying his weekly off or has proceeded on leave.

Sub-editor

The person who performs the job of editing in the news room in the true sense of the term is sub-editor. The functioning in a daily newspaper revolves around him/her. In view of the nature of his/her job, he/she is a silent but expectedly the most efficient and alert worker in a daily.

The significant position of sub-editor has been described by many known/unknown scholars and editors in various ways. To look at their expressions:

- Sub-editor is 'backbone of a newspaper'.
- Sub-editor is called 'surgeon of news'.
- Sub-editor is an 'unknown soldier'.
- Sub-editor is a 'creative artist'.
  – Mr. R.D. Bloomfield of *Daily Express*, Britain.
- Sub-editor is 'blacksmith, architect and sculpture'.
  — K.P. Narayanan.
- Sub-editor is a 'brave person, who is always remembered'.
  – Rolland E. Woolsley.
- Sub-editor is an 'unsung hero'.
  – Stainly Walker.

Qualities of a Sub-editor

(1) *Command Over Language*: A sub-editor must have a good command over the language in which he/she is working. He/she must not only be able to express his/her views in an easy and communicable language but also to turn the diffused, round about and grammatical incorrect language of others into direct, simple and lucid wording without changing its meaning.

(2) *Self-confidence*: A sub-editor must possess enough self-confidence to perform the job he/she has been assigned. He/she should not hesitate in changing, correcting or improving bad copies.

(3) *Decision-making*: A good sub-editor must be a good decision-maker. He/she is required to make selection of news and on occasions even at the eleventh hour. He/she also takes decision regarding the positioning of news stories on different pages.

(4) *Restrain*: A sub-editor must be mature enough to shoulder the responsibility of editing. He must show restrain while handling sensitive news.

Duties and Functions of a Sub-editor

News material pours into media organisations from various quarters. It is written by persons with different perceptions and for different purposes. It comes from an experienced special correspondent, from a raw stringer, a public relations man who wants to project something on behalf of his/her client or a government department or it could be propaganda material from information departments of embassies.

Inevitably, this material is written in a variety of style, size and sophistication. Editing is the business of fixing what is news and later making it fit to print. It is a process of refining the received material so that the finished product serves the goals of the newspaper as well as the interest of the reader.

As thousands of words flow into a newspaper office, the copy taster or the chief sub-editor applies the criteria for news, accepting only what is genuinely news. The path is full of pitfalls and disguised traps which may trip an unwary newsman. Once the credentials of the copy are established, material is passed on to sub-editors with appropriate instructions regarding the size of the item, the heading to be given etc. The actual business of editing begins at the sub-editor's point and is appropriately known as subbing.

The functions of sub-editor can be discussed likewise:

(1) The sub-editor, apart from the chief sub's initial screening, takes a deeper look into the news story, evaluates it from many angles, international, national, regional and local. A local dignitary might have received an international award. Or sometimes, an international celebrity has a local connection, like Lutiyan who designed New Delhi, or President Clinton who visited a Rajasthan village.

An intelligent sub unearths this local connection. This makes the story more acceptable to not only the local population but also to a new generation which does not know who Lutiyan was. Same about Raman Subba Rao who came to India as manager of the visiting English cricket team 20 years ago. He had an Indian connection. He had relatives in Andhra Pradesh because his father was an Indian. His visit to small towns in Andhra Pradesh became relevant to *The Indian Express* and the item was relevant to *Hindu* editions coming from that state. Making the item relevant to the reader is one of the most important jobs of the sub-editor.

(2) The sub has also to see if the news he/she is editing is part of a bigger story that is appearing in the newspaper. He/she must edit it so as to fit it into the bigger framework. A minor plane mishap in which two or three persons would have died can be bracketed with a bigger disaster story, say a train crash where the toll is 100. A minister resigns, the reaction to his exit must be part of the resignation story.

(3) The most important thing in editing is organising the structure of the story. Identify the lead element first and tag to it the other elements in order of importance. Take the Indian plane hijack to Kandhar. The reaction story must always begin with India's reaction.

(4) The sub-editor is always conscious of the policies and philosophy of his/her newspaper. Facts are sacred, comment is free is true. But there is no newspaper in the world which does not reflect its policies in news items. This is subtly done by a process of choice and elimination, through playing down, or up certain items or some elements of the story, through suggestive headings and the order of priorities in the organisation of the news story. Can any Indian newspaper be neutral in its news coverage when there is a war between India and some other country. Therefore, to say that newspapers treat news as sacred is an exaggeration and it is the bias in the presentation of news which distinguishes one newspaper from the other.

(5) Editing involves a deep knowledge of the language in which the paper is published, of places, personalities and politics of the area of publication and a hundred other

sundry things. A sub has to know nearly everyone and everything. When people prominent at one time but now no longer so die, the sub has to know them. He/she must be some kind of a know-all, knowing enough to place a person or a place or an event. The rest is taken care of by the library or research section.

Editing means an almost involuntary commissioning of all these skills. It is the sculpting of a story, to make it relevant to the reader, to stories of similar nature in the paper and highlighting it according to its importance. The sub-editor should not only be a student of current affairs but also be familiar with history and economics specially. More important is the mastery over the language in which the newspaper is printed. This is essential for successful communication. Lack of knowledge of the medium can result in comic and sometimes tragic situations.

14

Editing the Copy

Whatever we as readers read in a newspaper and other periodicals is exactly not the same, which was written by the reporter. The copy written by a reporter passes through many changes—minor to major before it finally goes to print. The person who makes the copy worth publishing or worth reading is known as copy editor designated as sub-editor/senior sub/chief sub-editor in many Indian newspapers.

Editing is a multi-farious job which is very difficult to define. It includes selection of the copy, taking out grammatical corrections, improving the expression, checking the facts and figures, adjusting the length, deciding the display or placement, putting the headline and so many other things which we will discuss in this chapter.

Meaning of Editing

Editing can be defined in so many ways. It includes:

- Preparing a piece of writing for publication.
  - Normally a piece written by another person.
  - Publication may be a book, newspaper or other periodical (magazine).
- Doing the work of planning and directing the publication
  - *Planning* involves the whole work plan like—(1) *length* or size of the item, (2) *nature* of item, (3) *display* of item, (4) *time* taken in editing, (5) *process* of editing and (6) *arranging* for *tools* of editing.
  - *Directing* involves—(1) issuing necessary *instructions* to subordinate staff, (2) *monitoring* the work assigned

to them, (3) *interacting* with the production staff, (4) *controlling* the quality of publication.

- Preparing a cinema film, video film, tape recording, or any kind of audio video programme by putting together parts in a suitable sequence.
- Arranging data for computer processing—related to research/survey.

Scope of Editing

Scope means the reach and it can be discussed in two ways—

- The areas covered.
- The jobs performed.

Areas Covered

1. Newspapers
2. Magazines
3. Books
4. Any other print publication
5. Cinema films
6. Video films
7. Tape recording
8. Any kind of audio-video programme
9. Research
10. Public opinion survey.

Jobs Performed

1. Taking up grammatical corrections:
   (*a*) Usage
   (*b*) Spelling
   (*c*) Punctuations
   (*d*) Capitalisation.
2. Making the expression clear, avoiding ambiguity.
3. Checking the accuracy of facts to avoid distortions.
4. Paragraphing appropriate length of each para.
5. Sequencing:
   - Continuation of thought
   - Fluency in reading, listening, watching.

6. Making proper use of mechanical devices.
7. Administering the process of publications or any other production.
8. Maintaining the quality of the product.
9. Data compilation and doing necessary corrections.
10. Data processing for the purpose of analyses and drawing inferences.

Objectives of Editing

1. To present an item or piece in a summarised or concise form.
2. To enhance the clarity of item.
3. To increase the understanding or comprehension of the item.
4. To ensure coherence of thought in the news item.
5. To maintain consistency or continuity in the news coverage.
6. To make the item readable and interesting.
7. To put the item in a presentable manner—layout, design etc.
8. To ensure that the item is in good taste.

Tools of Editing

Mechanical Tools

Pen, pencil, computer, editing machines, etc.

Human Tools

Editor's

1. Education
2. Intelligence
3. Wisdom
4. Knowledge
5. Sensibility
6. Capability
7. Motivation
8. Social orientation
9. News or literary sense
10. Artistic sense.

Copy Selection and Copy Tasting

The first and the foremost job done in a newspaper is copy selection i.e., selection of the news story. The selection can be of both—hard copy as well as soft copy, depending upon the infrastructure and the working pattern in a newspaper. If the conventional teleprinters are installed in the news room, the copy editor has to select from the pool of hard copies of agency reports. Also in the case of correspondents filing handwritten or typed reports, selection will be that of the hard copies of correspondents' reports.

In the case of availability of wire service online, the copy editor will sit on his/her PC to select the stories he/she wishes to take on his/her page/pages. Since most of the newspapers in India have gone for computerisation, the correspondents also file their reports directly on their PCs. In such a case, the News Editor or City Editor/ Metro Editor will make a selection from among the soft copies. This is part of on-line or electronic editing that has been discussed later in this chapter.

In the case of hard copies, the selection of news stories is a long process. The peon in the news room will tear the copies from the long roll of paper installed in the teleprinter and you as in-charge of main desk have to do the job of sorting i.e., taking out useful copies and keeping them in baskets of different sections/ desks like sports, business etc. Thus, the selection of stories will be done by chief sub-editor/copy editor, in-charge of respective desks. The stories for the front page will be selected by the chief sub-editor/copy editor in-charge of the main desk.

In the case of soft copies, the respective in-charge of various desks have to select their stories on their PCs. They can be asked to forward their copies in a folder to the news editor or editor for their perusal or approval. The computerised selection and editing is obviously convenient and time-saving.

Copy tasting is an inseparable part of copy selection. Copy tasting means weighing a copy and tasting it on its news value. The parameters of news value are well defined and have been discussed in detail in the initial chapters of this book.

In fact, the first tasting of a copy has to be done at the time of selection. The selection will be made only when the copy editor in-charge finds the copy of some worth, otherwise he can throw the copy in the dustbin.

But the real tasting is done when the copy is taken up for editing. The copy editor will assess the news value of the story to finally decide its length or size, its composing—single column, double column, triple column or multi-column, its placement on a particular page—front page or inside page, its display or projection on the page whether as first lead, second lead, third lead, box item, anchor or bottomspread, the headline, the font size etc.

Administering the Editing Job

I. Preliminary Preparations

(A) Manual
- Sorting
- Classification
- Selection.

(B) Mechanical/Online
- Availability of machines/computer
- Proper networking
- Handling of mechanical devices.

II. Improving the Copy

(A) Taking up grammatical corrections
(*a*) Usage
(*b*) Spelling
(*c*) Punctuations
(*d*) Capitalisation
(*e*) Abbreviating
(*f*) Writing full form.

(B) Making the expression clear
(*a*) Avoiding ambiguity
(*b*) Avoiding verbosity
(*c*) Replacing weak verbs with strong verbs
(*d*) Rewriting
(*e*) Restructuring/arranging
(*f*) Sequencing
- Continuation of thought
- Fluency in reading, listening and watching

  - Shifting the stress
- (*g*) Deleting
- (*h*) Adding
- (*i*) Making the copy tighter.

(C) Checking the accuracy of facts
- (*a*) Ensuring the accuracy of all data/figures
- (*b*) Cross checking to avoid any distortions or ambiguity
- (*c*) Conducting preliminary research
- (*d*) Consultation with colleagues
- (*e*) Dropping the portions of doubt.

(D) Structuring the story
- (*a*) Deciding the size
  - Importance
  - Space availability
- (*b*) Paragraphing—appropriate length of each para
- (*c*) Clubbing—joining two stories
- (*d*) Breaking the story in two stories
- (*e*) Headlining
  - Type
  - Font size
  - Suitable words
  - Non-use of words
  - Active voice
  - Catchy.

(E) Taking care of technical details
- (*a*) Mentioning the source (Correspondent/News Agency)
- (*b*) Datelining
- (*c*) Marking italic
- (*d*) Marking bold
- (*e*) Drop letter
- (*f*) Marking box/column composing
- (*g*) Quoting reliable/authentic source.

III. *Preparing Copy for the Press*

(A) Observing the deadline
(B) Page-making
(C) Marking necessary instructions for production purposes
(D) Display
(E) Placement/Positioning

Steps in Editing Process

I. Read the story three times,
   - once for familiarisation,
   - second for editing, and
   - third for rechecking.

II. Finally, check for errors of spelling, grammar, punctuations etc.

III. To work upon the process of inverted pyramid, if the story is exceeding, then condense it.

IV. To check for the right lead and the presence of 5 Ws and one H.

Copy Tightening and Fine-tuning

Copy tightening means condensing the copy in view of the news value of the story. The news value changes with the time. The story might be getting a triple column in seven paragraphs in the city edition of the daily but it might be reduced to a single column in two paras in the late city edition if the news value of that story has diminished.

The news value of a story is a relative thing and an assessment has to be made in view of the news value of other stories. If more important stories need to be taken on the page, the copy editor might be compelled to further tighten some story.

In newspapers, unlike Indian satellite news channels, the concept followed is that no story should be given more space than what it deserves. Also it has to be edited in a manner that it carries right words with right expression. The copy should be free from verbosity, nothing unwanted will make the copy tight.

For fine-tuning, a story has to be re-checked, re-edited before it goes for print. Some of the following steps can be taken for re-checking:

- Accuracy
- Balance
- Right credibility
- Attribution to right source
- Fairness of the context
- Focus, clarity

- Objectivity
- Facts and figures
- Language
- Style.

Style Sheet: Its Importance in a Newspaper

- Style sheet is the document that prescribes editorial instructions for editorial staff in a newspaper or magazine.
- It details the guidelines which the editorial staff need to follow while undertaking editorial assignments or performing editorial responsibilities.
- It carries guidelines or instructions for both—sub-editors and reporters. It tells them the precautions which are to be taken while writing the copy or editing it.
- Every newspaper has its own style sheet which is prepared and developed by the Editor in consultation with senior editorial staff. This helps the newspaper in maintaining its own distinctive style.
- The basic purpose of style sheet is to ensure uniformity and harmony in the working of the editorial staff and in the overall quality of the newspaper.
- Style sheet guides the editorial staff whenever they are stuck somewhere, motivates them to improve the copy and produce a presentable newspaper which is complete and perfect in every respect.

A Model Style Sheet

Indian Institute of Mass Communication (IIMC) has developed a model style sheet for its students.

Style Sheet/Editorial Instructions for Editorial Staff in the Magazine/Newspaper Office

Note: It's not necessary that you or your editorial staff should follow all the instructions contained in this paper. However, you should pick and choose those areas that suit your needs or are necessary for your type of newspaper/magazine. But once decided, you yourself and your staff must follow all these editorial instructions strictly. This will give personality to your journal and prestige to it.

This style sheet is intended to be actively used in the production of the paper/journal by writers, sub-editors, reporters and correspondents not just to be looked through and laid aside.

So here they are:

Editorial Instructions

- Use the short word instead of the long: the concrete instead of the abstract; the simple instead of the complex.
- Use the active voice instead of the passive.
- The essence of the news story must be in the first paragraph: the subsequent paragraphs must be in the descending order of importance. The idea is that wherever the story is cut from the bottom, it should be complete. Follow Inverted Pyramid.
- Sentences should be short and crisp. Paragraphs should be short. Do not get involved in a sentence. Split long sentences into two or three. Do not alter the sense. A good rule to follow is that no paragraph should exceed six or seven lines in print, that is 40 to 50 words.
- Remember you are working to produce a bright magazine or newspaper, not a gazette. You must give the reader the essence of the news in easily understood terms. If you drive the reader to the dictionary, most probably he will drive you out of your job.

City Reports

City reports, including special correspondents' stories will not have a dateline (as in the case of "The Statesman" and " Patriot") the day will be mentioned in the first or second paragraph of the report.

All other reports will carry the dateline this way—Lucknow, January 15, March, April, May, June and July will not be shortened in the dateline. Write them fully. In the body of the reports, write the months fully but put the date after this, "January 15", if that is the paper's style.

City reports by our reporters will carry this byline—"By Our Special Correspondent" or "Our Staff Reporter." Names of staff writers will appear with special stories, city and other features. A special political story may also carry the name of the special correspondent concerned as the Editor may decide.

City reports from agencies (These will be kept down to a minimum) will carry the name of the agency at the end of the first or second para, thus "... reports PTI (or UNI)."

Other Reports

In all reports other than city, mention the news agency with the dateline; LUCKNOW, January, 15, (PTI) or in the end.

When reports from two or more agencies are combined, it will be (PTI, UNI), or (Reuter, AP).

In a dateline, avoid mention of the country except where it is absolutely essential—when a country has to be mentioned do not put it in brackets. Put it in commas, thus—"Britain, Jan. 15 (Reuter)..."

Towns: Mention the state in the first para of a report unless the town is well-known.

No abbreviations are allowed in the body of a report except where well-known organisations and companies are mentioned in capitals. For the United Nations and its agencies always use the UN, UNESCO. Unicef only with the "U" in capitals. Defence alliances like the Seato, Cento will be written thus. For Indian companies and organisations like the Tisco, only the first, letter will be in capitals. All other names, HAL, HMT, DVC—all caps, (No full stops to be used in such abbreviations).

The Government of India is "the Indian Government" when you refer to it in the international context; or it in the international context: or the Government. The Central Governments or the Centre in the national context.

Do not use "Mr." Nehru. Call him either the Prime Minister (not the Prime Minister of India) or Jawaharlal Nehru.

Say—the President, Mr. R. Venkataraman, or President Venkataraman.

Designations of ministers should come before their names—Finance Minister, S.B. Chavan. In further references to him, in the same report, only Mr. Chavan. If we are reporting what Mr. Chavan has said or done in any capacity other than as a Minister, we need not identify him so as the Finance Minister. "The Finance Minister told... a women's cookery meeting" is absurd. Mr. Chavan is enough in such a context.

Numerals

Write ten and numbers over ten in figures less than ten in words.

1,00,000 is one million—use the word in all such cases, like lakhs and crores. Lakh is better than putting it in figures, but where the fraction is less exact, figures should be used.

No sentence should start with figures.

Put commas in Indian money and weight figures in units of hundreds, thousands, lakhs. Put commas in units of thousands for figures of foreign money and weights.

When you refer to weight in pounds, change it into lb: lb is both singular and plural.

When you refer to the pound sterling (British currency) say £ (and the U.S. dollar $). (Try to remove quotes from news stories as far as possible. Quotes should be kept in only when they are really necessary, say when reporting a controversial statement of view. Normally, when you begin saying "Jawaharlal Nehru said..." much of what follows need not be in quotes. Quotes obstruct the clarity and the readability of a sentence.

Avoid

Avoid informed sources, circle, etc., in any report.

Kill sentences like this: "With regard to the discussion which took place at yesterday's meeting in reference to the position arising out of the present situation, the result, so far as the practical point of view is concerned, was of a purely negative character."

"Nothing came of yesterday's discussions" is enough.

The Editor does not wish to see these words in the news columns.

ANTICIPATED—Not to be used for "expect".

AS COMPARED WITH—often means "than".

AS A RESULT OF—is not to be used after a verb. Not "die as a result of"; death can be the result.

AS TO—never use "as to whether" "as to when." Use the ordinary proposition. "Whether" "when" should be enough.

AVOID—should not be used for "avert" when it is a question of the future. We avoid a traffic jam but avert or prevent a collision.

CATER—means a supply food.

CAVALCADE—means a procession of horsemen.

CENTRE ROUND—is a geometrical impossibility, say "circle round" or "centre in" or "converge upon."

TALK OUT—Need not be used to describe, define, indicate, or explain would do.

COMPARATIVELY and RELATIVELY are often unnecessary, "Few people saw the accident" not "comparatively few." Again, "comparatively cold weather" means "colder weather."

CONSIDER—should not be used for "think." It implies deliberation.

CONSIDERABLE—a feeble, over worded adjective, better left out.

DEAL WITH—a dreary verb. Find a better one.

DEFINITE and DEFINITELY often unnecessary; e.g. "a definite decision." All decisions are definite.

DECIMATE—means kill one in ten and nothing else. It is not a synonym for exterminate.

DUE TO—is not an equivalent of "because of" e.g., "he is confident due to what he hears." "Due" is an adjective and so there must be a noun somewhere to which it refers. "His absence was due to illness" or "he was absent due to illness."

ELIMINATE—should not be substituted for "destroy", "abolish" and such other words. ELIMINATE means remove at the outset before the real difficult is approached.

EX—is often attached to the wrong element of a compound phrase. A socialist ex-member has lost his seat and ex-socialist member has lost his principles.

EXPERIENCED—dreary VERB "rain is experienced" for "rain falls."

FOLLOWING—is a bad substitute for "after" or "in consequence of." A man dies after (not following) an accident.

GALORE—do not use it.

GAMBIT—is a technical term meaning sacrifice (in chess).

GOVERNMENT—is in singular: The Government has (is).

HE, SHE, IT: HIM, HER, IT, THEY, THEM—For these simple useful words, a needless repetition of the proper name or nouns is substituted.

INTERESTING—A feeble adjective, better left out.

INTERENCINE WAR—means war to the death, not necessarily civil war. In this connection always redundant; score it out.

LARGE—try not to substitute it for "big", "many", etc. Also remember no distance or number is large.

MAJOR—often wrongly used for "great" or "big".

METICULOUS—substitute "scrupulous" unless the notion of exactitude is essential.

NOSTALGIA—is not a sentimental regret for the past. It means homesickness.

OBLIVIOUS OF—means "forgetful of" not "ignorant of" or "not knowing that".

OCCUR—"happen" is often better.

OFFING—there is nothing in the offing. Don't put anything into it in your paper at least.

ONE—is much too often used after an adjective and is hardly ever necessary in that position, e.g. "The game was a keenly contested one." "The game was keenly contested" is much better. "The picture was a beautiful one, "—" The picture was beautiful," and so on.

ONUS—don't use in headlines. Onus means only responsibility; There is no onus of responsibility except for people who are irresponsible about words.

OPERATE and OPERATION—"operate" should be avoided as much as possible, and the appropriate verb substituted; and the noun "operations", it will be found, can often be left out as from "mining operations", "building operations" and the like.

OWING TO and DUE TO—often used wrongly, for "because of" or "by reason of".

PARTIALLY—should not be used far "partly".

PORTION—very often means only "part".

PER—if this Latin preposition is used, it should be followed by another Latin word—e.g., per annum: otherwise we ought to say "a year", "a pound", "a mile", etc.

PERCENTAGE—wrongly used when it is not a matter of percentage—e.g., "a large percentage of parents"—many parents. 50 per cent—Often better as half.

25 per cent—often better as quarter.

80 per cent—four-fifths.

But numbers like 19, 79, 98 per cent imply measurement, not to be accurately expressed otherwise.

PICK and PICK UP—A man "picks" a quarrel: he does not "pick up" one. He picks up something he has dropped or found—(fountain pen, stone, a corn). A taxi driver "picks up" a fare (passengers). A man is "picked" to lead, say, an expedition to Everest. A man is "picked out" at an identification parade.

PERSONNEL—is to be avoided. Say STAFF, or MEN, or CREW, or whatever word may be necessary.

POINT OF VIEW—VIEW POINT and STAND POINT—from "so-and-so's point of view", etc., should be avoided.

POSITION AND SITUATION—both very dull and much overworked, words meaning often nothing at all, as in "the coal position is unchanged."

POSSESSIVE CASE FOR PLACE NAMES should be avoided thus "Delhi water supply" not "Delhi's water supply".

PROBLEMS—everything can be turned into a "problem" which has to be "solved", whenever you see the "solution of the problem", or the problem to be "solved" suspect it as useless jargon.

PROTAGONIST—means "leading actor", not "Champion" or "active". There cannot be two protagonists in one play.

PURPOSES—often needlessly added, as in "land for development purposes." "Water for washing purposes."

QUALITY—is a noun, not an adjective; "good quality silk" is shopkeeper's jargon for "good silk" or "silk of good quality."

QUESTION OF WHETHER—prefer "question whether."

QUOTA—means an allotted number, and must not be used as in the following sentence: "The Moghul Gardens had its full quota of visitors." No number of visitors is assigned to the gardens.

QUOTATION MARKS—are often quite needless. If the writer is shy or ashamed of the word, let him find another; but if the word is part of the regular vocabulary of any branch of human activity though perhaps not familiar to all, it is fit to be used without quotas. When a word has not got into the language, quotes are desirable if the word must be used.

RANGING FROM—not to be used except when a range is possible as in "ranging from three to 12 years." But a crowd, the components of which range from priests to golf professionals is incorrectly so described.

RECEIVE—injuries can be received, but broken limbs: heads, legs, etc., ought not to be. For "he received or sustained a broken leg", say "his leg was broken" or "he had his leg broken."

RESPONSIBLE—persons bear responsibility, but not things. Thunderstorms are not "responsible" for damage; they cause it.

RESULT IN—is perhaps the laziest of all verbs. It should be suspect, and an equivalent should be ready. By a thoughtless writer, RESULTED IN can be made to do duty for all the verbs in the following sentence—"The outbreak of plague CAUSED many deaths; it CREATED alarm; it EVOKED public clamour; it LED

TO investigations; it BROUGHT about thoroughgoing reforms, etc." It too often happens that so-and-so is said to have resulted in so-and-so when the result is only an accident. A football match cannot be said to result in a player's broken leg; the result of the game is the score, though a player may have his leg broken.

SHAMBLES—means a slaughter house, not a scene of bloodless disorder.

SHOPKEEPERS' LANGUAGE is often bad: e.g., "quotation" should be "prince".

SITUATION—often meaningless when added to another noun, e.g., the food situation, the war situation, etc., etc. Another and more appropriate word can generally be found, e.g., the food supply, the course of the war.

SO FAR AS SO-AND-SO IS CONCERNED—this is nearly always used wrongly and is best avoided. A turn of the sentence sometimes will make it unnecessary; again, sometimes only an ordinary preposition is wanted. "The subject is unknown so far as astronomy is concerned" "is unknown to astronomy."

SUBSEQUENTLY—prefer "afterwards."

TAKE PLACE—a dull substitute for too many verbs which would import life to a sentence.

TERRIFIC and TREMENDOUS—too often used when no terror or fear is created.

THE ABOVE—is not adjectival, Use "the foregoing", or some other word as may be necessary word.

VERBS—are for use, and not for suppression: and the right verb is preferable to a verb which is not so right. For instance, it is better to say that "an exciting race was run" rather than "seen", because the race is more important than the fact that it was seen. Many nouns can be turned into verbs to the advantage of vividness, e.g., "he batted well, bowled cleverly, and fielded smartly is better than "his batting was good, his bowling clever, and his fielding smart."

VERY—"very" hardly ever strengthens an adjective, and often exaggerates. A very cold wind is in all probability only a cold wind; not Arctic. We might save two or three columns yearly by excluding "very". But in giving up "very" we must not turn to "most", or "highly" or similar words by way of compensation.

WEATHER—is not an adjective—"weather conditions" should be "weather."

WITNESS (Verb)—writers too often say that events are witnessed or seen when it is unnecessary to bring in spectators. Thus "an exciting race was witnessed" should be "an exciting race was run, or rowed."

WITH A VIEW TO (in order so)—"To" is usually enough.

WORLD—Avoid the "sports world", the "theatre world", the "fashion world".

Capital Letters

Capital: too many words are honoured with capital letters. Watch it. The following illustrations are not exhaustive; when you are in doubt ask for a ruling.

Ayurveda, unani, allopathy, homeopathy, all in the lower case.

Avoid the word High Command with reference to the Congress. (The High Command is the Congress Parliamentary Board).

"A" of the "Ambassador" in caps. In specific cases the British Ambassador, but the ambassador. Use the man's name after the first reference.

The Bill—when referring to a particular legislative Bill, the 'B' will be in caps.

Chairman of the Rajya Sabha and Legislative Councils—'C' in Caps (All other chairmen in lower case).

Congress—is the U.S. Congress. The Congress—is the Indian National Congress. When we talk about the U.S. Congress say U.S. Congress.

Delhi corporation is the Corporation.

The 'e' of "embassy" in l.c. except in specific cases as in "The US Embassy", but the "embassy was stoned."

Editor—"e" will be in l.c. except for the editor of the *Indian Express* or the *Free Press Journal*.

Government—'G' is in capital letter in "the Government of India." "The Government is considering...." but popular government, local government.

Ideologies—in lower case; communism, socialism.

Political parties: The Praja Socialist Party—and later references the party.

Leader of the House 'L' and 'H' in caps. Leader of the Opposition—'L' and 'O' in caps.

Central Budget—it will be the Budget. State and municipal budgets will be in lower case.

Minister—the 'M' in caps when giving it full and in l.c. after that. "The Indonesian Foreign Minister, Mr. ... expressed the hope that the Sino-Indian border dispute would be settled through negotiations. The minister was speaking...." But try to avoid referring to anybody as the minister. Use the man's name after clarifying his ministerial position.

National Development Council has N.D.C. in capital letters. In the body of the story, it can be referred to as the council (with the 'C' in l.c.)

'N' of the "note" in l.c. as in the Chinese note.

Names of all papers in Roman letters. The TELEGRAPH will be in caps and small caps.

The Opposition—'O' in caps (the Opposition leader).

The "p" in specific five-year Plans in caps, e.g., The first five-ear Plan; the third Plan. India's five-year plans.

Power as in "power blocs" in l.c.

The President of India has the 'p' in caps. All other presidents, including the Congress President, in lower case. The presidents of other states will be in caps.

'p' of the "press" in l.c. Legislative Council L and C in caps, but legislatures with 'L' in l.c.

'p' of the "press" in l.c. as in the press enjoyed vast powers than the press not.

Pradesh Congress committee only 'C' of the Congress in caps. But PCC, DCC, etc., all in caps.

Panchayat, bhoodan, municipality, etc., all in lower capital case.

This style sheet is, however, not the final word about instructions which should be ideally followed by the editorial staff in a newspaper. The IIMC style sheet reproduced above is simply a specimen as lot of things have changed in newspaper English and style since the time the above style sheet was developed.

Editorial Instructions for Improving the Copy

Almost every newspaper develops a style sheet so as to issue necessary instructions to its editorial staff. Following are some editorial instructions given in a newspaper with regard to use of words.

FOLLOWING—is a bad substitute for "after" or "in consequence of." A man dies after (not following) an accident.

GALORE—do not use it.

GAMBIT—is a technical term meaning sacrifice (in chess).

HE, SHE, IT; HIM, HER, IT; THEY, THEM—for these simple useful words, a needless repetition of the proper name or nouns is substituted.

INTERESTING—a feeble adjective, better left out.

INTERNECINE WAR—means war to the death, not necessarily civil war. In this connection always redundant; score it out.

LARGE—try not to substitute it for "big", "many" etc. Also remember no distance or number is large.

MAJOR—often wrongly used for "great" or "big".

METICULOUS—substitute "scrupulous" unless the notion of exactitude is essential.

NOSTALGIA—is not a sentimental regret for the past. It means homesickness.

OBLIVIOUS OF—means "forgetful of" not "ignorant of" or "not knowing that."

OCCUR—"HAPPEN" is often better.

ONE—is much too often used after an adjective and is hardly ever necessary in that position, e.g.

"The game was a keenly contested one." "The game was keenly contested" is much better. "The picture was a beautiful one",—"The picture was beautiful", and so on.

OPERATE AND OPERATION—"Operate" should be avoided as much as possible, and the appropriate verb substituted; and the noun "operations", it will be found, can often be left out as from "mining operations", "building operations" and the like.

PARTIALLY—should not be used for "partly".

PORTION—very often means only "part".

PER—if this Latin preposition is used it should be followed by another Latin work—e.g., per annum; otherwise we ought to say "a year", "a point", "a mile", etc.

PERCENTAGE—wrongly used when it is not a matter of percentage—e.g., "a large percentage of parents"—many parents.

50 per cent—often better as half.

25 per cent—quarter.

80 per cent—four-fifths.

But numbers like 19,79,98 per cent, imply measurement not to be accurately expressed otherwise.

Avoid		*Always Prefer*
sustained injuries	...	was hurt—got hurt
on the part of	...	by
abrasions and confusions	...	scratches and bruises
in spite of the fact that	...	although
commence, commencement	...	begin, beginning
he was in poor circumstances	...	he was poor
made good their escape	...	escaped
in the field of education	...	in education—or with education
or with education in order to	...	to
prior to, preparatory to	...	before
in the majority of instances	...	mostly
a large proportion of his experience was of a terrifying nature	...	he was terrified
the deceased, the defendant	...	prefer the man's name
in the neighbourhood of	...	near, almost
with the result that	...	so that
at the present time	...	now
in the event of	...	if
owing to the fact	...	because
continue to remain	...	stay
majority of	...	most of or nearly all
carry out	...	do
expensive	...	dear, costly
purchased	...	bought
is of the opinion	...	believes
assistance	...	help
the result so far achieved	...	the results
the capacity for implementation	...	what can be done
of the order of	...	about
under preparation	...	being prepared
from out of the	...	out of OR from
draw the attention of	...	remind
sufficient consideration	...	enough thought
inform, acquaint	...	tell
to continue in existence	...	to continue

(*Contd.*)

Avoid		*Always Prefer*
at present	...	now
at an early date	...	soon
proceed	...	go
residence	...	home
reside	...	live
under active consideration	...	being considered
in addition to with the	...	beside OR as well as
minimum delay	...	as soon as possible
a portion of	...	some
accommodation	...	seats, rooms
as at	...	on
as from	...	from
as to	...	often means about OR of
in many cases	...	often
was in collision with	...	collided with
implement	...	carry out, fulfil
likewise	...	similarly OR also
an entire absence of, a complete absence of	...	no, hardly
on account of the fact that, owing to the fact that	...	since, because
practically anterior to, prior to	...	almost, very nearly
previous to	...	before
category	...	kind, class, sort
in addition to	...	also

Your Story Sounds Better if you could Avoid These Clichéd Words/Phrases.....

	Cliché	*Alternatives*
1.	actively considering	is thinking of
2.	affirm	said
3.	as requested	EDIT OUT
4.	assert	said
5.	auspices	organised by
6.	bedlam	confusion
7.	bilateral relations	ties between the two countries

(*Contd.*)

	Cliché	*Alternatives*
8.	called upon	asked
9.	constituted	set up
10.	created mayhem	rioted
11.	deteriorated	worsened
12.	dignitaries	EDIT OUT
13.	elaborate security arrangements	tight security
14.	emphasised	pointed out/said
15.	employment opportunities	jobs
16.	engagements	schedule
17.	ex-gratia payment	compensation
18.	floral tributes	offered flowers/offered homage
19.	harmoniously	smoothly
20.	ill-fated	EDIT OUT
21.	inclement weather	bad weather
22.	increase	hike
23.	instituted	set up
24.	law and order situation	security situation
25.	making a submission	told the court/house
26.	massive combing operations	a search is on
27.	minimise	cut down
28.	miscreants	those involved/unknown persons
29.	pak-occupied	pakistan occupied
30.	pak-sponsored	pakistan sponsored
31.	Pandemonium	disorder/chaos
32.	peace and harmony	peace
33.	reaffirm	repeated
34.	reduction	slash/cut down
35.	reiterated	has again said
36.	relief and rescue operations	relief efforts/rescue efforts
37.	resource crunch	lack of funds
38.	solarium	compensation
39.	speaking on the occasion	EDIT OUT
40.	stressed	pointed out/said
41.	Supremo	leader
42.	tense but under control	peaceful though still tense
43.	untoward incident	violent incident
44.	various issues/the issue of	EDIT OUT

Copy Editing

The quality of writing and editing is a major area of concern in dailies as well as periodicals. This reinforces the vital role of the copy editor. Comparatively few stories, when they have been completed by the reporter, are perfect. Most writers need some careful checking and expert editing. After all, good editing helps make good writing.

The copy editor's main function is to read the story carefully, eliminate mistakes, improve the language and write the headline. As the last person to check the story before it is set in type, the copy editor must be the watchdog for the newspaper and something of a guardian for the reporter, although reporters often do not see it that way. Often reporters accuse copy editors of butchering stories and destroying creativity, while copy editors believe reporters need to be reminded that they do not have a licence to kill the English language. Despite their differences, reporters and copy editors have one thing in common: the readers of their newspaper.

Copy editing is one of the most important and painstaking jobs on a newspaper because the number of possible errors in a news story is great. Many of the most common ones that need to be corrected are a result of carelessness on the part of the reporter. Other errors are far more complicated. That is why a copy editor must have a commitment to accuracy, a knowledge of and respect for the English language; the ability to grasp not only what a story says, but also what it fails to say; and enough sense to know the difference between good, tight, creative editing and butchering.

The Copy Editor

1. *Checks the story for accuracy*: A careful and well-informed reader of the newspaper, the copy editor should know the background of most news events or where background information can be found. Doubtful statements should be checked automatically. In addition to familiarity with the city—its streets, buildings, leading citizens and officials—such standard references as the city directory, dictionary, atlas, encyclopaedia, clippings and other information

should be readily available. Personal knowledge and reference material help the copy editor catch most errors unless the error has to do with a fact that can be verified only on the scene or at the source of the story.

2. *Makes corrections of grammar*: Haste and carelessness on the part of the writer often result in grammatical errors. The copy editor makes certain that standards of good English are observed in all newspaper stories.
3. *Eliminates verbosity in newspaper copy*: Newspaper writing style should be lean and crisp. The copy editor, by killing one word or even a complete paragraph, can often make a dull, wooden story come alive.
4. *Eliminates libellous statements*: Potentially libelous statements should be toned down or eliminated. "When in doubt, leave it out" is an excellent guideline if a statement in a story could be interpreted as libellous. Of course, no copy editor can catch libellous statements resulting from erroneous reporting.
5. *Simplifies the story*: All confusing or ambiguous statements and all words that will not be understood by the lay person are eliminated. Technical terms or professional jargon is replaced or defined.
6. *Eliminates editorialised matter in news stories*: Editorial opinion should not be included in news stories. If a story is by-lined, however, a certain amount of editorial expression is sometimes permitted when the writer is relating a first-hand account.
7. *Checks all stories for adequacy*: If the reporter evidently has omitted certain essential facts, the copy editor often returns the story to the city desk. The story might be given back to the reporter or to a person on the rewrite desk for completion.
8. *Sometimes trims or shortens a story*: If the story is longer than the news editor desires, the copy editor might be instructed to cut it down to a certain length by eliminating the least essential paragraphs.
9. *Makes the story conform to the newspaper's style*: Each newspaper has certain rules covering optional forms of punctuation, abbreviation, capitalisation and spelling, and the copy editor sees that every story observes those rules.

10. *Attempts to polish and improve the story*: Generally, copy editors should not completely rewrite a reporter's story unless it is hopeless. However, they should try to transform every story into a smooth and lively account by inserting or deleting certain words and phrases or by rearranging paragraphs and sentences.
11. *Writes identifying labels and instructional notes*: For each story, certain codes, labels and instructions must be provided to expedite processing through the computer in the mechanical department. They include identifying labels for each story, codes for fonts and instructions for type face and size of the headlines to be used on the story. Some newspapers include the section and page number where the story will appear. Each paper, however, has its own set of codes and instructions. While they might be similar in a number of ways, each has its own particular way of handling stories edited by the copy editor.

At most newspapers, the copy editors work at computer terminals grouped in one section of the newsroom, still referred to as the "copy desk". Copy editors generally handle all stories for the paper. However, at larger newspapers some special sections such as "Sports" and "Lifestyles" may have their own copy desks. Some newspapers have been experimenting with assigning copy editors to other sections of the paper as well.

Electronic Editing

Computers dominate the newsroom of newspapers these days. Reporters write their stories on computer terminals and save copies there only. City editors and section editors use computer networking to call the story up from storage for review and preliminary editing. Copy editors use them for the final editing and headline writing.

The so-called front-end system will vary from newspaper to newspaper, depending on the particular equipment purchased. However, most computers are quite similar and once a reporter or copy editor has learned one system, using a different one requires very little adjustment.

Personal computers are considered a blessing by some copy

editors. Others still are not. There is no question that a computer is more flexible than a typewriter. A copy editor can perform the following functions on PC:

1. Delete characters, words, lines and paragraphs as well as move entire blocks of copy within a single story.
2. Delete the entire story.
3. Add new text at any location in the story being displayed on the computer screen.
4. Instruct the computerised typesetting machine how wide to set the copy and what font size and typeface to use for a particular story.
5. Write the headline for the story.

A wide range of electronic editing systems are available, and they are being refined and made more sophisticated every year. The functions that can be performed depend entirely on how sophisticated the equipment is. Some, for example, have split-screen capabilities that allow two stories to be shown at the same time should a copy editor want to compare or possibly combine the stories.

It is important to remember that the computer terminal is the central device for the system. The codes a reporter and copy editor must learn will vary from newspaper to newspaper, and the keyboard on the terminal may vary slightly. However, all systems are essentially the same.

A number of newspapers have named "systems editors" whose responsibility is to know everything about the particular computer equipment used in the newsroom and the editorial department. The systems editor serves as a trouble shooter for the editorial staff when glitches develop in the computer system.

Wire News

Most copy coming into newspaper offices from wire services like Press Trust of India (PTI) and United News of India (UNI) now is fed directly into the newspaper's computer, eliminating the need for clattering teletype machines and reams of paper copy. Copy editors retrieve the wire stories from the computer on their PCs and complete the editing and headline writing process there itself.

Generally speaking, newspapers follow the style set in the PTI stylebook, so wire stories may not require extensive editing to make them conform to the style in such matters as spelling, grammar, punctuation, use of titles and the like. However, a number of newspapers have their own style, which may differ from PTI or UNI style. In such cases, the copy editor follows the newspaper's style as enumerated in the style sheet.

Copy editors often have to shorten wire copy, rewrite stories to emphasise a local angle, or combine several wire stories into one.

It should be noted that some reporters do use PTI or UNI hard copy. A number of PTI or PIB features are also mailed to newspapers. This material generally is entered into the computer by a DTP operator and edited on the PC like other wire copies.

A few newspapers and some special publications, newsletters and journals are still edited by pen rather than on PC. For the convenience of persons who edit by pen, a set of standard copy editing symbols have been mentioned in this chapter.

Rewriting Stories

On many occasions, stories need to be rewritten by the reporter, if time allows, or by someone assigned "rewrite" duties by the city desk because the original has serious flaws in construction, organisation or perhaps tone. Occasionally, copy editors may be called on to rewrite a story. However, most newspapers prefer to have the reporter who wrote the original story do the rewrite after consulting his or her editor.

Thus, editing also includes rewriting which is taken up by copy editors in case of need. Mostly, newspapers have backup systems—the city or section desk and the copy desk. Many errors in news stories—such as those involving grammar, style, spelling and punctuation—can be corrected by a copy editor if they slip past the city or section editor. However, some errors are so serious they require that the story be rewritten. Whenever, the original writer of the story is not available and the story is being pushed because of an upcoming deadline, the story is turned over to another writer who is assigned rewrite duties. Those given such duty are among the newspaper's most experienced staff members and write with skill, grade and speed.

The Main Feature might not be Stressed in the Lead

The choice of the news hook of any story generally is a matter of opinion. Generally, the most important point of the story is obvious. The reporter's sense of news values is usually an excellent guide in selecting the facts to feature in the lead when there are several to choose from.

However, reporters sometimes overlook what is undoubtedly the outstanding feature and may bury it deep in the story. For example, suppose a reporter wrote a lead about a fire in a nursing home, using two or three paragraphs to describe the scene and mentioning for the first time in the fourth or fifth paragraph that 11 persons died in the fire. The story, or at least the lead, probably would be rewritten in most newspapers to emphasise the 11 deaths in the opening paragraph, if not the opening sentence.

The Story might be Poorly Organised

In some stories the main feature may be handled properly in the lead, but the body of the story may be jumbled and confusing. Or the reporter might not support the lead with information until five or six paragraphs into the story.

In other stories, it may be that the reporter jumps too quickly into a chronological account of the event, forgetting to summarise all features before relating details. Sometimes only a few paragraphs need to be changed, and this might be done by an editor or the copy desk by simply rearranging the paragraphs on the computer. But other times a completely new and rewritten version of the story might be needed.

The Story might be the Wrong Type

Deciding just how to handle a story properly can present a problem for some reporters. Obviously, some stories should be handled as a feature, but the reporter—especially one not accustomed to writing features—will ignore that approach and produce a lackluster hard news story.

At other times, the reporter may try to write a feature about an event that should be handled as straight news. The results often appear strained, and that may be obvious to the reader. The switch from straight news to feature or feature to straight news usually requires a complete rewriting of the story. Generally, a major rewrite can be avoided if the reporter discusses the story with the editor before starting to write it.

Rewriting should not be done capriciously, and the rewritten version of the story should always be better than the original. If the reporter cannot handle the rewrite, the person assigned to do it should first read the story carefully to get a clear picture of what the story is about and how it is organised.

During the rewriting process, the reporter should be consulted to make certain the new version is an accurate representation of what took place. Special care must be taken during the rewriting process not to make errors of fact. The person doing the rewriting should never assume anything and never guess. When in doubt, questions should be asked and facts checked. If a fact cannot be verified, it should not be used.

Persons assigned to rewrite and copy editors often are assigned to combine several stories into a single one. Although some try to blend the stories by moving paragraphs around, the most effective way to handle this type of assignment is simply to rewrite the facts from the stories into a single new one.

Preparing Copy

Most newspaper reporters write their stories on their personal computers and follow a set of guidelines for preparing their copy that have been developed for that particular newspaper in the form of style sheet. In many ways, there are quite similar to the instructions for preparing a piece of copy on a typewriter.

For those writers who still use typewriters or get the copy typed by the DTP operator, here is how your copy should be prepared:

1. Begin every story on a new sheet of paper.
2. Place your name at the upper left-hand corner of every page.
3. Write the guideline or slug for the story in the same line with your name or in the line below it. This line is a brief identification of the story, such as "fire" for a fire story or MCD for a report of MCD meeting.

4. Number every page at the top, following the slug.
5. On the first page, leave ample space between the slug and the first paragraph—from one-fourth to one-third of the page.
6. Leave margins of at least two cm on both sides.
7. Double-space all copy.
8. Type on one side of the paper only, or take the printout on one side only.
9. Indent five spaces to begin a paragraph.
10. Do not underline.
11. Four-line paragraphs are optimum.
12. Do not split a word at the end of a line.
13. Do not split sentences between pages, and avoid splitting paragraphs between pages.
14. Write "more" or draw a short down-pointed arrow in the center at the end of each page when the story continues on another page.
15. Place an end mark (# or 30) in the centre of the page at the end of the story.

Copyreading Symbols

Copy editors use a standard set of symbols that in most instances allow them to indicate changes without using words. Following is a list:

Symbol	*Definition*	*Example*
⊗ or ⊙	Period mark	He was there ⊗ He was there ⊙
^,	Comma	Therefore, he will...
∨'	Apostrophe	I'll let you know...
∨"	Quotation marks	I'll let you know...
≡ or ~	Make capital letter	later that monday...

(*Contd.*)

Symbol	*Definition*	*Example*
/	Make lowercase letter	Later in The day...
○	Abbreviate or spell out word or number	Doctor Kapoor said... Dr. Kapoor said... The 2 men were... The twelve men were...
⌊ or ⌋ or ¶	Start new paragraph	The end of the... The end of the... ¶The end of the...
no ¶	Do not make this a new paragraph	no ¶ The end of...
] or [	Indent on left or right	This symbol may be used on either side of the page or on both sides. If used on both sides, it indicates that the material should be centered.
|	Separate letters	Some of our students...
⌒	Bring letters together or close space	So me of the students... Some of the students...
Line from one word to the beginning of the following word.	Bring copy together or join paragraphs	Four men ~~who were found~~ were found adrift near...
(≡)	Delete letter, word, or phrase	Saailing on ... Sailing on the...

(*Contd.*)

Symbol	*Definition*	*Example*
(delete mark)	Delete letter, word, or phrase	Saailing on ... Sailing on ~~on~~ towards...
∧ Or ∧	Insert letter, word, or phrase	Sling on... Sailing on ∧ the...
(transpose mark)	Transpose letters, words, or phrases	Salling on... Sailing to on the...
Stet	Restore original text	Four ~~of the~~ men...
(wavy line)	Set in boldface text	New residents here...
———	Set in italics	The habeas corpus case

Correcting Copy

Although stories written on PCs are corrected electronically, it is still useful for reporters to learn the standard copy editing symbols. The following are examples of the symbols that are used universally whenever written material is corrected by hand.

Delete letters:

Two men werre in the car...

Delete word or words:

Two men were ~~were~~ in the car ~~behind us~~ with...

Transpose letters or words:

Tow men in were the car with...

Spell out or abbreviate (same symbol in both cases):

2 men were in the car with Mister Jones.

Insert word or words:

Two men in the car with Mr. Jones.

Capitalize letter:

two men were in the car with...

Make letter lowercase:

Two Men were in the car...

Period mark (either of two symbols):

To men were in the car with Mr Unnikrishnan

Separate letters with space:

Two men werein the car...

Bring letters together:

Two men we re in the car...

Restore copy that has been marked out:

Two men ~~were in the car~~ with Mr. Unnikrishnan.

In deleting copy or more than one line, mark out all the deleted material and draw a heavy line directly from the beginning to the end of the deleted material:

Located in the centre of the little island is a log cabin, ~~built perhaps 100 years ago through no one knows for sure and there is no way of finding out~~ and back of the cabin is the site of the old Indian village.

In correcting misspelled words that have only one or two letters wrong, mark out each misused letter and place the correct letter above it. If a word is badly misspelled, mark out the whole word and write it correctly above:

The bay walked ~~selinlty~~ into the room.

Proof-reading

Error-free newspapers simply do not exist. Despite the concentrated efforts of writers, editors and proof-readers, errors still appear in every issue of every newspaper.

Critics, both inside and outside the newspaper profession, insist that the advent of computerisation has resulted in the elimination of "backshop" proof-readers who generally make the final check on a story after it has been set in type and just before the pages are made up. There is some evidence that the critics may be right.

The object of proof-reading is to eliminate any errors made during the editing and typesetting process. Although proof-reading and copy editing are similar in that their chief purpose is to catch errors, the responsibility of the proof-reader is to see that the proof follows the original copy—that no words, sentences or paragraphs are jumbled or omitted—and that there are no typographical errors. However, proof-readers generally correct misspelled words, incorrect English and other blunders that might have slipped past reporters and copy editors.

Proof-readings involves the following:

(1) *Follow copy*: After the compositor has composed the matter, a proof of the copy is taken out, and passed on to the proof-reader. The proof-reader compares the proof with the manuscript/original copy, detects the mistakes in the proof copy and marks the corrections. This is known as 'follow copy'.

(2) *Correction of grammatical mistakes*: The proof-reader also corrects the mistakes in spellings, grammar and punctuation, etc., if these are lying in the manuscript. He also uses some prescribed terms to indicate capital letters, italics, paragraphs, divisions, etc.

(3) *Correction of editing mistakes*: The proof-reader also corrects those mistakes which are left in the original copy/manuscript due to some lapse on the part of the sub-editor. Thus, he contributes to the editing work.

(4) *Correction of factual mistakes*: In addition to the above, the proof-reader is expected to correct the factual mistakes as well. This can, however, be done only by a knowledgeable and aware proof-reader.

Advantages of Proof-reading

Proof-reading helps in the following:

- It ensures the publication of an error free material.
- It brings clarity and comprehension in the published material.

Basics of Proof-reading

There are two kinds of corrections made at the proof-reading stage.

- Signs of error.
- Signs of amendments.

Normally, both these signs are put together to mark the corrections. This is known as 'Tracking'. Since it is easy and convenient, most of the newspapers practice it. In this process, the proof-reader draws a line from the place of the error to the left or the right side space and put the required mark there.

Precautions Required in Proof-reading

1. If the proof-reader feels that there are not much errors in the copy and it is worth printing after minor corrections, he can mark on the top of the proof copy—"print off."
2. If he finds too much (mistakes or errors in the copy, he will mark necessary corrections but write on the top of the proof copy—"send another copy."
3. If the proof copy is illegible, he should send the copy back to the composing department with the remark—"send clean proof."
4. The proof copy lying on the table of the proof-reader is known as "Green proof."
5. After marking the corrections, the proof-reader should put his signature at the bottom of the copy.
6. Proof marks should be entered in the margins—never on the type itself/and invariably in the order in which the lines occur.
7. Proof marks should follow standard practice and be clear and unmistakable.
8. Only a clear proof gives full protection.
9. Corrections are made in the left hand margin for errors occurring in the left half of the column, and the right margin for errors in the right half of the column.
10. When more than one error is found in a single world, it is always sound practice to delete the entire word and substitute the complete correct word.
11. It is always safer to line out a figure such as a sum of money, and write the correct figure in the margin than to indicate the correction by means of transpositions marks or other symbols.

Using Proof-reading Symbols

Many proof-reading symbols are similar to copy editing symbols but there is an important difference in their use. The copy editor uses symbols within the body of the story, making changes at the point in the text at which the error occurs. The proof-reader places all of the proof-reading symbols in the margin of the proofs, indicating at which point changes are needed in the story. This is the process of correcting errors after the story is in type. The person correcting the mistakes need only scan the margins, not read the entire story word for word.

Two methods are used by proof-readers to indicate that corrections are needed:

1. The correction is noted in the margin directly to the right or left of the line in which the error appears, with an additional symbol within the line pointing out the error. The correction should appear in the margin closest to the error.

   # **A 33-year-old tribalwoman was accused of killing her husband...**

   If the line contains several errors, the correction symbols are placed in sequence and are separated by slanting lines.

   l.c./ **A 33-year-old tribal Woman was acsued of killing her husband...** tr

   The correction is noted in the margin with the correct symbol marking the point of error.

   A 33-year-old tribal woamn was accused of killing her husband... tr

Corrections requiring words and short phrases usually can be handled in the margin by either of the two methods just illustrated. However, if a complete line of copy has been omitted or jumbled, the proof-reader may mark "See copy" in the margin and return the original copy with the corrected proof. The proof-reader must indicate exactly where the words and phrases are to be changed or added. For example:

A 33-year-old tribal woman was accused of/her husband... killing I

the error is only a single letter, the correction can be made this way:

h **A 33-year-old tribal woman was accused of killing fer husband...**

As an additional duty, the proof-reader must check the method of dividing words between lines and correct the words that are not divided between syllables according to accepted usage. A dictionary is usually the best guide for this purpose. Split-word corrections are made as follows:

Suit filed in Sup-
p^ **reme Court.**

The more common proof-readers' symbols are given below:

Symbol	*Definition*	*Example*
X	A defective letter	Civil liberty is freedom from restraint by any law, save that which conduces in a greater or
∂	Delete material	less degree to the general welfare.
6⁊	Letter is inverted	To do what I will is natural liberty. To do what
#	Insert space	I will, consistently with equal rights of others, is
w.f.	Wrong font	civil liberty, the only liberty possible in a state of civilized society.
stet	Do not make change. Let copy stand as it is.	If I wish to act, in every instance, in accordance with my own un-restrained will, I am made to reflect that all
(;)	Insert semicolon	others may do the same in which case I shall meet
⌢	Close up space	with so many checks and

Symbol	Definition	Example
tr ∿	Transpose	obstructions to my own will my that liberty and hapipness will be far less (tr, tr)
^,	Insert comma	than if I, with the rest of the community^ were
⊙	Insert period	subject to the restraints of
¶	New paragraph	reasonable law: applying to all So it is, that proper and (⊙ ¶)
Cap ≡	Capital letter	adequate laws are essential to the well-being and good order of civil society. but (Cap)
l.c. /	Lowercase letter	legal restraint, for no other Reason than mere restraint, (l.c.)
Rom ++++	Use Roman type	is certainly unphilosophical, and ininherently wrong, because it amounts to a deprivation of *natural* (Rom)
Ital —	Use italics	liberty without any compensating benefits to (Ital) the public at large.
(:)	Inserted colon	James C. Carter, in his "Origin and Function of Law," says^ (:)
] or [	Move to right or left, as indicated	"It is the function] of government to define the limits or sphere
⌴ or ⌐ ¬	Move down or up, as indicated	in which the individual may act as a member of
eq# ˇˇ	Equalizing spacing	the social state, without at the same time encroaching upon the freedom (eq#)
^"	Insert quotation marks	of others.^
spell out ○	Spell out circled word	It follows, therefore, that to live under civil (gov.) is to (spell out)
^'	Insert apostrophe	surrender a portion of our natural liberty for the publics good, in order that that which

(Contd.)

Symbol	*Definition*	*Example*
↓	Push down slug that prints	remains to us may be the better safeguarded by the ↓ strong arm of the law. But
!/	Insert exclamation mark	liberty may be destroyed by law. The Romans furnish a concrete example^ The !/
b.f. ~~~	Use boldface type	prevailing ethos or national spirit of the Romans was law. b.f.
?/	Insert question mark	Did not law regulate everything^ A citizen could ?/ not fix a price upon his own
=/	Insert hyphen	goods. It was the oppression of law which cheap^ =/ ened the desire for life.

Journalistic Terms

Ad. Advertisement.

Add. Copy to be added to a story already written.

Advance. A preliminary story concerning a future event.

A.M. Morning paper.

Angle. The aspect emphasised in a story.

Art. All newspaper illustrations.

Assignment. Reporter's task.

Banner. A page-wide headline (also called "streamer").

Barline. A one-line headline.

Beat. The reporter's regular run.

Blind interview. Interview that does not give the name of the person interviewed.

Blurb. A short statement used to promote the sale of a new book or publication.

Body type. Small type in which most of the paper is set.

Box. An enclosure of line rules or borders.

Break. (1) The point at which a story is continued to another column or page; (2) as a verb, refers to the time a story is available for publication.

By-line. The author's name at the start of a story—"By John Smith."

C. and L.C. or clc. Capital and lowercase letters.

Canned copy. Publicity material.

Caps. Capital letters.

Caption. See Cutlines.

City editor. Person in charge of local news; also called "Metro editor" in some papers.

Clip. Newspaper clipping.

Col. Column.

Copy. All typewritten material.

Copy desk. Where stories are edited and headlines written.

Copy editor. One who edits and headlines news stories.

Correspondent. Out-of-town reporter.

Cover. To get the facts of a story.

Credit line. Line acknowledging source of a story or picture.

Crusade. Campaign of a newspaper for a certain reform.

Cub. A beginning reporter.

Cut. To reduce the length of a story.

Cutlines. Explanatory lines describing a picture or illustration, usually under the picture; also called "captions".

Dateline. Line at the beginning of a story that includes both date and place.

Deadline. The time all copy must be completed in order to make an edition.

Deck. Part of a multibank headline.

Desk. The copy desk.

Double truck. Two adjoining pages made as one.

Down style. A newspaper headline style calling for a minimum of capitalisation.

Dummy. Diagram of a page for use in making up a page.

Dump. Changing stored material from one computer unit to another.

Ear. Small box in the upper corners of the nameplate (flag).

Edition. Issue for one press run, as "Dak edition", "City edition", "Late city edition".

Editorialise. To include opinion of the writer in copy.

Embargo. A restriction, such as the precise date and time, placed on the release of news.

Filler. Short news or informational items used to fill small spaces in a page.

Flag. Name of paper appearing on first page.

Flash. A short message briefly summarising a news event.

Fold. Place where paper is folded.

Folio. Page or page number.

Follow or Follow-up. Story giving later developments of an event already written.

Follow copy. Instructions on copy to set story or word exactly as written, used often to indicate that word is purposely misspelled or that spelling is unorthodox.

Folo. Short for "follow".

Font. Type face of one size and style.

Fotog. Short for photographer.

Future file. File in which stories coming up at later date are kept.

Guideline. A slug line, giving title of the story for convenience of makeup editor and compositors.

Hammer. See Kicker.

Head. Short for "headline".

Headline schedule. All of the headline combinations used by a newspaper.

Hold for release. Instructions to hold copy until editor orders it printed.

Insert. Copy that is to be inserted in a story already sent to the compositor.

Itals. Italics.

Jump. To continue a story from one page to another.

Jump head. Headline above a continued story.

Jump lines. Lines such as "Continued on page 6" or "Continued from page 1" to identify a continued story.

Kicker. A short one-line head, sometimes underlined, either centered above or slightly to the left of main head, usually in type about one-half type size of main head; also called "hammer".

Kill. To delete or exclude copy.

Layout. (1) Diagram of page (see Dummy), showing where stories and ads are to be placed; (2) arrangement of pictures on picture page.

L.C. or lc. Lowercase type.

Lead (leed). The first paragraph of a news story.

Leg man. Reporter who gathers news, phoning it in instead of going to newspaper office to write it.

Library. Newspaper morgue or files of clippings, photographs, prepared obituaries, biographies, etc.

Localise. To emphasise the local angle in a story.

Log. City editor's assignment book.

Make-over. Rearrangement of stories on page to provide for new copy or to change the position of stories.

Makeup. Arranging stories, pictures, ads, etc., on a page.

Masthead. Editorial page heading that gives information about the newspaper.

More. Used at end of a page of copy to indicate story is continued on another page.

Mug shot. Head-and-shoulders photograph of an individual.

Must. Instructions that story must be used on that day without fail.

Nameplate. Name of paper on page 1 (also called "flag").

Newsprint. The grade of paper used in printing newspapers.

Obit. Obituary.

Offset printing. Process of printing that uses a rubber roller that takes the impression from a metal plate and transfers it to the paper.

Op-Ed. Page opposite the editorial page featuring comment, cartoons and other editorial matter.

Overline. Caption above a cut. Also another word for kicker.

Overset. Type in addition to that needed to fill a paper.

Pasteup. Method of making up a page for the camera in the offset process—pasting in proofs of headlines, body type, line drawings, etc.

Pix. Picture.

Plate. A stereotyped page of type, ready to lock in press.

Play up. To emphasise.

P.M. Afternoon paper.

Policy story. A story showing directly or indirectly the newspaper's stand on an issue.

Precede. Material to precede the copy already set in type.

Proof. An imprint of set type used in correcting errors.

Proof-reader. Person who reads proof to correct errors.

Puff. Editorialised, complimentary statements in a news story.

Q and A. Question-and-answer copy, printed verbatim.

Quad. A type character or space equal in width and height.

Query. Question on an event sent by a correspondent to a paper or by a paper to a correspondent.

Queue. Order of priority in scheduling; each schedule is known as a "queue".

Quote. Quotation.

Release. Instructions on the time to publish a story, as "Release after 3 p.m. Feb. 6."

Rewrite. (1) To write a story again to improve; (2) to write a story that already has been reported in a competing newspaper; (3) to write a story from facts given by another reporter (sometimes from a leg man over the telephone).

Run. A press run (edition).

Run in. Instructions to make a series of sentences, names, etc., into one paragraph, if each one of the series has been set-up as a separate short paragraph or line.

Runover. Part of a story that is continued on another page.

Sacred cow. News or promotional material that the publisher or editor demands be printed in a special manner.

Schedule. List of assignments.

Scoop. An exclusive story.

Slant. To emphasise a certain phase of a news event.

Slot. The place occupied by the head of the copy desk (on the inside of horseshoe-shaped desks). Slot man is also called "copy desk chief."

Slug. (1) The guideline at the beginning of the story, to make it easy to identify (see Guideline); (2) a strip of metal, less than type height and used to space between lines; (3) a line of type cast by the typesetting machine.

Sort. Arranging material in a specific sequence.

Squib. A brief story.

Stet. Restore text of copy that has been marked out. (This is a copy-readers' and proof-readers' sign.)

Streamer. Headline stretching completely across a page (also called "banner").

String. Newspaper clippings pasted together.

Subhead. Small, one-line headline in the body of a story.

System. The computer and computer programmes used in a news room.

Take. A section of a running story.

Terminal. Common name for PCs used by reporters and editors.

Thirty. The end of a story (numeral usually used).

Tie-back or Tie-in. That part of the story which reiterates past events to remind the reader or to give background for the latest developments.

Time copy. Copy that might be held over and used when needed.

Top heads. Headline at top of a column.

Trim. Reduce length of story.

U.C. and L.C. Uppercase and lowercase type.

15

Headlining

Every news story has a headline except what are called fillers which are used to fill gaps. Since the use of fillers has almost vanished after the arrival of DTP, every story deserves a good headline, whether it is a lead or an anchor piece. The good hard lead deserves a headline at least as good as its basic facts, otherwise it can be killed by a dull, vague headline and, it will not arouse readers interest. The story of less-obvious interest observes a good headline if only as a form of improvement.

Importance of Headlines

Headlines are like a label. They tells us what is inside the story. Earlier newspapers had no headlines at all but merely such indications as "Indo-US Agreement". "Nuclear Test" or "Public Occurrences." Perhaps words like "Public Occurrences" were being used to distinguish news items from articles or editorials.

Today an average Indian newspaper has 20 pages and is full of news from abroad, home and the city from where the newspaper is published and in such a situation, we cannot even think of a news item without a headline.

Defining Headlines

Headlines or heads as they are called are the display windows of newspaper. They have the kind of relationship with the news story as form has with content.

Headlines are any line or collection of lines of display type/font that precede and summarise a story. They are different from picture captions. Label headlines are not headlines in the strict sense of the term. They are called binders, like "Text of Agreement."

Headlines are an advertisement for the story. A good headline will reach out and attract the reader. When it is bright, informative, clear and accurate, the readers are hooked. They read on, that's the basic objective behind headlining.

Functions/Purpose of Headlines

What is the purpose of a headline? What function it performs? As has been mentioned above, early newspapers had no headlines. It is a later addition which the reader accepted for good reasons. With heavy industrialisation and consequent job opportunities, readers had lesser time to read in full their favourite newspapers. It was almost impossible for a reader to read completely all the news items carried by a newspaper before he/she left for his work station. With the introduction of headline system, the reader had the choice to read the news in full or limit to the headlines.

Basically, a good headline must do these things:

1. Tell the reader what the story is about;
2. Give this information in quick and easy form; and
3. Make the reader want to follow on to the story and 'read all about it.'

The basic purpose/functions of headlines can further be discussed likewise:

1. *Enticing the readers*: The main aim of a headline is to attract reader's attention. The reader must be lured to read the full text of the news on reading the headlines. When a reader glances through a page, he/she first looks at headlines and hence it is a challenge for headline writers to tell the story in a flash, in an artistic manner.
2. *Indexing/Grading*: Headlines grade the news symbolically by highlighting the importance or prominence given to certain stories. The headlines guide the readers to stories in which they are interested and steer them away from stories that are of marginal or no interest to them.
   Headlines help the reader to pick and choose. Now-a-days, newspapers have different pages for different sections—

Foreign/International, Local, States, Parliament, Sports, Business etc. Headline saves the reader's time. A reader can straightway take upto the cricket story he/she wants. This is called the indexing function of headlines.

3. *Gist of the Story*: Headlines summarise the story for the readers. They must convey, concise and accurate information for headline scanners (persons who limit their reading of current affairs and other news items to headlines only). Most of the readers have little time in the morning to settle down for reading the newspaper. So, headlines help them to choose from the mass of information newspapers provide.
4. *Visual Appeal*: Headlines help in making the newspapers more attractive. The headline in its various forms is essential to assembling eye-catching, yet coherent news pages. Headlines can add visual appeal to the newspaper. For this headlines need to be used as an element of layout—as part of the overall design.
5. *Identity of Newspapers*: Headlines give the newspaper character and stability. The consistent use of familiar headline structures gives the newspaper a relatively familiar and welcome personality. Through the choice of type families fonts, they give the newspaper a distinct identity.
6. *Seriousness of News*: Headlines give relative seriousness of the news as well. For example, italics and various decorative devices such as boxes, star, dashes and so on, indicate that a story is primarily included for some value other than the significance of the news it conveys.
7. *Sale Value*: Headlines help the newspaper to sell. The screamy headlines of tabloids contribute to a great extent in its roadside sale. You can always find catchy headlines on the cover of weeklies tempting you to buy the magazine from the sales outlet.

Characteristics of Headlines

The practice of headline writing varies from one newspaper to another but they have some common distinguishing characteristics. The three important characteristics of headlines are:

- Summariness
- Use of present tense
- Predetermined typographical style.

The characteristics of headlines can further be discussed likewise:

1. Headlines are sentences built around action verbs.
2. They are adjusted to predetermined space and typographical style.
3. They are skeletonised to save space. Omitting articles and other unnecessary encumbrances leaves room for more detail in restricted space headlines are allowed. Skeletonising contributes to a sense of urgency, the rationale being that no word should be wasted in getting the latest intelligence to the readers as quickly as possible.
4. They use the present tense to convey immediately and also to save space. Usually present tense forms of verbs are shorter than past tense forms.

Features of Headlines

What makes a good headline? VIDURA, the prestigious magazine on journalism and mass communication has attempted an answer to this.

The good headline:

- prefers active verb to passive verb
- prefers sentence form to label form
- deals with the most interesting part of the story
- can be understood at first reading
- uses language that is apt for the paper—and its readers
- places the most interesting words early
- is specific, rather than general
- avoids splitting words that belong together
- ends lines with a noun or verb: not preposition or article or adjective
- avoids accidental double-meaning
- avoids proliferation of nouns as adjectives
- makes the reader want to read on (to the story)

— omits the articles and auxiliaries, except where they are needed
— tries to avoid punctuation and abbreviation
— tries to avoid useless place names
— looks good
— contributes to design success.

Headline Types/Patterns/Trends

With an occasional exception, headlines were essentially label until the industrial revolution and the development of widespread reading habits of people.

In modern typography the trend is towards simplicity. This means shorter main heads and fewer, if any, secondary headlines. Some newspapers have eliminated decks completely. Others still use them. And some mix them up. Many newspapers have introduced a variety of headline techniques, often similar to those used in magazine make-up and even advertising.

1. *Cross Line/Bar Line*

This is a pattern of label headline. It consists of a single line centred over the body.

Example

Letter from Prime Minister

Here, nothing is said about the contents of the letter or its importance or to whom it has been written.

Example

Heavy bombing in Lebanon

Here also, we do not get much idea about the story.

Example

Parliament meets

Here, it is not clear which session of Parliament, when it has been convened and what is its significance.

Cross line headlines may be used in single column, double column or even spread to more columns.

On occasions even a single line can serve the purpose of headlining. For example—Winter session of Parliament begins.

2. *Double Cross Line*

Such headline consists of two lines centred over the body. This headline is mostly used in single column or double columns. Sometimes it may be used in three columns but never more than this number. Depending on its length, the line may be touching the edges of the column/columns or may be set in the midst of the column/columns.

Examples

S/c | Three MLAs
...quit Congress... |

D/c | Kesri fails to attend
Sonia's rally in Ranchi |

3. *Flush-Left*

The flush-left headline is the most common in modern newspaper typography because it is based on the instinctive pattern in which the reading eye moves from left to right. The following are several examples of flush-left headlines:

New Delhi sets record
with 1,500 murders

Ceasefire in Lebanon,
Deployment of UN
Peacekeeping Force soon

Muslim world
unites against
US presence
in Iraq

In flush-left, the lines remain aligned to the left of the column and run ragged on the right side. The structure gives more freedom in the variation of length.

Many newspapers, however, use a variation on the flush-left theme. These pattern are mentioned below.

4. *Inverted Pyramid*

This consists of a number of lines, mostly two or three lines, with each line shorter than the previous one, and centred. The resulting tapering structure makes the inverted pyramid.

Examples

Ambush by tribal
group kills 11
in Assam

Heated exchanges in
Parliament over
demolitions in
Capital

This is now used mostly for single-column headline though in the past it was used for two or three-column display. The character count in each line is meticulously reduced to give the inverted pyramid appearance.

5. *Drop/Stepped Lines*

This pattern consists of two or three lines, each approximately of the same length. The lines are symmetrically staggered like flight of steps. In the case of two lines, the first line is set flush to the left of the column and the second line is set flush-right.

Example

India goes to polls
ahead of schedule

In the case of three lines, the top one is flush left, the second line is indented one space and the third line is indented two and is flush right.

Examples

Steps soon to
curb budget
deficit: PM

Bush condemns
explosions in
Mumbai locals

6. *Inverted Stepped Lines*

This is opposite to stepped lines headline. In this pattern, the first line is spread to the whole width of the column/columns, the second line is shorter than the first and the third line is shorter than the second. Both the second and the third lines are flush-left. Thus, they form inverted steps.

Examples

Red alert sounded
in New Delhi
on R-Day

For war on dengue,
Vietnam offers a
few good tips

7. *Hanging Indentation*

This pattern carries two, three, or four lines, the first line is longer than other lines and flush left. Other lines are equal and are indented to an identical number of spaces at the left. Since the second and third lines start a little off left, it gives the impression that they are hanging on the first line.

Examples

Weak regulations, greed...
blamed as investors,
institutions lose out

Hizbollah, Lebanon agree
to ceasefire in...
war-torn areas...

8. *Flush-Right*

The above mentioned flush-left patterns are no doubt popular but on many occasions, we find departures from the practice. Flush-right is one such pattern. Here, all the lines are flush-right and run ragged on the left.

Examples

Indian Railways suffer
heavy losses due
to accidents

Maintenance for
illegitimate child
upheld

9. *Square Indentation*

In this pattern, the headline runs into three or four lines. All the lines remain equal and indented uniformly on left and right. The headline gives the impression of a square. This type of headline is more used in single column stories.

Examples

Parliament
calls for a
special meet

Kim Davy will
be back, but
conditions apply

10. *Roller/Waist Line*

In this pattern, the first and third lines are of equal length while the second line is shorter and centred. Thus, it creates the impression of roller—the cylinder-shaped object of wood, or waist of a person.

Examples

New Delhi Summit
crucial for
NAM countries

Bad loans of Japan
banks surpass
official estimates now

11. *Kicker/Overline/Shoulder Line*

Kicker is a subordinate line placed on top of the main headline. Use of kickers is a popular trend in many newspapers. The kicker normally is about one-third the width of the main headline and should be approximately one-half the type size/font size of the main head. A 60-point headline should have a 30-point kicker.

Kickers most often are used on multi-column headlines, though they can be used on one-column heads if they are kept short. With a kicker, the main head should not have more than two lines. The main head under a kicker should be indented several spaces but the kicker is set flush or centred over the main head. The combination of the kicker and the indention of the main head creates white space around the mass of type/letters in the head, and white space tends to attract the reader's eye.

Examples

Jeep scandal case
Accused found guilty
On six charges

Indo-US Nuclear Deal
No compromise on national interest,
PM reassures Parliament

<u>Fighting in Lebanon</u>
UN intervenes for ceasefire,
Deployment of peacekeepers

12. ***Reverse Kicker/Hammer***

The use of kicker has led to the introduction of a reverse kicker, also called a hammer. In this style, the headline writer simply reverses the size of the main head and the kicker. The reverse kicker usually is twice the size of the main headline and it is set flush left. It should be no wider than half of the headline space, which means it should not be attempted too often in two columns of space and never in one. The main head under a reverse kicker also is indented to help balance the area of white space at the right created by the kicker.

Examples

BARGAIN SOURCE
... Postal service auctions packages
that can't be delivered, returned

INTENSE FIGHT IN IRAQ
US forces working hard
to capture Saddam Hussain

Kickers and reverse kickers allow the headline writer to expand the ideas to be conveyed in the headlines. However, they are difficult to write and unless done with care can be pointless. Even when excellent kickers are written, the reader should be able to get an accurate message from the main headline alone.

13. ***Banner Headline***

This is merely an extended bar line to cover all the columns on the page. This type of headline is used on special occasions on the front page. The lead item on the front page is given this headline. It is the top headline under the masthead.

The use of this type of headline has considerably increased recently. Though the headline is spread in seven columns these days as most of the newspapers have reserved the extreme left column for news-in-brief. The type size/font size used in this headline is normally 60 pt and above.

Example

→ Earthquake hits Gujarat, 2000 dead
→ Indira Gandhi shot dead

14. *Skyline*

This pattern of headline is used under extraordinary circumstances. In this pattern, the masthead is pushed down and the headline is given over the masthead on top of the page.

This type of headline is mostly used in case of the death of some stalwart or the deceased number being too high. In any case, it is used once in few years.

Example

Latur quake claims 10,000

The Times of India

The variety of headlines used by newspapers is endless. Four and even five-line heads are showing up frequently. Headlines in all capital letters are used more often now than they were 20 years ago, even though they are considered more difficult to read than those written in capital and lower case letters.

Whatever has been mentioned in this chapter are only the patterns emerged over a period of time. There is no one who has said the last word on headlines. Limiting factor for headline writing is only the imagination apart from the style of the house.

The use of headline patterns varies from country to country and newspaper to newspaper. In Indian newspapers, the most commonly used patterns are various forms of flush-left, which include inverted pyramid and inverted stepped lines. Hanging indentation is generally used for box items. As compared to a daily, periodicals have more variety. In a magazine you can find most of the patterns talked about above if the editor is innovative and believes in experimentation.

Headline Schedule

Headlines can be either all caps and lower case. The choice will make a difference in the number of units of space in the headline, depending on the size of the type—the smaller the type, the more letters and spaces. The headline writer must compose a headline that will fit into that limited space allotted for the headline.

Although the headline count will vary from newspaper to newspaper depending on the type family used, the following is a typical schedule. For heads set in capital and small letters, use this unit count:

One-half Unit

Small i and I, capital I, numeral 1
Punctuation marks (except dash and question mark)
Spaces between words

One Unit

All small letters except i, l, m and w
All figures except 1
Dash and question mark

One and One-half Units

Small m and w
All capitals except M and W (and I, which 1/2)

Two Units

Capital M and W
For all-capital heads the following applies:

One-half Unit

I, numeral 1
Punctuation marks (except dash and question mark)

One Unit

All letters except I, M and W
All figures except 1

Spaces between words
Dash and question mark

One and One-half Units

M and W

To enable the headline writer to work swiftly, all newspapers provide headline schedules. The schedule is nothing but printed forms showing the varying sizes of types available and the number of units that will fit in any given number of columns. We have already discussed the head counts. Here is an example of headline schedule prescribed in a newspaper.

HEADS IN ALL CAPITAL LETTERS

M and W	2 units
I	½ unit
All Other Letters	1 unit

HEADS IN CAPITAL AND LOWER CASE LETTERS:

Capital M and W	2 units
Capital I	½ unit
All other Capital Letters	1½ units
Lower case m and w	1½ units
Lower case f, l, i, t, r	½ unit
All other Lower case Letters	1 unit

OTHER ELEMENTS IN CAPITAL AND LOWER CASE LETTERS

Symbols ($, % £)	1 unit
Punctuation	½ unit
Quotation Marks (Single in Headlines)	½ unit
Numeral 1	½ unit
Other Numerals	1 unit
Space between words	½ unit

Thus, if the headline schedule shows that the unit count of a No. 5 Headline (All-Cap, 2-line, 2-column) must be 18 to 21, and this headline will fit.

1½ 1½ 2 1½ 1½ 1½ 1½ ½ 1½ 1½ ½ 1½ 1½ 1½ 1½ = 21
R E M O V A L O F K T D C

2 1½ ½ 1½ 1½ 2 1½ 1½ 1½ 1½ 1½ = 16½
M D D E M A N D E D

The same headline in capital and lower case letters has a slightly different unit count total:

1½ 1 1½ 1 1 1 ½ ½ 1 ½ ½ 1½ 1½ 1½ 1½ = 16
R e m o v a l o f K T D C

2 ½ 1½ ½ 1½ 1 1½ 1 1 1 1 1 = 13
M D D e m a n d e d

This is an accepted method of counting in headlines but headline writers do not always follow the system carefully. Many writers count each letter and space as one unit. In many cases, such headlines will fit the space, but sometimes they must be rewritten because they are too long.

An able copy editor will have many synonyms filed away in his mind. They are among his principal tools. His headlines vocabulary includes many short words:

accord for agreement
balk for impede or halt
bar for prevent
bare for expose or reveal
bid for ask, invite, or request
blast for criticise strongly
body for committee or commission
cite for accuse, charge or enumerate
curb for limit or restrain
dip for decline or decrease
ex for former
fall for defeat
flay for criticise strongly
foil for thwart
hike for increase
hop for flight
job for appointment or position
kill for murder
mum for silent
O.K. for accept, adopt or approve
pact for agreement or contract
post for appointment or position
probe for investigate
put off for postponed
quit for resign
quiz for question
raze for destroy or wreck
Reds or **Russ** for Russians
rift for separation
row for argument or wrangle
rule for decision

scan for examine
score for criticise
seize for arrest
set for arrange or schedule
shift for transfer
slay for murder
spark for encourage
state for nominate, arrange, or schedule
tell for inform or reveal
tiff for argument or quarrel
try for attempt
up for increase
urge for advocate or propose
verdict for judgment
vie for compete
void for nullify
vow for pledge or promise

At the same time, the perceptive copy editor recognises the small shades of meaning. He will understand that there are differences in the degree of meaning. He will grasp the difference between "criticise" and "condemn". He will know that "state", "opine", "exhort", "expostulate", "pontificate" and "conclude" are not simply different ways of writing the word "say".

Types/Fonts and their Sizes

As discussed above, headline writers have certain constraints. The space available and the letters that will fit in a line are the primary limitations. That is why an 'enquiry' becomes a 'probe', a child becomes a 'kid', an attempt becomes a 'bid', agree becomes 'okay', request becomes 'plea', prohibition becomes 'ban' and so on and so forth.

A knowledge of types available and their appearance and impact when printed should be the basic strength of the copy editor. Every newspaper has at its disposal a variety of types to choose from, such as Cheltenham, Century, Caledonia, different varieties of Bodoni like Light, Roman, Italic, Bold, Bold Italic and an imaginative sub-editor uses the right one for a beautiful display. The sizes of types generally used in newspapers are:

A	A	A	A	A	A	A	A
5.5	6 pt.	7 pt.	8 pt.	10 pt.	15 pt.	18 pt.	24 pt.

A	A	A	A	A	A
30 pt.	36pt.	42 pt.	48 pt.	60 pt.	72 pt.

The type books available with the newspapers can be used by the sub-editors to select types suitable for the story in hand.

With the entry of computer in the news-room hot metal types and the above described point systems and the type family have gradually lost their importance. Newspapers passed though Photo Type Setting (PTS) to finally reach at Desk Top Publishing (DTP). And in this age of computer editing and offset printing, the complex type size and counting system has been replaced by smooth and convenient font system.

In DTP, manual counting has been replaced by mechanical operations where computer provides a helping tool in the selection of font and its size. The measurements are available on the computer and the copy editor needs not to worry for them.

Using DTP softwares, you can even 'squeeze' the headlines by very slightly reducing the headline's point size. The squeezing is also possible by reducing space between letters and words, or lines, or by pressing the line vertically.

Writing Headlines

Many believe that writing headlines is easy. All you have to do is make them accurate, fair, clear, precise, punchy, thoughtful, inviting, relevant, urgent and readable and do it in half a dozen words, often in three or four minutes. Obviously, that's stretching the point. The truth is, headline writing is often the most difficult and demanding part of a copy editor's job. What a reporter said in 30 words or more in a lead, a headline writer might have to say in six words or less. But it can be done. It requires skill and a command of the language. Most of all, it requires imagination.

If you have understood the basic purpose of headlines, the task becomes easy. However, the job must be done clearly and intelligently in a small amount of space, within the additional restrictions placed on the headline writer by the required type size/font size.

Generally, the headline on most straight-news stories should be drawn from the lead. The headline should be the lead translated into sharp, punchy, dramatic words. Material from the body of the story is used in the secondary head, or deck, if the newspaper's headline style permits decks. If a headline writer has to go into the body of the story for the headline on a straight-news story, chances are the lead needs to be rewritten.

Some headline writers are intimidated by the limited space they have to work with. They tend to think first of something to fit the space rather than the idea they want to convey. As a result, their headlines often are dull, little more than vague labels.

Advice on how to write good headlines abounds. Some suggest that you get what you want to say down on paper first without worrying about headline then refine and polish those words. One copy editor suggests: Write the headline, then imagine swinging open a barroom door and shouting it. Depending on many heads turn, either set it or forget it.

A good headline does not require translation. The reader should understand it immediately, unlike the following example (that was actually used):

BN VP at BS

It translates "Boys Nation Vice-President at Boys State." Although that is an extreme example, many headlines are almost as difficult to grasp because they are vague, such as:

Trip Needs Volunteers

What trip? Where? How many volunteers? Actually, it referred to a trade mission to Malaysia. But you'd never know from that vague headline. Some copy editors read their headlines aloud to make certain they "read" smoothly. If the copy editor stumbles over his or her own headline, then the reader will almost certainly do the same.

Reading the following headlines aloud could have spared the writer and the newspaper some embarrassment. They are from Columbia Journalism Review's "The Lower Case" page:

Lawmaker
backs train
through Iowa

Another Body Found Missing

Guidelines for Writing Headlines

Most newspapers have a list of guidelines for writing headlines. Although they often are quite similar, some vary according to the particular views of the editor and copy desk chief. Here are the rules followed by a prominent newspaper:

1. Make the headline say something; don't write non-heads.
2. No headline may start with a verb.
3. Conjunctions, prepositions and modifiers in headlines may not be placed at the end of the line.
4. Commas or semi-colons may be used at the end of a line in multi-deck heads. Single-line heads may have commas or semi-colons, but they should be used sparingly.
5. Do not pile modifiers one after another.
6. Do not split the parts of verbs from one line to another.
7. Do not use pronouns alone and unidentified.
8. It is NOT always necessary to use a verb in a headline. But when you do not, the omission must help make a better headline.
9. Do not use "hit" or "flay" or "rap" or "score" or "blast" or anything in that category of verbs, unless the word means precisely what it says.
10. Fill out the lines in your head.

The paper then tells its copy editors to "break the rules" if it will help make a better headline. Substance outranks form. Copy editors are given considerably more freedom in writing straight-news heads now than they were in the past.

Copy editors have always had greater freedom in writing headlines for feature stories than they had for straight-news stories. That doesn't mean they can take an "anything goes" approach. After all, the feature head should reflect the tone of the story, and it should not necessarily summarise the facts as a straight-news head would. Moreover, feature heads should not divulge a story's surprise ending or unusual twist.

Selecting the Headline

The practice will vary from newspaper to newspaper, but the responsibility for evaluating news stories and deciding what size headline should be written for each is the job of the news editor, which he often assigns to copy editors.

How does an editor determine what headline should go on a story? In general, the importance of the story or the local interest in it dictates the size of the headline on the story. The position the story will occupy on the page also influences the headline size. Longer stories frequently get larger headlines, partly out of reader interest, but also because a large head on a long story generally makes the page more attractive. Stories compete with each other, not only for length and headline size but also for position in the paper. A short news story may be the most significant that given day and may end up with a large headline, prominently displayed on the page. So length does not automatically ensure a large headline.

News is inconsistent. A fairly interesting story may get a rather large headline on a day when outstanding stories are scarce. On other days, several leading stories might be of equal importance, but the editor cannot use the same type and size of headline for all of them. In such a case, the editor attempts to make all of them approximately equal but uses a variety of typefaces and headline combinations to signify to the reader their relative importance.

The importance of the story should always dictate the approximate size of the headline. Although planning is necessary, stories should not be greatly overplayed or underplayed to meet space requirements or a predetermined page design.

Here are a few suggestions for selecting heads:

- Nearly every page will need a few large heads with one more dominant than the others.
- Double-column and other multicolumn heads improve the appearance of the newspaper's pages.
- Both Roman and Italic typefaces are available and should be used. Italic type is generally used to break the monotony of the darker Roman type often used for headlines on hard-news stories.

Some Rules of Headline Writing

Writing appropriate headlines to the news stories, features or articles is a difficult job performed by copy editors. The sub-editor who can bring a wooden story to life with a few strokes on the key board of the computer is prized everywhere, but he/she must do more. He/she will be more sought after if he/she has the expertise to compose headlines that crackle and lure the reader immediately into the mood of the story.

There are certain rules which a headline writer must follow. These could be enumerated likewise.

Dos

1. Make the headline based on the first few lines or the first paragraph of the story.
2. Try to put important facts in the headline.
3. Write the headline in historical present tense.

Correct	*Incorrect*
VIPS team wins debate	VIPs team won debate

4. Use the sentence form with a verb.
5. Use an action verb.
6. Share at least one verb in one deck

Poor	*Better*
Faculty codifies absence rules	Regulations for absentees

7. Prefer active voice over passive voice

Active	*Passive*
Student Council gives first party	First party given by student council

8. Headlines need to be specific.

Poor	*Better*
Ramdoss emphasises new A—Energy use	Ramdoss calls A—Energy new key to good health

9. Prefer infinitive form than proper time and date while using future tense.

Poor	*Better*
Mayor speaks Sunday on taxes	Mayor to speak on tax hike

10. Use only familiar and well-known abbreviations and acronyms.
11. Capitalise the first letter of the first word in the beginning of the headline and all other principal words.
12. Use numerals or spell out as convenient for spacing and easy reading, but spell out 'one'.

Don'ts

1. Avoid vagueness and ambiguity in headlines.
   No unnecessary word should be added but at the same time the headline writer should not leave out a word which will confuse the readers.

   Example

   US planes attack cities

   This headline is vague as it does not mention cities in which country. The US is facing a lot of problems in Afghanistan and Iraq and this is bound to confuse the readers about the location. It should have been something like—

   US planes attack
   Iraqi cities

2. Don't use articles, prefixes or conjunctions.
   Inclusion of *a, an* and *the* create obstruction and their removal adds speed to the headline.

   Example

   Injunction against strike vacated

   Wages revised for newspaper staff

3. Don't use question mark.
   The repeated use of question marks can shake the confidence of readers in the newspaper. It can, however, be used sparingly in case of dire need.

   Example

   Arjun Singh asked to resign?

   This means that confirmed authoritative report has not come. Thus, by putting a question mark the newspaper can reduce the risk of losing credibility.

4. Don't repeat words i.e., using the same word thrice in a headline.
5. Avoid structural repetition.
6. Don't separate adjective from the noun.
7. Don't break a verb in two lines.
8. Don't separate proper nouns between lines.
9. Don't end lines with prepositions (thus separating the preposition and its object).

10. Don't separate an objective and the word it modifies between lines.
11. Don't use 'and', instead use a comma.
12. Avoid verb in the beginning of the headline.
13. Avoid using names of odd places in the headline.
14. Don't be flippant.
15. Avoid editorialising the headline.

Poor	*Better*
Local dairymen seeking fair milk price share	Local dairymen seeking 'fair' milk price share

The above-mentioned rules are general guidelines for making headlines. It is not always possible to rigidly conform to these rules for various reasons. We can find newspapers not following many of the above-mentioned rules if they do not adhere to their style or the breaking/overlooking these rules could help in making a good imaginative headline.

Verbs in Headlines

Verbs occupy the most important place in headlines since no headline is possible without a verb. While creative use of a verb can shape, use of a wrong verb can spoil the headline. Moreover, a verb used in a headline has to be in conformity to grammatical rules.

Lot has been said about verb in the above-mentioned rules of headline writing. It is the verb which converts a label into a headline. Here, we are trying to discuss verb in a headline to a greater length so- as to help the headline writers.

The verb is vital—but it need not be expressed. It can be understood. The verb "is" is understood in this good headline: "Space-ship with Indian launched." All forms of the verb "to be" should be deliberately omitted in the headline. "Is" and "are" should not be used, unless for clearness. A headline is much more emphatic without them and can be understood. For instance, heading "20 students arrested" rather than "20 students are arrested", reads better.

Make your headline verb active if you can. This means the verb should have a present tense or future; the past tense is dead for headlines, though it is sometimes necessary. For instance, "Mr. so and so dies" is better than "Mr. so and so has died."

When writing headlines ensure only present tense is used. Suppose there was an accident the previous day. The tendency is to use past tense to be correct time-wise.

48 Died in Stampede
At Kumbha Mela

As the stampede occurred the previous night the sub-editor is technically correct in writing the headline as above. But in the process he has taken away the excitement of the story. The reader should be given a sense of active presence at the spot when the incident really occurred. So it is more appropriate to write.

48 Die in Stampede
At Kumbha Mela

There is yet one further accepted rule about the verb in the headline. Better headlines are written in the active voice of the verb, rather than the passive. In other words, prefer to use headlines with somebody saying something or doing something, rather than having it told to them, or done to them. Compare: "RAJIV URGES MORE AID TO ASIA" with the same headline in the passive voice, "MORE AID FOR ASIA URGED BY RAJIV."

Active voice increases the urgency of headline rather than passive voice:

Elephant Crushes
Mahout To Death

is better than

Mahout Is Crushed To death
By Elephant

Words in Headlines

Headline words must be short, striking words. English has many of these good words. Given accuracy, always prefer the short word. In English the headline writer will always keep a mental note of short alternative words. He will use *banned* for prohibited; *talks* for negotiations; *lose* for defeated; *changes* for amendments; *neutral* for uncommitted; *urges* for advocates. There are hundreds more. Make it a rule never to use polysyllabic words in a headline if you can. The effect will be striking. This does not mean doing violence to the contents, of course. The headline must stay strictly true to the facts of the story. Here are some examples, in all of which the preferred alternative would have fitted the available space.

Here is a thick head: "Rehabilitating Nepal Economically." The story was about increased water and power to yield increased crops. That should have been the headline point: *"More water and power for Nepal."* Here is another dud: *"Phenomenal progress by L.I.C."* Try and say, "Phenomenal"—and that is a good test of headline. Does it trip lightly off the tongue? Say it aloud. If it trips you up, try writing another. In this case, a far better headline would have been; *"Many more insure lives."*

Again: *"More Commodities to be Exchanged"* is too long in its wording. "Goods" is better than commodities. Avoid loading a headline with unnecessary words. Not just unnecessary parts of the verb "to be"—but things like this: "130 Feared Dead in Boat Tragedy." Here it's not necessary to say "tragedy". The death roll tells its own story.

Avoid euphemism. Don't say "car mishap on road" when you mean there has been a crash. Never write a venue into a headline. Only the significant must go in the headline.

Principles of Headline Writing

Good headline writing is an art practised under the pressure of deadlines. Every headlines writer will develop individual techniques, but a study of headlines, good and bad, will show that there are some general principles usually practiced in all newspapers.

1. The headline should tell the story's essentials and tell them accurately. It should be based on the lead in the case of news stories and should give as many of the five W's as necessary, playing up the proper W. Each head should be a complete sentence with unnecessary words omitted.

Poor	*Better*
Man Sustains A Fatal Injury	Guard Killed In Gun Fight

2. The symmetry of line length required by the style of a particular headline should be achieved. The lines must not appear to be too crowded with type or too empty. They should not appear grossly unbalanced:

Poor	*Better*
Nagendra to Head CBI Office	Nagendra Named CBI Director
Poor	*Better*
Mayor Urges Crackdown	Mayor Urges Crackdown

3. If a headline is made up of several different forms, each part should be a full statement and should stand alone:

Poor	*Better*
Huge Oil Slick 100 Km Long	Huge Oil Slick Threat to Coast
Reported by Coast Guard	Covers 100 Km Reports Guard

4. A thought should not be repeated. Each deck or bank should advance the story with additional information:

Poor	*Better*
Heavy Truck Bill Postponed	Heavy Truck Bill Postponed
Truck Weight Increase Sought	Public Hearings Planned for Fall

5. Involved, confusing or ambiguous heads should be avoided:

Poor	*Better*
Aged Fight Pension Plans for Future	Aged Group Fights New Pension Plans

6. Feature stories should have feature headlines:

Poor	*Better*
Horse Is Favourite at President House	Horse riding at the President House
Poor	*Better*
Patrons Borrow Free Umbrellas Permanently	Free Umbrella Idea Picked up Quickly

7. Each headline should contain a verb in order not to appear as a mere label. The verb should be in the first line if possible, but the headline should not start with a verb:

Poor	*Better*
Metro Mall	Metro Mall Opens
—	—
Urge Milk Fund For City's Needy	Milk Fund Urged For City's Needy

8. Headlines generally should be written in the active voice, not the passive, for impact:

Poor	*Better*
Strikers Warned by Minister	Minister Warns Rail Strikers

9. Headlines should be written in the historical present tense (or future). However, some newspapers permit past tense in headlines:

Poor	*Better*
Two convicts escaped from jail van	Two convicts escapes from jail van

10. The headline should use vivid, fresh language; avoid dull and trite words:

Poor	*Better*
Parliament Studies Arms Control Again	Parliament Takes Aim At Arms Control Again

11. Words should not be repeated in the headline:

Poor	*Better*
Strike Conference Ends Coal workers strike	Meditation Session Ends Coal workers strike

12. Headlines should be specific. Try to find the exact word to convey a thought:

Poor	*Better*
Youth Injured In Knife Battle	Youth Slashed In Knife Fight

13. Peculiar slang expressions should be avoided:

Poor	*Better*
Stockers Sales Cut in Half	Local Cattle Sales Drop 50 Per Cent

14. The headline writer cannot use simplified spelling (such as "tho") unless it is the style of the newspaper:

Poor	*Better*
Rain to Continue Thru Another Day	Rain to Continue Through Tomorrow

15. Single quotation marks should be used in headlines:

Poor	*Better*
Kidnapped Boy "Buried Alive"	Kidnapped Boy 'Buried Alive'

16. Abbreviations should not be used unless standard, conventional and generally understood, such as CBI, SBI:

Poor	*Better*
500 of ASE At Meeting Here	500 Engineers Convene Here

17. Words, phrases consisting of nouns and adjective modifiers, prepositional phrases and verb phrases should not be split between lines:

Poor	*Better*
Centre Approves Trade Tax Despite Protest	Trade Tax Approved Despite Protest

18. Opinion headlines should be attributed or qualified:

Poor	*Better*
Taxes Too High On Businesses	Taxes Too High Say Businessmen

19. Articles and other unnecessary words should not be used, except with names of books and other proper titles:

Poor	*Better*
Fireman Saves A Little Puppy	Fireman Saves Dog from Blaze

20. "Half truths" must be avoided. Sometimes such heads can be libelous or misleading.

Poor	*Better*
Bina Ramani Sought In Jessica Lal Case	Bina Ramani Sought As Eyewitness

Decks

If we scan newspapers published two decades ago, we find most of the important stories having headlines in multiple decks. Any news story of some significance had a minimum of two or three deck headlines. *The New York Times* is reported to have used 24 decks when it reported the story of Lincon's assassination.

Decks can be used in different types/fonts and sizes.

Example

US PLANES BOMBARD LIBYAN CITIES
HUNDREDS KILLED AND INJURED
GADDAFI PLANS RETALIATION

The multiple deck headline has almost disappeared from our newspapers. Today, the style is to give one-line headlines that take less space and help in page layout. But this change has put an additional burden on the sub-editor who has to find new ways and means not only to make the headline snappy, but meaningful and complete in itself. This is any day a harder task.

Some sub-editors circumvent this by giving a shoulder headline left flush, with or without a rule underneath, to strengthen the main headline.

WORST-EVER DISASTER IN MEXICO
THOUSANDS FEARED DEAD
IN VOLCANIC ERUPTION

OR

Arjun Singh Issue
Walk-Out And Uproar
In MP Assembly

The shoulder headlines are always in smaller types than the main head. One-line headlines help considerably in designing the page apart from saving space.

POWER-CUT LIKELY IN MP
OR
BANK STAFF TO STEP UP STIR

Contains essential information about the news story and they can be set for three column story or two-column story by suitably displaying them.

At present in India, newspapers prefer single-deck headlines for all items except the lead story or the second lead story. A second or a third deck is unnecessary if the first can tell all. Most of the D/C and T/C stories today are in single deck. And to avoid a second deck, you can always use a shoulder headline.

Some Caution

Lot has been discussed about headline writing. A great caution is demanded on the part of headline writer. Also the style sheet of the newspaper has to be in tune with the changing patterns and the demand of profession.

Take for example the trend of using 'By' in credit lines and bylines.

It is debatable whether the use of the 'by' is necessary or not. Or else there can be headlines as the one below the kind of which often appears even today in one of the leading dailies in India.

14-YEAR-OLD GIRL RAPED

By Our Staff Reporter

The headline and the byline give the impression that the reporter of the paper himself has raped the girl.

No doubt, copy writers undergo tremendous strain in framing attractive and suitable headlines.

But, for any reason they should not abuse the language. Nor they should make the headline a pun on words.

See the Examples:

DENGUE EPIDEMIC IN DELHI
Motion Disallowed in Parliament

A grammatical error in 48 Pt may be worse than half a dozen language errors buried in the body type.

1. **Couple <u>Needs</u> Help With <u>Their</u> Sex Life**

Both singular and plural are used in the heading.

2. **Woman <u>Reports</u> She <u>Is</u> Robbed**
   By Man Posing As Inspector

Here the present tense 'reports' is correct. However, the second verb should be 'was' to show that she is reporting a previous event.

So, read and understand the story before writing the headlines.

Get the key-words, the most important element of the story and be specific. Give punch to the headline by using snappy verbs, action verbs and colourful verbs.

Subheads

Subheads are boldface lines of type used to break up the body type used in long news stories. They are a typographical device to relieve the greyness of long columns of type. As a general rule, they start after the first three paragraphs of a story and are placed evenly three or four paragraphs apart throughout the story. The last one generally is placed three paragraphs before the story ends. Some newspapers set their subheads in all caps, boldface type slightly larger than body type. Others use boldface-cap and lowercase subheads. The general principles of headline writing apply to subheads. They should not fill the entire line, nor should they be too short.

A number of newspapers have eliminated subheads in favour of other devices to break up the monotony of large masses of solid body type. One is to boldface whole paragraphs, parts of paragraphs, or even parts of sentences—the first four words of a sentence, for example. Others take sentences or paragraphs right out of the story, set them in larger type and insert them into the body of the story with ample white space around them.

Trends in newspaper headlines come and go just as they do in the overall design of newspapers. But the principles of headline writing remain the same. Good headlines say something.

Experimentation in Headlines

It is futile to search for uniformity in the pattern of headline writing in different countries or even in different newspapers in a country. Despite all rules framed, headline writers do experimentation.

There would be innumerable kinds of headlines if we try to categorise them on the basis of the style of writing. However, few writing styles we can talk about.

1. Factual Headline
   - Six independents too extend support to BJP in UP
   - BJP needs support of 30 more MLAs in UP
2. Conclusive Headline
   - BJP govt. in UP a distant dream
   - BJP govt. in UP a remote possibility
3. Humorous Headline
   - Preity Zinta gets work "Kabhi Bhi Kaisa Bhi"
4. Colourful Headline
   - In Lucknow, it is film star versus political stalwarts
5. Curiosity Arousing Headline
   - Guess who is coming to town
6. Hard Hitting Headline
   - G for Gujarat, Gandhi and Genocide
7. Poignant Headline
   - Millions mourn their queen of hearts (Headline given on the death of Princess Diana)
8. Intelligent Headline
   - Nine months of President rule delivers new Ministry in Manipur

Some More Examples

On December 5, 2000, the disciplinary committee of the Board of Control for Cricket in India (BCCI) imposed life bans on former Indian Captain Mohammad Azharuddin and former cricketer Ajay Sharma and five-year ban on Ajay Jadeja and Manoj Prabhakar. The Committee exonerated Nayan Mongia.

The Times of India put the following headline on this news item spread in six columns as front page lead.

THE VERDICT: LIFE BAN ON AZHAR, FIVE-YEAR BAN ON JADEJA, AJAY SHARMA, MANOJ PRABHAKAR; MONGIA EXONERATED

Alvida Azhar, An revoir Jadeja, Attaboy Mongia

In January 2001, during Mahakumbh in Allahabad, *The Times of India* firstly gave Sanskrit shlokas in praise of Ganga with English translation and underneath was given the photograph and the main headline.

Index